THEOLOGICAL ESSAYS.

PRINTED BY R. CLAY, LONDON,

FOR

MACMILLAN & CO. CAMBRIDGE.

London: GEORGE BELL.
Dublin: HODGES AND SMITH.
Edinburgh: EDMONSTON AND DOUGLAS.
Glasgow: JAMES MACLEHOSE.
Oxford: J. H. PARKER.

THEOLOGICAL ESSAYS.

BY

FREDERICK DENISON MAURICE, M. A.

CHAPLAIN OF LINCOLN'S INN.

Il s'en faut peut-être que le christianisme, à cette heure qui nous paraît si avancée, ait produit dans la conscience et dans la vie de l'humanité toutes ses applications, ait exprimé toute sa pensée, ait dit son dernier mot. Dans un sens, il a tout dit dès l'abord; dans un autre sens, il a beaucoup à dire encore, et le monde ne finira que quand le christianisme aura tout dit.—VINET.

Second Edition.

WITH A NEW PREFACE, AND OTHER ADDITIONS.

Cambridge:

MACMILLAN & CO.

1853.

TO

ALFRED TENNYSON, ESQ.

Poet Laureate.

MY DEAR SIR,

I HAVE maintained in these Essays that a Theology which does not correspond to the deepest thoughts and feelings of human beings cannot be a true Theology. You writings have taught me to enter into many of those thoughts and feelings. Will you forgive me the presumption of offering you a book which at least acknowledges them and does them homage?

As the hopes which I have expressed in this volume are more likely to be fulfilled to our children than to ourselves, I might perhaps ask you to accept it as a present to one of your name, in whom you have given me a very sacred interest. Many years, I trust, will elapse, before he knows that there are any controversies in the world into which he has entered. Would to God that in a few more he may find that they have ceased! At all events, if he should ever look into these Essays, they may tell him what meaning some of the former generation attached to words, which will be familiar and dear to his generation, and to those that follow his,—how there were some who longed that the bells of our churches might indeed

> Ring out the darkness of the land,
> Ring in the Christ that is to be.

Believe me,

My dear SIR,

Yours very truly and gratefully,

F. D. MAURICE.

ADVERTISEMENT.

A Lady, once a Member of the Society of Friends who died some years ago, desired me in her Will to apply a small sum to purposes in which, I 'knew that she was interested.' It was not difficult to comply with the letter of this command, as she was interested in many benevolent undertakings. But I was aware that the words of her bequest had a special meaning, and that she intended to lay me under the obligation of writing, or procuring to be written, some book especially addressed to Unitarians.

I have made several efforts to execute this task, but have never done anything which gave me the least satisfaction. A mere controversial work I felt that I could not compose. Such works, so far as my experience has gone, do little else than harm to those who write, and to those who read them. Still it has been a great weight on my conscience, that I was neglecting a request so solemnly conveyed to me.

Some months ago I seemed to see a way in which I might acquit myself of the obligation. A series of Discourses which had occurred to me as suitable for my own Congregation, in the interval between Quinquagesima Sunday, and Trinity Sunday, might, I thought, embrace all the topics which I should wish to bring under the notice of Unitarians. It was suggested by a friend that I should throw each discourse into the form of an Essay, after it had been preached. By following this advice, I have been able to avail myself of criticisms which were made on the sermons when they were delivered; to introduce many topics, which would have been unsuitable for the pulpit; and at the same time, I hope, to retain something of the feeling of one who is addressing actual men with whom he sympathises, not opponents with whom he is arguing. I did not allude to Unitarians while I was preaching. I have said scarcely anything to them in writing, which I do not think just as applicable to the great body of my contemporaries, of all classes and opinions. Nearly every Essay has been re-written, and greatly enlarged in its passage out of the sermon state. Two were originally composed in their present form.

Though I have printed the Essays one after another,

before the whole work was completed, that I might be compelled to perform a task which I had deferred so long, I cannot ask for any toleration on the plea of haste. The book expresses thoughts which have been working in my mind for years; the method of it has not been adopted carelessly; even the composition has undergone frequent revision. No labour I have been engaged in has occupied me so much, or interested me more deeply. I hope it may be the means of leading some to a far higher knowledge than their guide has ever attained.

May 24, 1853.

PREFACE TO THE SECOND EDITION.

A CRITIC of these Essays in the November number of the *Prospective Review*, observes that I have "not the art of convincing" him; but then, "that it is startling to think how few writers ever do radically overturn any mature system of belief." I certainly never suspected myself of possessing this 'art.' I do not know whether there is such an 'art.' If there is, and if I had it, I am not certain that I should wish to exercise it. To overturn "radically a mature system of belief" is the very last object of my ambition. There are some Unitarians, and some Trinitarians also, who are not very mature in their convictions, not very settled in their belief, who have tried systems, and are not content with them. To such I addressed myself. By some of these I have been understood. They have responded to my words with more sympathy than I had any right to expect. For they have perceived that I have not wished to unsettle them in their opinions, or to bring them to mine, but to show that God has laid a foundation for them and for me upon which we may stand together.

I should wish these weary and earnest seekers to read the Article to which I have referred, and to ask themselves whether they find there what they are looking for. The Review is written with much gracefulness and eloquence. It contains the latest message of the new Unitarian school. It undertakes to expose the feebleness of my analysis, and the unsatisfactoriness of my logic. Very likely it may have succeeded. But the question at issue between us is not that at all, not whether they are good reasoners and I am a bad one, but what Gospel they have to bring to mankind, what light they have to throw on all the questionings and yearnings of the human spirit, what they can show has been done for the deliverance of our race and of its members, what hope they can give us of that which shall yet be done. On that issue I am willing to put their creed and mine. That which is true in itself, that which the God of Truth declares to his creatures, can, I am sure, bear the test. What proceeds from man will never satisfy man.

I have no cause to complain of the Writer of this Article for want of courtesy to me personally. On the contrary, he has paid me compliments to which I am not entitled, and which I am bound to disclaim. He thinks that I have some good and genial qualities of my own; that I should probably prefer truth to a lie, if I had not set myself to defend certain Articles of Faith. That necessity leads me into "miserable juggling," and makes me an object of the Reviewer's deepest compassion. It is very agreeable thus to get all honours for oneself, and to have all one's crimes attributed to an unfortunate position. I feel the temptation to accept a distinction which sets the conscience so much at ease, and gives one's vanity such a pleasant stimulus. But I cannot do so without proving myself not to be what the Reviewer is kind enough to say that I am, but the very opposite of it,—without being guilty of a conscious and inward falsehood. I *know* that the Creed which leads me, as the Reviewer thinks, to contradict my better nature, gives me an interest in my fellows, a sympathy with mankind, which I have not naturally, and which I find it exceedingly hard to maintain. I know that that Creed has led me to desire truth in my inward parts, and to resist those tendencies to 'juggling' and trickery into which the Reviewer supposes that it tempts me.

I know, moreover, that the belief in fixed Articles respecting the relations and acts of God has enabled me, and does enable me, to believe that the world is progressive, and not stationary; just as the belief in the fixed article respecting gravitation has given an impulse to all the inquiries of natural students. If, after nearly 6,000 years of man's existence, we assume that nothing is known respecting the questions which men have felt to concern them most, we shall not expect that anything will be known. I contend that articles do not crush inquiry, but awaken it; that they do not hinder education, but show how we may avoid superstitions which have hindered it most effectually; that they do not oblige us to be harsh or repulsive to any men of any sect, but qualify us to understand them, to sympathise with them, to justify their opposing thoughts, to reconcile them.

These doctrines I maintained in the first book which I wrote after I took orders.* The experience of nineteen very eventful years in English Ecclesiastical history has led me to change some of the opinions which I expressed in that book.

* Subscription no Bondage; or, the Thirty-nine Articles guides in Academic Education. Oxford. 1835.

I would not impose our Articles upon the students in our Universities, because I see that by doing so we tempt them to dishonesty, and lead them to dislike a document which I believe they ought to love. But the other convictions which I maintained then, instead of being shaken, have been confirmed by all I have seen, heard, thought, and regretted since. I am more than ever persuaded that they whose zeal for progress leads them to preach that the Bible is a collection of obsolete Hebrew stories, are seeking to defraud the world of the treasure to which it has owed its past and will owe its future progress;—that those who tell us that we may not express the facts and principles of the Bible in popular Creeds and teach them to our children, leave us at the mercy of coteries, where men and women prostrate themselves before some newspaper oracle which allows them no freedom whatever;—that those who would take from us our intellectual formularies, under pretence that if we cast them off we shall do greater justice to the earnest convictions of those who dissent from us, are not just to these convictions themselves, but very intolerant of them; and that, on the contrary, *we* are *bound* by those forms, in spite of our own natural narrowness, sectarianism, and dogmatism, to recognise and honour the strivings after truth of every man whatsoever, even of the man who scorns us and hates us most.

In connexion with this subject, I shall allude to an event of which it would be affectation to suppose that the readers of this book are altogether ignorant. Most of them will have heard that the publication of it has led to my expulsion from a College connected with the Church of England. The inference has been readily drawn, that I shall now feel the position which I have taken up as a defender of the Church and its formularies to be untenable, that I must have learnt in myself how galling that yoke is which I have wished that other men should endure.

I do not know whether I shall be suspected by some of a base motive for what I am going to say; but I know that there are those who will believe that I am speaking solemnly, deliberately, as in the presence of God. I affirm, then, that during the thirteen years which I passed in that College, I never was restrained from uttering one word which I thought it would be good or right to utter before my Class, by the obligation under which I had laid myself to teach according to the formularies of the Church of England; that I *should* have suppressed, in obedience to what have been called my "sectarian timidities," many words which I did utter, if those formularies had not given me boldness, had not raised me to a higher point of view than my own, had not warned me against the peril and guilt of accepting the opinions of the age as my guides. I declare that if I have ever been able to see any method in history, civil or ecclesiastical, or to make my pupils see it, the Bible and these formularies have shown me that method. I declare further, that if I have been able to teach my pupils,—and I have tried diligently to teach them,—that they are to reverence the convictions of all men of all sects and schools, and to show them sympathy, I have done what I should not have been encouraged to do, or have thought it safe to do, if I had not taken these Articles as my own teachers and helpers, and if I had not considered that it was my duty, as far as I could, to impregnate those who would afterward be ministers in the Church with their spirit.

Once more, the fact that I had accepted these Articles and had bound myself to teach according to them, made me comparatively indifferent about the question, whether my view of the right method of education was the same with that of my superior for the time being. I had announced over and over again in various forms of language, that I did not look upon our Articles as marking out a close and narrow line between two opposite schools, and as authorizing us to denounce both; but as announcements of a higher truth, which should lead us to deal fairly with the strongest assertions of both. I could not lecture on Church History without telling my pupils that Creeds and Articles do not and cannot stifle opinions, seeing that the decrees of the Nicene Council were the beginning, not the end, of the Arian controversy, and that the proclamation of James I. against discussions upon Election and Predestination, was the signal for the most furious war between Calvinists and Arminians ever waged. The Principal of King's College had, I believe, declared himself the conservator of a *via media;* he probably expects results from Articles which I should consider most undesirable, even if they were not unattainable. But if, in the face of my statements, he could accept me as a fellow-worker, even invite me to become one, my conscience was clear. I could teach with perfect freedom, knowing that I was trying to obey the laws which we both confessed, not feeling that I was more tied to the habits of his mind, than he was to mine. It might be reasonable to expect that such a connexion would at some time or other terminate. But it would have terminated much sooner,—it would have been immeasurably less satisfactory while it lasted,—if there had been no common rule to which all the members of the College did homage. In that case, the fear of saying something which a superior would disapprove if he knew it, must be continually tormenting the mind of a teacher. He works in that most fretting of all chains, the sense of some unexpressed, implicit obligation to abstain from acts which his duty to his pupils, to the Church, and to God, would urge him to perform.

I cannot pretend that any recent experience of mine, either in a College or in the Church, has in the least changed my opinion, that our formularies are the best protection we have, against the exclusiveness and cruelty of private judgments. If our Catechism did not bear a continual witness to our children that Christ has redeemed them and all mankind, how could we resist the dictation of writers who pronounce it a heresy to say that our race is redeemed at all, that it is not lying under God's curse? If our Articles did not put forth the doctrine of Christ's Godhead and Manhood as the ground of Theology, before they speak of the Fall and the depravity of man, how could we withstand the popular theory, so plausible, so gratifying to all the selfish instincts of religious men, that the Gospel is only a scheme for saving *them* from the ruin which God decreed for the universe when Adam sinned? If the Articles had not refused to dogmatise on the meaning of the word Eternal, and on the endlessness of evil, what could prevent the doctrine, that an immense majority of our fellow-beings are in an utterly hopeless condition, from being regarded as *the characteristic* doctrine of CHRISTIAN Divinity? I am sure that it has been so regarded by multitudes of our lay brethren, and that therefore the consciences and hearts to which we ought to present our message are closed against it. They understand us to say that God has sent His Son into the world, not to save it, but to condemn it.

I count it the highest blessing of my life that I have been permitted to become a witness, that the Church of England gives not the faintest encouragement to so horrible a contradiction of God's word. I receive the cordial and generous sympathy which has been shown to me by persons from whom I had no right to expect it, who would naturally have regarded me with prejudice and suspicion, not as rendered as to me, but as a proof how much affection towards the Church there is still in the hearts of our countrymen, how glad they are to believe that she is not what her sons sometimes represent her to be. And though opinions, which, merely as such, are a thousand times weightier than mine, are in favour of forcing our Church to say what as yet she does not say, I believe they will not succeed in putting a new yoke upon our necks. I believe the English clergy will assert the freedom which God has given them,—the freedom of being silent where He has not spoken, being well assured that if they do not, they will soon be compelled to keep silence when He *has* spoken, nay, to deny that He wishes that all men should be saved, though He has declared that He does.

In the present Edition of these Essays, I have altered some passages which were said to be obscure, and have erased some which have caused unnecessary offence. In the Essay on the Atonement, besides some changes in my own language, I have made one omission with very great reluctance. I had quoted the beautiful Collect for the Sunday before Easter. I quoted it simply to show, by the most living instance, that the Church referred the Sacrifice of Christ to the 'tender love of God to mankind.' I never even alluded to the clause which speaks of our 'following the example of his great humility,' not because I did not prize it, or believe that it stood in the closest connexion with the rest of the prayer, but because it did not concern the special truth of which I was speaking. Yet I read with my own eyes, in one of our religious newspapers, the charge that I had appealed to this Collect because I regarded Christ's death not as a sacrifice, but simply as an example: and because I wished to fix that opinion upon the Church! As the Church believes, and as I believe, in Christ's Sacrifice, not in a narrower or more 'attenuated' sense than that in which this religious newspaper believes it, but in an infinitely wider and deeper sense,—as I believe it to be a real sacrifice made by the Son, of His whole spirit, soul, and body, to the Father,—as I believe it is a sacrifice which takes away sin, a sacrifice, satisfaction, and oblation for the sins of the whole world,—I have deliberately blotted out a sentence which was worth all the rest of the Essay together, rather than even seem to sanction so monstrous an inference. But I have not, of course, modified in the slightest degree the principles which I maintained in that Essay.

The Church does not maintain in one prayer, but in all its prayers, that the love of God is the only root and ground of Christ's Atonement, and that the perfect submission of the Son to the will of the Father constitutes the deepest meaning of the Sacrifice. These principles belong to the essence of our faith. In life, in death, I hope I may never abandon them or shrink from confessing them, and from repudiating any notion which sets them at nought or weakens them. I have perceived that the *fact* of the Atonement, which is *the* fact of the Gospel, is lost to numbers of people who are very earnest and who desire to be thoroughly Christian, through the restless efforts which their understandings make to apprehend the *cause* of it. They do not believe the Atonement, but an explanation of the Atonement which they have received from others or devised for themselves. And so they do not actually feed upon the Sacrifice which is given for the life of the world, but on some dry notions about the Sacrifice, which cannot give life to any human being. But this is not all. These explanations, being exceedingly plausible, seeming wonderfully to conspire with the experiences of a sin-sick soul, being such as a Heathen would use to defend the Sacrifices which he offers to a malignant power, come into the most frightful collision with those which the Scripture gives for the Sacrifice wherewith God is well pleased. There may be myriads of aspects of this cardinal doctrine which I have perceived very imperfectly, and into which I shall rejoice to enter more deeply. But they must be such aspects as do not interfere with and invert the very nature and meaning of the Sacrifice. The more unspeakably precious we consider it to each man and to all mankind, the more vehement shall we be in protesting against misrepresentations of it, which are leading more than we know or can count, to cast it out of their thoughts altogether.

I would make a similar remark in reference to the Essays on the Resurrection and the Judgment Day, which I have altered very slightly. It has been affirmed that I have sought to explain away the doctrines of the Resurrection of the Body, and of Christ's final Judgment; or at least, to throw an atmosphere of doubt over them. I affirm that I have endeavoured to bring forth these doctrines, which I hold to be most vital and necessary, out of the atmosphere of doubt, which popular theories, as it seems to me, have thrown over them. I do not say in any case who does or does not hold these theories, or any modification of them. But I find that they have darkened and are darkening the faith of multitudes in the articles of the Creed, and are destroying their practical effect on many more. Therefore I have spoken. Unitarians are probably less pleased with my words on these subjects than any other persons. I did not write to please them, or anybody, but to maintain what I think is the truth. And I ask any serious person whether those who say that the doctrines of the Atonement, of the Resurrection, and of the Judgment, can only be received in connexion with certain metaphysical, legal, or commercial explanations,—or I who say that they may be received simply as good news from Heaven, which suffering people on earth have need of, most deserve to be accused of Rationalism?

I have rewritten the Essay on Eternal Life and

Eternal Death, and greatly enlarged it. It has been supposed that I have argued for some mitigated notion of future punishment, as more consistent with the mercy of God than the ordinary one. To me the ordinary doctrine seems full of the most miserable mitigations and indulgences for evil. I plead for the Love of God, which resists sin, and triumphs over it, not for a mercy which relaxes the penalties of it. With continual effort, —only by the help of that revelation of God which is made in the Gospel of Christ,—I am able to believe that there is a might of Good which has overcome Evil, and does overcome it. To maintain this conviction, to believe in the Love of God, in spite of the appearances which the world presents and the reluctance of my own nature, I find to be the great fight of life; one in which we are continually baffled, but in which we must hold on, if we are not to become haters of each other, as we are always prone to be. I admire unspeakably those who can believe in the Love of God and can love their brethren, in spite of the opinion which they seem to cherish, that He has doomed them to destruction. I am sure that their faith is as much purer and stronger than mine, as it is than their own system. But if that system does prevent me from believing that which God's word, the Gospel of Christ, the witness of my own conscience, the miseries and necessities of the universe, compel me to believe, I must throw it off. I do not call upon them to deny anything they have been wont to hold; but I call upon them to join us in acknowledging God's Love and His redemption first of all, and then to consider earnestly what is or is not compatible with that acknowledgment. As it is, we are desired to believe the popular tenet respecting the future condition of the world absolutely, and God's love to mankind *in a sense.* I appeal to every devout man, to every preacher of the Gospel especially, dares he adopt this order in his convictions? Must he not confess that he has no good news for mankind if he does?

I have expanded the Theological part of the Essay on Regeneration, and have added to that on the Trinity some observations respecting the Unitarian notions of Prayer. I have also added some passages at the end of the Essay on Inspiration, the purpose of which has been perhaps more misunderstood than that of any in the book. It is against the very low notion of the worth of the Bible and of the nature of Inspiration which seems to prevail in the religious world, that I have there protested. I hold the Bible to be the Book of Life; I see it turned into a Book of Death. It is treated in a way in which no other book is treated. The divine method of it is despised; it is reduced into a collection of broken sentences; these are used in the most reckless irreverent manner by any one who has a notion of his own to defend, or a notion of an adversary to attack. The posture of students and learners towards it is abandoned by those who yet profess to accept it as their only guide and authority. There must be something very wrong in our belief, when this is our habitual practice. Have we not lost the faith in Inspiration, while we have been talking about it and inventing theories about it? Have we not lost our faith in the Inspirer? I trust to show shortly, in a book which I have been writing for several years on the Gospels and on the Epistles of St. Paul, that I do not receive the words of the Bible less literally, or regard it less as a whole, or submit to it less as an authority, than those who have complained of me because I cannot bear to see their sons driven into hopeless infidelity by their hard and cruel attempts to substitute a tenet concerning Inspiration for the Divine Word.

I ought not to conclude this Preface without

referring to the kindness and generosity of the new Bishop of Natal, who chose a moment when he knew that my character was in disgrace with the religious public, and when any acknowledgment of me might be perilous to him, for dedicating to me a volume of admirable Sermons. The very great delight which I felt at receiving such a testimony from such a man, would have been no compensation for my sorrow, that he should have risked his own reputation for the sake of a friend, from many of whose opinions he had expressed his dissent, if I had not seen in this act a pledge of his possessing those qualities of courage and indifference to self, which are so especially needed in a Chief Pastor of the flock, and which have very remarkably characterized our Colonial Bishops. For the events which followed this Dedication I cannot feel anything but thankfulness. Though Dr. Colenso had proved by his Sermons that he believed in the endlessness of future punishments, he had asserted most broadly and distinctly his conviction, that we are living in a world which God loves, and which Christ has redeemed, and had affirmed that this was the message which he was called to bear to the natives, as well as to the colonists, of South Africa. Those who think that the world is *not* redeemed, that God's love is limited to a few, felt that a golden opportunity was afforded them of obtaining from the authorities of the English Church, a practical contradiction of the doctrines which they abhor. The attempt was made, and it failed. Bishop Colenso is permitted to carry to the English and the Zoolus, the same Gospel, which St. Paul was denounced by his countrymen as a heretic and blasphemer, for carrying to Jews and Gentiles, in Greece and Asia Minor. May the message be as mighty and effectual in the nineteenth century as it was in the first!

LONDON, *December 9th*, 1853.

CONTENTS.

ESSAY I.

ON CHARITY.

ST. PAUL says, *Though I have all faith, so that I could remove mountains, and have not Charity, I am nothing.*

Many a person in this day has exclaimed, when he has heard these words, 'If the Apostle Paul always 'adhered to that doctrine, how readily one would listen 'to him,—what sympathy one would have with him! 'For this one moment he confesses how poor all those 'dogmas are, on which he dwells elsewhere with so 'much of theological refinement; faith, which he told 'the Romans and Galatians was necessary and able to 'save men from ruin, shrinks here to its proper dimen- 'sions, and in comparison of another excellence is 'pronounced to be good for nothing. It is for divines to 'defend his consistency if they can; we are only too 'glad to accept what seems to us a splendid inconsis- 'tency, in support of a principle which it is the great 'work of our age to proclaim.'

I have been often tempted to answer a person who spoke thus, in a way which I am sure was foolish and wrong. I have been inclined to say, 'The Charity 'which the Apostle describes is not the least that tole- 'rance of opinions, that disposition to fraternize with 'men of all characters and creeds, which you take it to 'be. His nomenclature is spiritual and divine, yours 'human and earthly. If you could look into the real 'signification of this chapter, you would not find that 'you liked it much better than what he says of Faith 'elsewhere.'

This language is impertinent and unchristian. We fall into it partly because we look upon objectors as opponents whom it is desirable to silence; partly because we suppose that there is a spurious Charity prevalent in our time, which must be carefully distinguished from real and divine Charity; partly because we think that the interests of Theology demand a more vigorous assertion of those distinctive Christian tenets which are often confounded in a vague all-comprehending philosophical Theory. I have felt these motives and arguments too strongly not to sympathise with those who are influenced by them. It is in applying them to practice that I have found how much I might be misled by them.

1. I know I *can* silence an objector by telling him that the Bible means something altogether different from that which it appears to mean. He does not care to

discuss any question with me when he has understood that there is no medium of communication between us; that I am speaking a language which I cannot interpret to him. He believes the book I honour above all others to be a book of Cabbala, and he throws it away accordingly. And if I afterwards refer to any passages of beautiful human morality which I think may impress him in its favour, he tells me plainly, that I know the intention of those passages is not what the words indicate, and that the conscience of mankind responds to their apparent, not to their real, signification.

I have done this service to him by that method of mine. What have I done for the Bible? I have practically denied that its language is inspired, and that the truth which the language expresses is divine. I must suppose that inspired language is the most inclusive and comprehensive of all language; that divine truth lies beneath all the imperfect forms of truth which men have perceived,—sustaining them, not contradicting them. If a particular temper or habit characterises a man, or a country, or an age, the believer in a Revelation would naturally conclude that there must be an affinity between this temper or habit, and some side of that Revelation;—he would search earnestly for the point of contact between them, and rejoice when he recognised it. He might find the temper or habit in question often confused, often feeble, often evil. His only hope of removing the confusion, strengthening the feebleness, counteracting the evil, would lie in the power which seemed to be given him of connecting it with that wider and deeper principle from which it had been separated. Every, even the slightest, inclination on the part of persons who were habitually suspicious of that which he regarded as truth, to acknowledge a portion of it as bearing upon their lives, he would eagerly and thankfully hail. So far from complaining of them because they fixed upon a certain aspect of the Revelation, remaining indifferent or sceptical about every other, he would consider this a proof that they were treating it in the most natural and sincere way,—accepting what in their state of mind they could most practically apprehend and use. If another side of it was for them lying in shadow, he might,—provided he had any clear conviction that God has His own way of guiding His creatures,—be content that they should not, for the present, try to bring that within the range of their vision. At all events, he would feel that his work was clearly marked out for him. In this, as in all other cases, he could not hope to arrive at the unknown, except through that which is perceived, however partially. He would not quench the light by which any men are walking, under pretence that it is merely torch-light, lest he, as well as they, should be punished with complete darkness. If I have failed to act upon these maxims, I am certain that my faith in God's Revelation has been weak.

2. I do not deny that there is much in the feelings

which we of this age associate with the word *Charity*, that is artificial, fantastical, morbid. Most will admit this respecting the charity of others,—some about their own. I do not deny that the talk about charity, the sensation about it, even the attempt to practise it, is compatible with a vast amount of uncharitableness. That also will be generally admitted; perhaps, the confession is more sincere than any other which we make. It is equally true that each school has its own notion of charity, that the definitions of it are unlike, that the limitations of it are various and capricious. The point to be considered is, whether all these diversities, subsisting under a common name, do not prove, more than anything else, the tendency of the time in which they are found,—the direction in which our thoughts are all moving. The conscience of men, asleep to many obligations, is awake to this. All confess that they ought to have charity of some kind. Portraits of dry, hard, cold-hearted men, who have in them, possibly, a sense of justice and right, are sure to produce a revolting, as from something profoundly and essentially evil, even in spectators who can look upon great criminals with half-admiration, as gigantic and heroical. The formalist has become almost *the* name for reprobation among us; that from which every one shrinks himself, and which he attributes to those whom he execrates most, precisely because it denotes the man in whom charity has been sacrificed to mere rule. The more you look into the discussions of different parties in our time, the more you will find that, however narrow and exclusive they may be, comprehension is their watchword. We separate from our fellows, on the plea that they are not sufficiently comprehensive; we strive to break down fences which other people have raised, even while we are making a thicker and more thorny one ourselves.

If there is any truth in the observations which I made under the last head, these indications might appear almost to determine the course which a divine in the nineteenth century should follow, though by adopting it he departed from the precedents of other times. The same motive which might have led one of the Reformers to speak first on Faith,—because all men, whether Romanists or Anti-Romanists, in some sense acknowledged the necessity of it,—should incline a writer in this day to begin his moral or theological discourses from Charity, at whatever point he may ultimately arrive. But there would be no deviation from precedent. The doctors of the first ages, and of the middle ages, continually put forth the Divine Charity as the ground upon which all things in heaven and earth rest, as the centre round which they revolve. And this was done not merely by those who were appealing to human sympathies, but in scientific treatises. What is more to our purpose, the compilers of our Prayer-book, living at the very time when Faith was the watchword of all parties, thought it wise to introduce the season of Lent with a prayer and an epistle, which declare that the tongues of men and of angels, the giving all our goods to feed the poor, the giving our bodies to be burnt, finally, the faith which removes mountains, without Charity, are nothing. This Love was to be the ground of all calls to repentance, conversion, humiliation, self-restraint; this was to unfold gradually the mystery of the Passion, and of the Resurrection, the mystery of Justification by Faith, of the New Life, of Christ's Ascension and Priesthood, of the Descent of the Spirit, of the Unity of the Church. This was to be the induction into the deepest mystery of all, the Name of the Father, and of the Son, and of the Holy Ghost. If it is asked what human charity can have to do with the mysteries of the Godhead, the compilers of the Prayer-book would have answered, 'Certainly nothing 'at all, if human charity is not the image and counter-'part of the Divine; if there can be a charity in man 'which beareth all things, believeth all things, endureth all 'things, unless it was first in God, unless it be the nature 'and being of God. If He is Charity, His acts *must* 'spring from it as ours *should;* Charity will be the key 'to unlock the secrets of Divinity as well as of Hu-'manity.' As a Churchman, I might, perhaps, venture to follow out a hint, which rests on such an authority and comes to us supported by such a prescription, without being suspected of innovating tendencies.

3. But I know why many will think that such a course may have been adapted to former days, and yet

be unsuitable for ours. I shall be told 'that it was very 'well to speak of Charity, divine or human, when the 'importance of dogmas and of distinguishing between 'orthodox and heretical dogmas, was admitted, nay, if 'that is possible, exaggerated; but that now, when all 'dogmatic teachings are scorned, not by a few here and 'there, but by the spirit of the age; when it is the 'minority who plead for them and feel their necessity; 'and when the popular cry is for some union of parties 'in which all barriers, theological, nay, it would seem 'sometimes, moral also, shall be thrown down:—at such 'a time to speak of putting Charity above Faith, or of 'referring to Charity as a standard for Faith, is either 'to palter with words in a double sense, pretending that 'you agree with the infidel, while you keep a reserved 'opinion in your own heart which would repel him if 'you produced it;—or else it is to give up your arms to 'him, owning that he has vanquished.'

I feel as strongly as these objectors can feel, that this age is impatient of distinctions—of the distinction between Right and Wrong, as well as of that between Truth and Falsehood. Of all its perils, this seems to me the greatest, that which alone gives us a right to tremble at any others which may be threatening it. To watch against this temptation in ourselves, and in all over whom we have any charge or influence, is, I believe, our highest duty. In performance of it, I should always denounce the glorification of private judgment, as fatal to the belief in Truth, and to the pursuit of it. We are always *tending* towards the notion that we may think what we like to think; that there is no standard to which our thoughts should be conformed; that they fix their own standard. Who can toil to find, that which, on this supposition, he can make? Who can suffer, that all may share a possession which each man holds apart from his neighbour?

But Dogmatism is not the antagonist of private judgment. The most violent assertor of his private judgment is the greatest dogmatist. And, conversely, the loudest assertor of the dogmatical authority of the Church, is very apt to be the most vehement and fanatical stickler for his own private judgments. His reverence for the Church leads him to exercise in his individual capacity, what he takes to be her function in her collective capacity. He catches what he supposes to be her spirit. He becomes, in consequence, of all men, the most headstrong and self-willed. There must be some other escape than this from the evils of our time; this road leads us into the very heart of them.

It seems to me that, if we start from the belief,—'Charity is the ground and centre of the Universe, God 'is Charity,'—we restore that distinctness which our Theology is said to have lost, we reconcile it with the comprehension which we are all in search of. So long as we are busy with our theories, notions, feelings about God—so long as these constitute our divinity

—we must be vague, we must be exclusive. One deduces his conclusions from the Bible; one from the decrees of the Church; one from his individual consciousness. But the reader of the Bible confesses that it appeals to experience, and must in some way be tested by it; the greatest worshipper of the Church asks for a Bible to support its authority; the greatest believer in his own consciousness perceives that there must be some means of connecting it with the general conscience of mankind. Each denounces the other's method, none is satisfied with his own. If Theology is regarded not as a collection of our theories about God, but as a declaration of His will and His acts towards us, will it not conform more to what we find in the Bible—will it not more meet all the experiences of individuals, all the experiences of our race? And to come directly to the point of the objection which I am considering, will it not better expound all the special articles which our own Church, and the Christian Church generally, confesses? This at least is my belief.

I have tried to understand those articles when they have been interpreted to me by some doctor or apologist who did not start from this ground, and I frankly own I have failed. Their meaning as intellectual propositions has been bewildering to me; as guides to my own life, as helps to my conduct, they have been more bewildering still. But seen in this light, I have found them acquiring distinctness and unity, just in proportion as I became more aware of my own necessities and perplexities, and of those from which my contemporaries are suffering. They have brought the Divine Love and human life into conjunction, the one being no longer a barren tenet or sentiment, the other a hopeless struggle.

I wish that I might be able to set them before some whom I know, as they present themselves to me. I do not think that I have anything rare or peculiar to tell; I believe I have felt much as the people about me are feeling. I might therefore address myself to many of different classes with a slight hope of being listened to; but I have one most directly and prominently before me while I write.

The articles of which I shall speak are precisely those which offend the Unitarian; in defending them I shall certainly appear a dogmatist to him, however little I may deserve that name from those who regard it as an honourable one. He either repudiates these articles absolutely, and considers that it is his calling to protest against them; or he repudiates them as distinct portions of a creed, holding that all the spiritual essence which may once have been in them, departs when they assume this character. I differ from those who take up the last position quite as much as from those who maintain the first; but I have points, strong points, of sympathy with both, and I have profited by the teaching of both. I am not ashamed to say that the vehement denunciations of what they suppose to be the general faith of Christendom which I have heard from Unitarians,—denunciations of it as cruel, immoral, inconsistent with any full and honest acknowledgment of the Divine Unity, still more of the Divine Love,—have been eminently useful to me. I receive them as blessings from God, for which I ought to give Him continual thanks. I do not mean, because the hearing of these charges has set me upon refuting them;—that would be a very doubtful advantage; (for what does one gain for life and practice, by taking up the profession of a theological special pleader?)—but because great portions of these charges have seemed to me well founded; because I have been compelled to confess that the evidence for them was irresistible. And I have been driven more and more to the conclusion, that that evidence does not refer to some secondary, subordinate point,—which we may overlook, provided our greater and more personal interests are secured,—or to some point of which we may for the present know nothing, and be content to confess our ignorance: but that it concerns the grounds of our personal and of our social existence; that it does not touch those secret things which belong to the Lord, but the heart of that Revelation which He has made to us and our children. I owe it very much to these protests that I have learnt to say to myself:—'Take away the Love of God, and 'you take away everything. The Bible sets forth the 'Revelation of that Love, or it is good for nothing. The

'Church is the living Witness and Revelation of that 'Love, or it is good for nothing.'

I owe also much to those Unitarians, who, being less strong in their condemnation of the thoughts and language of books written by Trinitarians, and avowing a sympathy with some of the accounts which they have given of their own inward conflicts, nevertheless hate Orthodoxy, as such, with a perfect hatred, affirming it to be the stifler of all honest convictions, and of all moral growth. I have not been able to gainsay many of their assertions and arguments. I cannot say that I have not seen and felt these effects following from what is called a secure and settled profession. I cannot say that the events of the last twenty years in the English Church do not convince me that it is God's will and purpose that we should be shaken in our ease and satisfaction, and should be forced to ask ourselves what our standing ground is, or whether we have any. I cannot dissemble my belief, that if we are resting on any formulas, supposing they are the best formulas that were ever handed down from one generation to another, or on the divinest book that was ever written by God for the teaching of mankind, and not on the Living God Himself, our foundation will be found sandy, and will crumble under our feet. For telling me this, for giving me a warning which I feel that I need, and that my brethren need, I thank these Unitarians, and all others not called by their name, who have, in one form or another, in gentle or in rough language, united to sound it in our ears. I can say honestly in the sight of God, I have tried to lay it to heart, though not as much as I might have done, or as I hope to do. And now I wish to show that my gratitude for these benefits is not nominal but real, by telling the men of both these classes what they have *not* taught me,—what I have been compelled to learn in another school than theirs.

To the first, then, I say:—You have urged me to believe that God is actually Love. You have taught me to dread any representation of Him which is at variance with this; to shrink from attributing to Him any acts which would be unlovely in man. Well! and I find myself in a world ruled over by this Being, in which there are countless disorders: yes, and I find myself adding to the disorder; one of the elements of it. My heart and conscience demand how this is. I want to know,—not for the sake of a theory, but for the most practical purposes of life,—I want to know how these disorders may be removed out of the world and out of me. You are, I am aware, benevolent men, a great many of you eager for sanitary, social, political reformation. That is well, as far as you are concerned; but is the Ruler of the Universe as much interested in the state of it as you are? Has He done anything adequate for the deliverance of it from its plagues: is He doing anything? I have not found you able to answer these questions; and I do not think other people find that you are able. Men who have to sorrow, and suffer, and work, may accept your help in improving their outward condition, but they do not accept your creed: it is nothing to them. Atheism is their natural and necessary refuge, if the only image of God presented to them is of One who allows men to be comfortable,—who is not angry with them,—who wishes all to be happy, but leaves them to make themselves and each other happy as well as they can. They can meditate the world almost as well without *such* a Being as with Him. I say this, because it is true, and because the truth should be spoken. God forbid that I should say for a moment that it is true for you. I know it is not. I know the vision you have of God is consolatory to you; that it would be a loss to all of you,—to some, a quite unspeakable loss,—to be deprived of it. Not for the world would I rob you of it, or of one iota of strength and comfort which you derive from it. Not for the world would I persuade you that your belief in a God of infinite Charity is not a precious and divine gift. But, remember!—*infinite* Charity. Charity is described as bearing all things, hoping all things, enduring all things. Any Charity which is not of this character, I am sure you would cast out of your scheme of ethics; you would feel it could not be an ideal for men to strive after; you do wish, in your own case, not to give barren phrases to your fellows, but to 'suffer with your suffering kind.' I have a right to claim, that you should not think more meanly of the God whom you condemn other sects for misrepresenting, than you do of an ordinarily benevolent hero, nay, than you do of yourselves. It is all I ask of you before we engage in our present inquiry.

You, again, who think that there is some important truth in the doctrines we confess, but are convinced that *we* hold the shell of it, while *you* are possessing, or at least seeking for, the kernel; and that no fellowship will ever exist among human beings till they have been persuaded to cast the shell away; you who support this sentiment by evidence, all too clear and authentic, drawn from the records of the controversies between Churchmen, and from the feebleness of their present condition; you who bid us always keep our eyes upon some good time coming, when such controversies will cease, and another kind of Church will emerge out of those which you tell us are crumbling into dust; you, I have asked what the substance is within the shell; and the best answer I have got is,—'a certain religious sentiment—a 'tendency, that is, or bias or aspiration of the soul towards 'something.' And that is—what? Is it known or unknown, real or fantastic, a Person or an abstraction? It is not a trifle to me whether I know or not; the world, too, is interested in the question. We cannot be told that our words and phrases are worthless, and then be put off with other words and phrases, which are certainly not more substantial. You declare aloud how divided Churches are: will you tell us what has prevented them from being wholly divided; what has kept the members of them from being always at war? Has it been a religious sentiment;—has it been a philosophical abstraction? Are you afraid to join with me in considering that question?

Lastly, you look for a better day, and a united Church:—so do I. But I want to know whether the foundation is laid on which that church is to stand, or whether it is to be laid; whether the Deliverer and Head of mankind has come, or whether we are to look for another? Your speculations have left me quite in the dark on this subject. I cannot bear the darkness. Shall we try if we can grope our way into the light?

ESSAY II.

ON SIN.

CLERGYMEN seem to take it for granted that their congregations understand what they mean when they speak of SIN. I am afraid some of us do not ourselves quite understand what we mean by it. Perhaps, if we would attend more to the doubts and objections of others, they might assist in clearing and deepening our own thoughts.

They frequently take this form: 'We find a number 'of crimes, outward, palpable, interfering with the 'existence of society; these we try to check by direct 'penalties. We find that these crimes may be traced 'to certain habits formed in the man, beginning to be 'formed in the child; these we try to extirpate by some 'moral influences. There is scope for infinite discussion 'as to the nature, measure, and right application, of 'these direct penalties, and these moral influences; as to 'the evils which most demand either. But scarcely any 'one doubts that both these methods are necessary; that 'there are disorders which need the one and not the 'other. It is different when a third notion is thrust 'upon us, one which we can refer to the head neither of 'Legislation nor of Ethics.

'The Theologian speaks of SIN. What is this? 'You say it is committed against God. Does God, then, 'want anything for His own use and honour? Does He 'crave services and sacrifices as due to Him? Is not 'doing justice and mercy to the fellow-creatures among 'whom He has placed us, the thing which He requires 'and which pleases Him? If not, where would you 'stop? Do not all Heathen notions, all the most into- 'lerable schemes of propitiation, all the most frightful 'inventions and lies by which the conscience of men 'has been defiled and their reason darkened, and from 'which crimes against society have at last proceeded, 'force themselves upon us at once? What charm is 'there in the name or word "Christianity" to keep 'them off, if they are, as we know they are, akin to ten- 'dencies which exist in all men, whatever names they 'bear, and which, for their sakes, need to be abated, if 'possible extinguished, certainly not fostered? But, if 'once we admit good feeling and good doing towards 'our neighbour to be the essence and fulfilment of God's 'commandments, why are not the ethical and legal con- 'ceptions of evil sufficient? What room is there for 'any other?'

Those of us who have had these thoughts, and have

expressed them, have probably heard answers which have satisfied us very ill. We have been told, perhaps, 'that the Commandments speak of a duty towards God 'as well as of a duty towards our neighbour; that there 'is no reason why He, from Whom we receive all things, 'should not demand something in return; that, *a priori*, 'we could not the least tell whether He would or not; 'that if He did, it would be reasonable to expect that 'He would enforce very heavy punishments upon our 'failure,—especially if it might have been avoided; 'that those punishments may be infinite,—at all events, 'that we can have no reason to allege why they should 'not be; that if we have any authority for supposing 'they will be so, we ought to do anything rather than 'incur so tremendous a risk.'

There is something in us all which resists these arguments. I believe great part of the resistance comes from conscience, not from self-will. There is a horror and heart-shrinking from the doctrine that we are to serve God because we are ignorant of His nature and character. There is a greater horror and heart-shrinking from the notion that we are to serve Him because, upon a fair calculation, it appears likely that this course will answer better than the opposite course, or that that will involve us in ruin. He who says, 'I cannot be religious 'on these terms,—it is my religion to repudiate them,' may not prize the Commandments very highly. He may look upon them merely as the words of an old

Jewish legislator. But he will at least feel that this legislator meant more by duty to God than his interpreters suppose him to mean, nay, meant something wholly and generically different from this. He may not acknowledge the name of Christ, or may attach to that name quite another signification from that which we attach to it: but he will at least be sure that Christ did not come into the world to tell men that they cannot know anything of their Father in Heaven; or that He is to be served for hire, or through dread of what He will do to them.

Most earnestly would I desire that each man should hold this conviction fast, that he should suffer no arguments of divines or of lay people, however plausible, to wrest it from him. And if he does not yet perceive any reality in the word 'Sin,' or in the thoughts which his teachers associate with it, by all means let him not feign that he does. For the sake of the sincerity of his mind, for the sake of the truth which may come to him hereafter, let him keep his ethical or his legal doctrine, if he really has some grasp of it, not exchange it for any that has a greater show and savour of divinity. But I would conjure him also, for the sake of the same sincerity, not to bar his soul against the entrance of another conviction, if it should come at any time with a very mighty power, because he is afraid that he may be receiving some old tenet of Theology which he has dreaded and hated. At some moment,—it may be one of weakness and sorrow, it may also be when he is full of energy, and is set upon a distinct and decided purpose, —he may be forced to feel; '*I* did this act, *I* thought 'this thought; it was a wrong act, it was a wrong 'thought, and it was *mine*. The world about me took 'no account of it. I can resolve it into no habits or 'motives; or if I can, the analysis does not help me in 'the least. Whatever the habit was, I wore the habit; 'whatever the motive was, I was the mover.' At such a moment there will rush in upon him a multitude of strange thoughts, of indefinite fears. There will come a sense of Eternity, dark, unfathomable, hopeless, such as he fancied he had left years behind him amidst the pictures of his nursery. That Eternity will stand face to face with him. It will look like anything but a picture, it will present itself to him as the hardest driest reality. There will be no *images* of torture and death. '*What matter where, if I be still the same?*'—this question will be the torture, all death lies in that. Yes, brother, such a death, that you will gladly fly from it to any devices which men have thought of for making their Gods gracious, to any penances which they have invented for the purpose of taking vengeance on themselves. These are all natural,—oh, how natural!—there is not one of them which the coldest, most unimaginative man may not have coveted; there are few which, in certain periods of confused restless anguish, he may not have believed would be worth a trial. And why?

Because anything is better than the presence of this dark self. I cannot bear to be dogged by that, night and day; to feel its presence when I am in company, and when I am alone; to hear its voice whispering to me,—'Whithersoever thou goest, I shall go. Thou wilt 'part with all things else, but not with me. There will 'come a day when thou canst wander out in a beautiful 'world no longer, when thou must be at home with me.'

This vision is more terrible than all which the fancy of priests has ever conjured up. He who has encountered it, is beginning to know what Sin is, as no words or definitions can teach it him. When once he arrives at the conviction, 'I am the tormentor,—Evil lies not in 'some accidents, but in me,' he is no more in the circle of outward acts, outward rules, outward punishments; he is no more in the circle of tendencies, inclinations, habits, and the discipline which is appropriate to them. He has come unawares into a more inward circle,—a very close, narrow, dismal one, in which he cannot rest, out of which he must emerge. And I am certain he can only emerge out of it when he begins to say, 'I have 'sinned against some Being, — not against society 'merely, not against my own nature merely, but against 'another to whom I was bound.' And the emancipation will not be complete till he is able to say,—giving the words their full and natural meaning,—'FATHER, I have 'sinned against *Thee.*'

I know there are some who will say, 'There is no

'occasion for a man ever to be brought into this strange 'sense of contradiction. He need not be thus confronted 'with himself: he need not see a dark image of Self be- 'hind him, before him, above him, beneath him. Very 'few people, in fact, do pass through this experience. 'Some of a particular constitution may. But how ab- 'surd it is of them to make themselves the standards for 'humanity! How monstrous, that a few metaphysicians 'or fanatics should lay down the law for all the busy 'men, the merchants, tradesmen, handicraftsmen, who 'get through the world, and must get through it some- 'how, without ever knowing anything of these torments 'of conscience, internal strifes, or by whatever other 'names philosophers or divines like to describe them!'

Very well! but were not you complaining—have you not a right to complain—of those priestly inventions which interfere so much with the peace of society, which interrupt the merchants and handicraftsmen in their employments, which beget so many horrors, especially such dreadful anticipations of divine punishment and vengeance, in human hearts? Is it not your object to sweep these away as fast as you can, because you find them so troublesome, taking so many different forms, reappearing when you least expect them, in periods and countries whence they seemed to have been driven for ever? Do you not complain that Christianity gives you no security, that Protestantism gives you no security, against the invasion of superstitious terrors, and against all the sacerdotal powers which are acknowledged where-ever they prevail? Do you not say that they interfere with the progress of science, and that science needs an aid against them, which neither itself, nor civil rulers, nor public opinion can give? Would it not be well, then, to look a little more deeply into the matter, and instead of raving at certain pernicious effects, to examine from what cause they may have sprung?

I tell you the cause is here. That sense of a Sin intricately, inseparably interwoven with the very fibres of their being, of a Sin which they cannot get rid of without destroying themselves, does haunt those very men who you say take no account of it. This is not the idiosyncrasy of a few strange inexplicable temperaments. It is that which besets us all. And because we do not know what it means, and do not wish to know, we are ready for all deceits and impostures. They may come in various shapes. They may be religious impostures, or philosophical; they may appeal to our love of the outward world, or to our craving for mysteries; but they will not permit us to be at rest, or to be acquainted with our own hearts, or to understand one another. All you can boast is, that preachers of religion have not a monopoly of these influences in this time; that here, as elsewhere, there is unrestricted competition; that Mormonists, Animal Magnetists, Rappists, take their turns with us, and often work their charms more effectually than we work ours. As long as men are dwelling in twilight, all ghosts of the past, all phantoms of the future, walk by them : I want to know, as I suppose you do, how they can come out of the twilight? The passage is the same, friend, for them, as for you and me ; we are not of different flesh and blood from theirs : that within us which is not flesh and blood is not more different, but more closely akin, whatever you, in your philosophical or literary or religious exclusiveness, may think. The darkness which is blended with the light must, in some way, be shown to be in deadly contrast with it,—the opposites must be seen one against the other.

Think of any sermon of a Methodist preacher which roused the heart of a Kingswood collier, or of a dry, hard, formal man, or of a contented, self-righteous boaster of his religion, in the last century. You will say the orator talked of an infinite punishment which God might inflict on them all if they continued disobedient. He may have talked of that, but he would have talked till doomsday if he had not spoken another language too, which interpreted this, and into which the conscience rapidly translated it. He spoke of an infinite *Sin :* he spoke of an infinite *Love :* he spoke of that which was true then, whatever might become true hereafter. He said, 'Thou art in a wrong state : hell is about thee. God 'would bring thee into a right state : He would save 'thee out of that hell.' The man believed the words ; something within him told him they were true : and that for the first time he had heard truth, seen truth, been himself true. I cannot tell what vanities and confusions might come to him afterwards, from his own dreams or the crudities of his teachers. But I am sure this was not a delusion—could not be. He *had* escaped from the twilight : he *had* seen the opposite forms of light and darkness no longer miserably confused together. Good was all good ; evil was all evil : there was war in heaven and earth between them ; in him, even in him, where the battle had been fiercest, the odds against the good greatest, good had gotten the victory. He had a right to believe that the morning stars were singing together at the news of it; otherwise, why was there such music in his, the Kingswood collier's, heart?

If such processes are rare in our days, it is, I believe, because the descendants of these Methodist preachers, and we in imitation of them, fancy that the mere machinery, whether earthly or divine, which they put in motion, was the cause of them,—because we do not thoroughly understand or heartily believe that there is that war of Life and Death, of Good and Evil, now in every man's heart, as there was of old. Therefore, we do not speak straightly and directly to both. We suppose men are to be shown by arguments that they have sinned, and that God has a right to punish them. We do not say to them, 'You are under a law of love; you know 'you are, and you are fighting with it.'

Benevolent men wish that the poor should know

more of Legislation and Ethics and Economy. I wish heartily that they should. But I believe that you will never bring them to that knowledge unless you can point them to the deeper springs of humanity, from which both Ethics and Laws and Economics must be fed, if they are to have any freshness and life. I do not think it dangerous that any man should get any knowledge of any subject whatever; the more he has the better. And I often think, that what is sincerely communicated to him of Economics or Physics, may bring him sooner to a right moral condition,—may startle him into apprehensions respecting his own being, sooner,—than insincere artificial theological teaching. But yet I cannot help seeing also, that Legislation, Ethics, Economics, even Physical Science, may themselves contribute to the foundation of superstitions, if the man is not first called into life to receive them and to connect them with himself. I am sure, at all events, that an infinite responsibility rests upon *us*,—not to be interfering with other men, or to be checking their efforts, whatever direction they may take,—but to be calling forth, by that power which, I believe, we possess, if we will use it, the heart and conscience of men, so that being first able to see their Father in Heaven truly, and themselves in their true relation to Him, they may afterwards manfully investigate, as I am sure they will long to do, the conditions under which they themselves, His children, exist, and the laws which govern all His works. I am convinced, indeed, that the message will be, in some respects, different from that which the Methodists delivered, even when theirs is stripped of all its foreign and enfeebling accidents. Men are evidently more alive now to their social than to their individual wants; they are therefore more awake to the evils which affect society, than to those which affect their own souls. To him who merely, or mainly, preaches about the soul, this is a most discouraging circumstance, —to him whose purpose is to awaken men to a knowledge of God and a knowledge of Sin, it need not be discouraging at all.

For if God presents Himself to us as the Father of a Family, it is not necessary for the knowledge of Him, that we should force ourselves to forget our relations to each other, and to think of ourselves as alone in the world. And though, as I have admitted and asserted, the sense of Sin is essentially the sense of solitude, isolation, distinct individual responsibility, I do not know whether that sense, in all its painfulness and agony, ever comes to a man more fully than when he recollects how he has broken the silken cords which bind him to his fellows; how he has made himself alone, by not confessing that he was a brother, a son, a citizen. I believe the conviction of that Sin may be brought home more mightily to our generation than it has been to any former one; and that a time will come, when every family and every man will mourn apart, under a sense of the strife and divisions of the body politic, which he has contributed to create and to perpetuate. The preaching *Repent, for the Kingdom of Heaven is at hand*, has always been the great instrument of levelling hills and exalting valleys. It will be so again. The priest and the prophet will confess that they have been greater rebels against the law of love than the publican and the harlot, because they were sent into the world to testify of a Love for all, and a Kingdom for all, and they have been witnesses for separation, for exclusion, for themselves.

My Unitarian brother! You believe that, at least, respecting us. You have often told us so. And how is it *you* have no power to work on the minds and hearts of men, and to convince them of God's love, when, as you say rightly, we are forgetting or denying it? How is it, that in the last age you were in sympathy with all our feeble worldly tone of mind, and thought we were right in mocking at spiritual powers, and in not proclaiming a Gospel to the poor? Why did you talk just as we talked, in sleepy language to sleepy congregations, of a God who was willing to forgive if men repented, when what they wanted to know was, how they could repent, who could give them repentance, what they had to repent of? You had a mighty charm in your hands. You spoke of a Father. Why could you not tell men that He was seeking them, and wishing to make them true instead of false? You did not, you know you did not. Why was it? I beseech you, do not turn round and say, 'You were as guilty as we.' I have said already, 'We 'were much more guilty.' Every creed we professed, every prayer we uttered, told us that this Father was an actual Father, actually related to us by the closest, most intimate bonds. We did not believe much of those creeds and prayers; you wished us to believe less than we did. Thank God, neither you nor we could get rid of the witnesses which He had established, or of the deep necessities which corresponded to them. The earnest preachers of the day beat us both, because they believed in a Father, while we repeated His name, and you argued to prove that He was the One God.

And now you have, many of you, changed your language. You see that there is a spiritual power in the world; these preachers have proved that there is. You point out powerfully and skilfully, what dull, drowsy priests we were who denied it. But you say that those who asserted it were narrow, that they are worn out, that spiritual power is much more widely at work than they supposed, that it is to be felt everywhere. Be it so,—the lesson is most impressive; we accept it. But why are you still powerless? why cannot you stir the hearts of the people by your message more than your fathers did? Why must it be proclaimed, not exactly like theirs, in the ears of comfortable merchants and dowagers wanting a not too troublesome religion,—but at least in the ears of those chiefly, who crave for some new thing, not of those who are hungering and thirsting for life? The secret of both failures seems to me this. You, of the older school, knew something of transgression; almost nothing of Sin. But the transgression was of a rule rather than of a law; breaches of social etiquette and propriety, at most uncomely and unkind habits, seemed to compose all the evils you took account of, which did not appear in the shape of crimes. Those who must be treated, not as members of some class of men, but as men, have no ears for discourses about conventions and behaviour; if you cannot penetrate below these, you must leave them alone. You who believe in spiritual powers, do you yet acknowledge spiritual evil? Can you speak to us as persons? Can you tell me of myself; what I am; who is for me, who is against me? I have not found that you can. You have a religion for us, I know, apparently a graceful and a refined one. It is a luxury, if we can afford it. But we have an enemy who tries to deprive us even of necessaries. Unless you can teach us how to procure them, in spite of him, I and my fellow-fighters must for the present let your religion alone.

ESSAY III.

ON THE EVIL SPIRIT.

I SUPPOSE if any of us met with a treatise which professed to discuss the Origin of Evil, our first and most natural impulse would be, to throw it aside. 'The 'man must have great leisure,' we should say, 'or be 'very youthful, who could occupy himself with such a 'subject as this. After six thousand years' experience 'of Evil, and almost as many of hopeless controversy 'about its source, we may as well reckon that among 'the riddles which men are not to solve, and pass to 'something else.'

The resolution may be a wise one, as far as it relates to discussions philosophical or theological upon this topic. Possibly the chief good they have done is, that they have shown how little they can do; that they have proved how inadequate school logic is for the necessities of human life. But if we supposed, when we closed the book, that we had done with the question which it raised and which it tried to settle; if we thought it would not meet us again in the law-court and the market-place, and mix itself, most inconveniently, in all the common business of the world,—a little experience will have shown us that we were mistaken. We *must* consider the origin of Evil, whether we like it or not. We are debating it with ourselves, we are conversing about it with others, we are acting on some conclusions we have formed about it, every day of our lives. Take a few instances.

1. A man cannot help perceiving that the climate he is living in has some influence on himself, and upon all who are about him. It is an influence which directly affects his body, but it does not stop there; through this, it acts in a number of ways upon his thoughts and his habits. If it affects him less or more than others, the difference is caused by a difference of temperament; *that* must be set down as another influence which requires to be taken account of; one of which the workings are great, and in various directions. Add the conditions of luxury, mediocrity, or poverty, into which he is born, and he is conscious of a whole system of agencies working upon him from childhood upwards, modifying apparently, if not determining, his wishes, conceptions, purposes. He has not yet calculated the effect of association upon him, even taking that word in its simplest narrowest sense, to express his intercourse with his brothers, sisters, schoolfellows. If he enlarges the

word to comprehend all that he has received from the atmosphere of his country and his age, he may become well-nigh overwhelmed. For he begins to think what shape his moral code might have taken, if he had been born within certain degrees of latitude. He asks himself whether he should not almost certainly have been a Roman Catholic, if his lot had been cast in any part of the south of Europe;—a Hindoo or a Buddhist, or perhaps something worse, if he had grown up in some of the finest regions of Asia. Without plunging into these speculations, there is the obvious and undeniable operation of those who have educated him; the operation of all the thoughts, feelings, and habits, which had descended upon *them* from their instructors and ancestors.

These are but a few items in an enormous calculation, a few hints which might be expanded indefinitely. What is the result? As some evil tendency or temper, which exists in him, forces itself upon his notice, or is forced upon him by the criticisms and admonitions of others, he refers it to some of these circumstances by which he is hemmed in. Has he not a right to do so? Can he not prove his case? That effeminate, slothful disposition, —cannot he explain to himself clearly, what early indulgence, what ill-health, what inherited morbidness begot it in him? That gambling fever which is consuming him, does not he know where it was caught, who gave him the infection? That loss of truth in words and deeds, cannot he trace it up to frauds practised on him in the nursery; cannot he almost fix on the hour, the moment, when one of them seemed to undermine his soul and make it false? But for riches, would he have been so hard and indifferent to others? But for poverty and successive disappointments, would he have been so sour and envious?

In this way we reason about ourselves; we deliberately assign an origin to the evil within us; can we refuse the advantage of the same plea to our fellows? Do we not blush when we tell any man, 'You ought to have 'been so different?' Have not a thousand influences that we know acted upon him for evil, which have not acted upon us? May there not have been tens of thousands which we do not know? Our practical conclusion, if we are charitable, is, that we must make great allowances for him: his circumstances have been, or may have been very unpropitious; may not much of his wrong-doing be owing to these? Here we seem to be extending a doctrine concerning the origin of evil to men generally.

And if we are aroused to exertion respecting ourselves or our brethren, it appears as if we directly applied this doctrine to practice. We fly from old associations, we bring new ones about us; we assume that those who have erred will not be better unless we can give them a different education, another social position, positive restraints imposed by us, opportunities for restraining themselves, freedom from some shackles which appear to have operated injuriously. We do not scruple, any of us, to say that there are forms of government and forms of belief which we wish to see destroyed, because we suppose individual morality can scarcely exist under their shadow.

From these data it is not wonderful that some persons, anxious to set the world right, should have generalized the conclusion, that all evil has its origin in circumstances; that when you make *them* good, you make men good. It is not wonderful that they should strive to point out how the first object may be accomplished here and everywhere; how the second is necessarily involved in it. We must submit to be charged by them with great logical inconsistency, for going with them so far, and yet stopping short at what seems to them the inevitable consequence.

2. There is one great hindrance to the acknowledgment of that consequence; perhaps to some persons it is the only one. They cannot persuade themselves that human creatures would receive so many evil impressions from the surrounding world, if there was not in them some great capacity for such impressions. They cannot suppose that the bad circumstances produce the susceptibility to which they appeal, however they may increase it. How, they ask, did the circumstances become bad? Perhaps the elements are good, but they are ill-combined. What produced that bad combination? Who put them out of order? Or there is some one of them that was

bad and disturbed the rest. That one must have become so, independently of its circumstances. 'There 'must,' they say, 'be some evil, which was not made so 'by the accidents that invested it; you will be involved 'in a wearisome circle, an endless series of contradic- 'tions, if you do not admit this. And if you do, is it 'not more reasonable,' they ask, 'to say that this evil 'belongs to the very nature of man, that it is a corrup- 'tion of blood? Will not that account both for the 'growth of bad circumstances and for the reaction of 'them upon you, upon us, upon all? Confess that the 'infection you speak of is in us all, confess that we are 'members of a depraved race, and you can explain all 'the phænomena you take notice of; on any other 'hypothesis they are incomprehensible.'

This view of the origin of Evil is also pregnant with practical consequences; it never can become a mere theory. It must lead all who hold it to inquire, whether this corruption is necessary and hopeless, or may be cured; whether the cure may come by the destruction of the substance in which it dwells, or whether that may be reformed: in either case, what the seat of the malady is, how the amputation may be effected or the new blood poured in, and the man himself survive. The world's history is full of the most serious and terrible answers to these questions,—answers attesting how real and radical the difficulty was which suggested them. 'The disease 'is in my body, this flesh, this accursed matter;'—here was one often-repeated, never-exhausted reply; 'the 'flesh must be destroyed; till it is destroyed, I can 'never be better.' All the macerations and tortures of Indian devotees had this justification. 'No, it is not 'there; it is in the soul that you are corrupted and 'fallen; the body is but the tool and handmaid of its 'offences;'—that was another, seemingly a more hopeful conclusion. And this soul must try to recover itself, must seek again the high and glorious position which was once its own. By what ladder? 'It must think 'high thoughts of itself; it must not allow itself to be 'crushed and overpowered by low bestial instincts, it 'must refuse to be degraded by the mere animals in the 'form of men, among whom it dwells.' This was one prescription. 'Ah, no!' said the mystic, after bitter trial of that method; 'it must not rise, but sink; the 'soul must desire annihilation for itself; till it dies, it 'will never know what life is.'

These conclusions, we might fancy, affected only a few individuals. Oh no! the whole society in which they are found, is coloured and shaped by them. I do not deny that there may come a time when they may lose their power, when the large mass of notions and practices which they have created through a series of ages may begin to upheave, when a general unbelief may take the place of an all-embracing credulity. But out of that unbelief you will see forms arising which will prove that the old notions are not dead; that they cannot die.

They are about you while you are despising them; they are within you while you are denying them; if you can find no clue to them, no explanation of them, they will still darken your hearts and the face of the whole universe.

3. This is equally true, I believe, of another, an older, we may think quite an obsolete, method of accounting for the existence of Evil. The belief in Evil Spirits, in Powers of Darkness, to which the bodies and spirits of men are subject, which haunt particular places, which hold their assemblies at certain times, which claim certain men as their lieges, from whose assaults none are free: this belief we may often have been inclined to look upon as the most degrading and despicable of all, from which a sounder knowledge of physics and of the freaks and the capacities of the human imagination, has delivered us. Are we sure that the deliverance has been effected? Are we sure that fears of an invisible world,—of a world not to come, but about us,—are extinct, or that they may not rush in with great force upon rich and luxurious people, as much as upon the poorest and the least instructed? Are we sure that they may not press the discoveries of physical science, and the possibilities of the vast undiscovered regions above and beneath to which it points us, into their service? Are we sure that all our discoveries, or supposed discoveries, respecting the spiritual world within us, may not be equally appealed

to in confirmation of a new demoniac system? Are we sure that the very enlightenment, which says it has ascertained Christian stories to be legends, will not be enlisted on the same side, because if we will only believe *these* facts, it will be so easy to show how *those* falsities may have originated?

And why is this belief at least as potent as either of the others, often mixing with them and giving them a new character? Because there is in men a sense of bondage to some power which they feel that they should resist and cannot. Because that feeling of the 'ought,' and the 'cannot,' is what forces, not upon scholars, but upon the poorest men, the question of the freedom of the will, and bids them seek some solution of it. Has not every one wondered that the deepest problem in metaphysics, the one which so many professional metaphysicians relinquish as desperate, that respecting which divines cry out in pulpits, 'Ask nothing, it is so hard; 'there is some truth in each view of it,'—should exercise and torment peasants in ten thousand ways; that they should have listened, as they did when Covenanters and Puritans were preaching, to the most elaborate as well as the most startling expositions of it; that if they cannot have the knot untied for them, they always find some intelligible superstition wherewith to cut it? Oh! let us give over our miserable notion that poor men only want teaching about things on the surface, or will ever be satisfied with such teaching! They are groping about the roots of things, whether we know it or not. You must meet them in their underground search, and show them the way into daylight, if you want true and brave citizens, not a community of dupes and quacks. You may talk against devilry as you like; you will not get rid of it unless you can tell human beings whence comes that sense of a tyranny over their own very selves, which they express in a thousand forms of speech, which excites them to the greatest, often the most profitless, indignation against the arrangements of this world, which tempts them to people it and heaven also, with objects of terror and despair.

Here then are three schemes of the universe, all developed out of the observation of facts, or, if you like that form of speech better, out of the consciousness of men, all leading to serious results affecting our well-being in this as well as in other periods of history. Each has given birth to theories of divinity, as well as to a very complicated anthropology. They show no symptoms of reconciliation; yet they exist side by side, and gather new votaries from various quarters, as well as new confirmation from each of these votaries. Shall we ask what Christian Theology, not according to any new conception of it, but according to the statements which have embodied themselves in creeds, and are most open to the censures of modern refinement, says of them?

1. First, then,—there is no disguising it,—the assertion

stands broad and patent in the four Gospels, construed according to any ordinary rules of language;—the acknowledgment of an Evil Spirit is *characteristic* of Christianity. I do not, of course, mean, that the dread of such a Spirit did not exist in every part of the world, before the Incarnation of our Lord. Powers which are plotting mischief against men, enter into every heathen religion; gradually those religions came to signify little else than the conciliation of such powers; in the highest civilization of the Roman Empire, when unbelief in the Divine had become habitual, the fear of the devilish expressed itself in a devotion to magic and prophecy, which was as real as the devotion of frivolous people can be. The Jew was taught, throughout all his history, that there were enemies within as well as without, who were contending against him. He realized the conviction in his prayers to the God of his fathers. He could not believe that Philistines or Moabites were tormenting him in his chamber. He learnt that the secret impalpable enemies there, were his country's tyrants, even more than the visible ones. The Pharisee of later times, with no feelings for his country except as it reflected his vanity or ministered to his contempt of others, wrapt up in the desire to get what he could for himself in this world and the next, had wrought out of the hints which the living men of former days supplied him, a very extensive Demonology. Beelzebub, the prince of the devils, occupied a large place in his theory; *he* could always be resorted to for the explanation of any more than usually startling difficulty. And this being was unconsciously becoming the object of Jewish worship. All his features were gradually transferred by the imagination of the self-seeker to the God of Abraham.

When then I speak of the belief in the existence and presence of an Evil Spirit as characteristic of the Gospels, I mean this:—that in them first the idea of a spirit directly and absolutely opposed to the Father of Lights, to the God of absolute goodness and love, bursts full upon us. There first we are taught, that it is not merely something in peculiarly evil men which is contending against the good and the true; no, nor something in all men: that God has an antagonist, and that all men, bad or good, have the same. There, first, this antagonist presents himself to us, altogether as a spirit, with no visible shape or clothing whatsoever; there first the belief that Evil may be a rival creator, or entitled to some worship,—a belief, which every reformer in the old world had spent his life in struggling with,—is utterly put to flight; the vision of a mere destroyer, a subverter of order, who is seeking continually to make us disbelieve in the Creator, to forsake the order that we are in, takes place of every other. With these discoveries another is always connected; that this tempter speaks to me, to myself, to the will; that over *that* he has established his tyranny; that there his chains must be broken; but that all things in nature, with the soul and the body, have partaken, and do partake, of the slavery to which the man himself has submitted.

I simply state these propositions; I am not going to defend them. If they cannot defend themselves, by the light which they throw on the anticipations and difficulties of the human spirit, by the hint of deliverance which they offer it, by the horrible dreams which they scatter, my arguments would be worth nothing. But I am bound to show how this part of the divine revelation affects those two other hypotheses of which I spoke first.

2. That there is a pravity or depravity in every man, and that this pravity or depravity is felt through his whole nature, the Gospel does not assert as a principle of Theology, but concedes as an undoubted and ascertained fact of experience, which no one who contemplates man or the universe can gainsay. What it does theologically with reference to that experience is this;—as it confesses an Evil Spirit whose assaults are directed against the Will in man, it forbids us ever to look upon any disease of our nature as the ultimate cause of transgression. The horrible notion, which has haunted moralists, divines, and practical men, that pravity is the law of our being, and not the perpetual tendency to struggle against the law of our being, it discards and anathematises. By setting forth the Spirit of selfishness as *the* enemy of man, it explains, in perfect coincidence with our experience, wherein this pravity

consists; that it is the inclination of every man to set up himself, to become his own law and his own centre, and so to throw all society into discord and disorder. It thus explains the conviction of the devotee and the mystic that the body must die, and that the soul must die. Self being the plague of man, in some most wonderful sense *he* must die, that he may be delivered from his pravity. And yet neither body nor soul can be in itself evil. Each is in bondage to some evil power. If there is a God of Order mightier than the Destroyer, body and soul must be capable of redemption and restoration.

3. And thus this Theology comes in contact with that wide-spread and most plausible creed, which attributes all evil to circumstances. Every one of the facts from which this creed is deduced, it fully admits. Every husband, father, ruler, brings his own quota of selfishness to swell the general stock. It accumulates from age to age. The sins of the fathers are visited upon the children, to the third and fourth generation. The idolatrous habit, the sensual habit, goes on propagating itself, so that the cry,

> Ætas parentum, pejor avis, tulit
> Nos nequiores, mox daturos
> Progeniem vitiosiorem,

is the ordinary complaint of intelligent observers. And because it is so, the prudential alleviations of the evil to which, as I admitted, we all do and must resort, have the highest justification in principle. Take away from a man all the injurious influences that it is possible to take away; not because circumstances are his rightful masters, but because these influences lead him to think that they are, and to act as if they were. Take them away that he may know what has robbed him of his freedom, whose yoke needs to be broken if he is not always to be a slave. And since the man soon discovers,—since his worship of circumstances is itself an acknowledgment of the discovery,—that the tyranny which is over him is a tyranny over his whole race, we shall never give him any clearness of mind, or any hope, unless we can tell him that the Spirit of Selfishness is the common enemy, and that he has been overcome.

I cannot be ignorant, that in this Essay I have encountered one of the most deeply rooted aversions in the minds of Unitarians. They have always regarded the doctrine of the existence and personality of the Devil as the least tenable figment of orthodox theology. They scarcely think that any one who professes to hold it, in the present day, can be sincere. They are very tolerant, can give us credit for much invincible ignorance; but they do not believe that any man in the nineteenth century is quite fool enough for that.

I perfectly understand this feeling. I know that it is very widely diffused. I shrink with instinctive cowardice from saying, 'I maintain this dogma.' I should like exceedingly to hide it under some respectable periphrasis. I will tell you why I cannot. I believe that some of what seem to me the hardest, most mischievous theories of our modern popular divinity,—those which shock the moral sense and reason of men most, those which most undermine the belief in God's infinite charity,—arise from this timidity, of which I am conscious myself, and which I see in my brethren. When men in the old time would have said bravely, meaning what they said, 'We are engaged in a warfare with 'an Evil Spirit, *he* is trying to separate us from God, to 'make us hate our brethren,' *we* talk of the depravity of our nature, of the evil we have inherited from Adam. Now that every child of Adam has this infection of nature, I most entirely and inwardly believe. But to say that this infection forces us to commit sin, is to say what the Jews of old said,—what the Prophets denounced as the most flagrant denial of God,—*We are delivered to do all these abominations.* And it is the *very* close approximation which we make in some of our popular statements to this detestable heresy, which has called forth an indignant and a righteous protest from many classes of our countrymen, the Unitarians being in some sort the spokesmen for the rest. When we try to avoid this censure, it is by the very feeble and pusillanimous course of introducing modifications into the broad phrases with which we started, modifications that make them mean almost nothing. We maintain the 'absolute, universal, all-pervading depravity' of human nature; but then there are 'beautiful relics of the divine image,' 'fallen columns,' &c.;—pretty metaphors, no doubt; but who wants metaphors on a subject of such solemn and personal interest? Who can bear them when they reduce assertions, which we were told had the most profound signification, into mere nonentities?

What is pravity or depravity,—affix to it the epithets universal, absolute, or any you please,—but an inclination to something which is not right, an inclination to turn away from that which is right, that which is the true and proper state of him who has the inclination? What is it that experiences the inclination; what is it that provokes the inclination? I believe it is the spirit within me which feels the inclination: I believe it is a Spirit speaking to my spirit, who stirs up the inclination. That old way of stating the case explains the facts, and commends itself to my reason. I cannot find any other which does not conceal some facts, and does not outrage my reason. And of this I am sure, that when I have courage to use this language, as the expression of a truth which concerns me and every man, the whole battle of life becomes infinitely more serious to me, and yet more hopeful; because I cannot believe in a Spirit which is tempting me into falsehood and evil, without believing that God is a Spirit, and that I am bound to Him, and that He is attracting me to truth and goodness.

And thus another very unsightly, and to me quite portentous, imagination of modern divines, is shown to be utterly inconsistent with the faith which we and our forefathers have professed. There is said to have been a war in the Divine mind between Justice and Mercy. We are told that a great scheme was necessary to bring these qualities into reconciliation. When I attribute this doctrine to modern divines, I do not affirm that there may not be very frequent traces of it in the argumentative discourses of old divines; but I mean that, with the strong belief which they had, that an Evil Spirit was drawing them away both from mercy and righteousness,—was tempting them to be both unjust and hard-hearted—they had a practical witness against any notion of this kind, which we have lost, or are losing. They could not but feel that to be in a healthful moral state, they must be both just and merciful; that there must be a perfect unity and harmony between these qualities; that whatever puts them in seeming division, comes from the Evil Spirit; that it is treason to ascribe to the archetypal mind that which destroys the purity of the image. The God who was to deliver them from this strife, could not Himself be the subject of it. I believe, then, that the change which the Unitarians perceive in us, and which they consider the blessed effect of civilization and progress upon minds naturally averse from either, has introduced darkness into our views of God, feebleness into our struggles for good as men. As soon as we return to the practical faith of the old teachers, we shall fling their theories and our own to the winds when they interfere with the absolute righteousness and love of God; we shall know that there must be an All-Good on the one side, or that we shall be at the mercy of the All-Evil on the other.

And now, having applied this principle to our own condemnation, I have a right to turn round upon the Unitarian and ask him, whether the same causes are not at work upon him as upon us. I complained in my first Essay that the Unitarians of the last century substituted a mere amiable, good-natured Being, for a God of perfect Charity. I referred in the last to their superficial notions respecting Sin. I said that they could not tell us anything about the actual conflict of life; that the deepest wants of which human beings are conscious were unknown to them; that they could only teach us to preserve quietness and propriety, when there is little to ruffle the air or the sea. Is not that refinement which will not face the fact of an Evil Spirit,—the scorn of such a belief as vulgar,—at the root of a weakness which is alienating not merely other men, but the youthful and earnest members of their own sect, from them?

For these younger men, I know, do confess the reality of spiritual conflicts. Bunyan's 'Pilgrim's Progress' they regard as a book of great significance. They have no doubt that Christian must, in some sense, fight with

Apollyon. 'And who,' they ask, 'can object to an 'allegory which clothes so much of real experience in 'a robe of fantasy? Of course,' they continue, 'you 'would not take the whole of that story for gospel, 'would you? And if we are quite willing to take what 'is universal in it apart from its old Hebrew drapery, 'what more do you want? We allow there are abysses 'and eternities, with which men have to do,—valleys of 'the shadow of death, if you like that language. When 'you speak of the Devil, we suppose you mean that, or 'a conceit of your own, or a dream of the past.'

One word, dear friends, only one word, just that we may understand each other. If you *do* maintain the universal truth which lies in that story of Apollyon, I am thoroughly content: let all the outsides pass for what they are worth; let them be acknowledged as the mere dress suitable to a story, not to fact; to the seventeenth century, not to the nineteenth. But mark, it is the *outside* which I give up; to the inside I hold fast. I am very sorry to say, that these eternities and abysses of yours look to me very like outsides, mere drapery; the fashionable dialect of a certain not very earnest, rather fantastic, period. The dress of the old people being stripped off, as we are agreed it shall be, there remains—what? The history of some mental process, no doubt;—but the nature of the process? Is it a shadow-fight? Is it a game of blacks and whites, the same hand moving both? These are questions of some importance to the sincerity of our acts and thoughts. I tell you plainly you have not resolved them, as I have a right to demand, on my own behalf and on behalf of my kind, that they should be resolved. And though I would not for the world that you should anticipate by one hour the decision of your own consciences upon them; though I honour you for not adopting phrases of ours, or of the Bible, which do not express something substantial to you; yet I cannot conceal my conviction, the result of my own experience, that your minds will be in a simpler, healthier state, that you will win a victory over some of the most plausible conventionalisms of this age, that you will grasp the truth you have more firmly, and be readier to receive any you have not yet apprehended, when you have courage to say, 'We do verily believe that we have a world, and a flesh, and a DEVIL, to fight with.'

And before you believe it, or know that you do, I shall claim you as men who are actually engaged in this struggle, and I shall go on to show, that in your heart, as much as in mine, there is a witness for righteousness and truth, which world, and flesh, and Devil, have been unable to silence.

ESSAY IV.

ON THE SENSE OF RIGHTEOUSNESS IN MEN, AND THEIR DISCOVERY OF A REDEEMER.

Every thoughtful reader of the book of Job must have been struck by two characteristics of it, which seem, at first sight, altogether inconsistent. The suffering man has the most intense personal sense of his own evil. He makes also the most vehement, repeated, passionate, protestations of his own righteousness. It cannot be pretended that he defends his innocence as far as men are concerned, but that he confesses himself guilty in the sight of God. On the contrary, he appeals again and again from men to God. He calls for His judgment. He longs to go and plead before Him. There would have been no need of clearing himself before a human tribunal. His friends do not, as it has been customary to say, attack him. They try, in their way, to console him. They are as much astonished at the vehemence of his self-accusations as they are shocked at his self-righteousness. They are quite convinced that God is ready to forgive those who make their prayer to Him. That is what they would do, if they had fallen into Job's calamities. The ancients, who were much wiser than he or they, have assured them that it is the right course. Why does not the stricken man take it? Why does he indulge in such dreadful wailings, which must be offensive to the Judge who has afflicted him? Above all, how dares he talk, as if a man might be just before God? How could he, who complained that he possessed the sins of his youth, nevertheless declare, that there was a purity and a truth in him, which the Searcher of all hearts would at last acknowledge? What did this contradiction mean? How could he justify it against all their precedents and arguments?

He could not justify it at all. The contradiction was there. He felt it, he uttered it, he found in it the secret of his anguish. He could only tell his friends: 'Your precedents and your arguments do not clear it 'away in the least. I knew them all before. I could 'have poured them out upon you if you had been in 'my case. But when one is brought face to face with 'suffering, they prove to be mere wind. These words 'of yours buzz about me, torment me, sometimes leave 'their stings in me, but they have nothing to do with 'me. They do not show me where I am wrong and 'where I am right. I am before a Judge who does not 'appear to recognise your maxims and modes of procedure. Oh! that I might order my cause before Him!'

Nor was it only the self-righteousness of Job which

shocked Eliphaz, and Bildad, and Zophar. Their theory of the nature of pain was also thoroughly outraged by his language. I do not see any proof that they thought it merely a judgment from God for his transgressions. They would have been quite willing to call it, as we do, a merciful visitation. What offends them is, that Job groans under it as if it were an evil, that he seems to speak of it as if it came from an enemy. How can this be? Did not God send it? Is not all this suffering permitted, even ordained, by Him? What possible right can a poor creature, a worm of the earth, have to remonstrate and complain that anything is amiss?

Again it is clear that the friends have the advantage. Job cannot at all explain how it is that pain should seem to him so very intolerable, and yet that it should be from God. It is the secret he wants to discover. But the demands for submission which his friends make upon him are not the least helps to the discovery. He cannot satisfy these demands; he cannot do what they tell him to do. He must and will cry out. He is sure that all is not right, let them pretend to think so, as much as they will. This pain, however it may have come to him, is an evil. No one shall force him to belie his conscience by saying that it is a good.

It does not appear from the story that, in either of these points, Job grows into more consent with their opinion, as his discipline becomes more severe and his experience greater. His confidence that he has a righteousness, a real substantial righteousness, which no one shall remove from him, which he will hold fast and not let go, waxes stronger as his pain becomes bitterer and more habitual. There are great alternations of feeling. The deepest acknowledgments of sin come forth from his heart. But he speaks as if his righteousness were deeper and more grounded than that. Sin cleaves very close to him; it seems as if it were part of himself, almost as if it were himself. But his righteousness belongs to him still more entirely. However strange the paradox, it is more *himself* than even that is. He must express that conviction, he does express it, though he knows, better than any one can tell him, how much it is at variance with what he had been thinking and saying the moment before.

So also of the suffering. He has wonderful intuitions, ever and anon, of the mercy and goodness of God. He believes that He is trying him, and that He will bring him forth out of the fires. And yet, why does this happen to him? What is it all for? He will not cheat God and outrage His truth, by uttering soft phrases which set at nought the conviction of his heart. There is that about him from which he feels that he ought to be delivered, an anguish of body and soul, which he cannot reconcile with the goodness he yet clings to and trusts in.

There comes a moment in the life of Job when these two thoughts, the thought of a righteousness within him which is mightier than the evil, the thought of some deliverance from his suffering which should be also a justification of God, are brought together in his mind. He exclaims, '*I know that my Redeemer 'liveth; in my flesh shall I see God, whom I shall 'see for myself, and mine eyes shall behold, and not 'another*.'* He expects that this Redeemer will stand at the latter day upon the earth. But he evidently does not rest upon an expectation. It is not what this Redeemer may be or may do hereafter he chiefly thinks of. He lives. He is with him now. Therefore he calls upon his friends to say whether they do not see that he has the root of the matter in him.

At length, we are told, God answers Job out of the

* The force of this passage, as I understand it, is not in the least affected by the question whether the word 'Redeemer' should be exchanged for 'the Avenger of Blood.' I do not quote Job to prove a future state, or anything relating to a future state. The idea of an Avenger is inseparably connected with that of a Redeemer; he who believes there is one, believes there is the other. I make this remark in especial reference to an eloquent article on the book of Job, which has appeared in the *Westminster Review*, since the first edition of these Essays was published. To a great part of that article I must object, as containing what seems to me a wrong statement of facts. I cannot find, as I have explained more at large in my Sermons on the Old Testament, that the Jewish Scriptures exhibit that theory about Prosperity and Adversity which the Reviewer attributes to them. Every one of the heroes of the history, Joseph, Moses, David, is a sufferer. The chosen people is a suffering people. But this difference between us does not affect the Reviewer's interpretation of the text to which I have alluded. I am quite content that he should demolish any formal argument which has been deduced from it; its practical and spiritual significance become thereby the more apparent.

whirlwind. He shows him a depth of wisdom in the flight of every bird and in the structure of every insect, which he cannot dive into. He shows him an order which he is sure is very good though he is lost in it. Then he says, 'I have heard of Thee by the 'hearing of the ear; but now mine eye seeth Thee. 'Wherefore I abhor myself, and repent in dust and 'ashes.' A wonderful conclusion follows. God justifies the complaining man more than those who had pleaded so earnestly for His power and providence. They are forgiven when *he* prays for them. And the last days of Job are better than the beginning.

The early passages in the book of Job respecting Satan seem to anticipate what I said was especially New Testament theology. They do so only, I believe, because the story is more simply human, less Jewish, than any in the Old Testament. Job is represented as living outside of the limits within which the posterity of Abraham was confined. No words are used to identify him with them, or to show that he possessed any of the privileges with which their covenant and history invested them. We have here, therefore, what is at least meant to be a history of human experience. Whether it is biographical or dramatical, or, as I conceive, both, this must be the intention of it. Job is shown, and we are shown, by an *experimentum crucis*, what in him is merely accidental, what belongs to him as a man. Christendom has received the book in this sense. Doctors have taken pains to illustrate it, and have left it much as they found it. Plain, suffering men have understood it with all its difficulties much better than the most simple tracts written expressly for their use. You will see bedridden women, just able to make out the letters of it, feeding on it, and finding themselves in it. You will hear men who regard our Theology as a miserable attempt to form a theory of the universe, expressing their delight in this one of our theological books, because it so nobly and triumphantly casts theories of the universe to the ground. How it squares with our hypotheses they cannot imagine, but it certainly answers to the testimony of their hearts.

And I believe most clergymen, most religious persons, who have conversed at all seriously with men of any class, from the most refined to the most ignorant, in any state of mind, from that of the most contented Pharisee to that of the lowest criminal, have another test of the authenticity of the book as a record of actual humanity. They hear from one and all, in some language or other, the assertion of a righteousness which they are sure is theirs, and which cannot be taken from them. They may call themselves miserable sinners; some of them may feel that they are so; some may tremble at the judgment which they think is coming upon them for their sins. But in all there is a secret reserve of belief, that there is in them that which is not sin, which is the very opposite of sin. When you tell them that the feeling is very wrong, that 'God be merciful to me' is the only true prayer, that God's law is very holy, that they have violated it, and so forth,—they will listen, —they may assent. From prudence or deference to you they may suppress the offensive phrase, or change their tone. Those will not be the best and honestest who do so. The man who cries, *Till I die you shall not take my integrity from me*, and who makes his teacher weep for the fearful deceitfulness of the human heart, may be nearest, if the Bible speaks right, to the root of the matter,—nearest to repentance and humiliation. But be that as it may, the fact in each case is nearly the same. Each man has got this sense of a righteousness, whether he realizes it distinctly or indistinctly, whether he expresses it courageously or keeps it to himself.

Not less true is it that each man has that other conviction which Job uttered so manfully, that pain is an evil and comes from an enemy, and is contrary to the nature and reason of things; however from a stoical maxim, or a sense of duty, or a habit of patience, he may submit to it; however much, to please his teacher or to get rid of him, he may assent to phrases which appear to affirm an opposite doctrine. The witness of the conscience,—of the whole man,—on this point, is too strong for any cool, disinterested reflections. It is no time for school distinctions about soul and body. Both are confounded in one mortal anguish.

And when the man sends forth a bitter cry towards heaven, when he expresses his faith that he has a Deliverer somewhere, it is not a Redeemer for his soul that he asks, more than for his body. It is from the condition in which he finds himself that he cries to be set free; he feels that he has a kind of right to be set free from it. To be as he is, is not, he thinks, according to nature and order. He asks God, if he asks at all, to show that it is not according to His will.

If we did believe that there is a divine process, such as the Book of Job describes to us,—if we might take that book as an inspired history of God's ways to men,—we should not surely stop at this point of the application. We should suppose God was really answering his creature and child out of the whirlwind; and by wonderful arguments, drawn, it may be, from the least object in nature, from the commonest fact of the man's experience, or from the whole Cosmos in which he finds himself, addressed to an ear which our words do not reach, entering secret passages of the spirit to which we have no access, was leading him,—the instincts and anticipations of his heart being not denied but justified,—to lay himself in dust and ashes. When a man knows that he has a righteous Lord and Judge, who does not plead His omnipotence and His right to punish, but who debates the case with him, who shows him his truth and his error, the sense of Infinite Wisdom, sustaining and carrying out Infinite Love, abases him rapidly. He perceives that he has been measuring himself, and his understanding, against that Love, that Wisdom. A feeling of infinite shame grows out of the feeling of undoubting trust. The child sinks in nothingness at its Father's feet, just when He is about to take it to His arms.

But it is a *Father*, not a vague *world*, before which he has bowed. Oh! if we would preserve our brethren from a dark abyss of Pantheism, when their spirits are beginning to open to some of the harmonies of the universe, let us not pause till we understand how it should be the end of God's discipline to justify Job more than his three friends; how it can be possible for Him to sanction that conviction of an actual righteousness, belonging to the man himself, which we were so anxious to confute. I believe, for this purpose, we must lay the foundations of our faith deeper, not than they are laid in the Scriptures or in our Creeds, but very much deeper than they are laid in modern expositions. We say we wish to bring the sinner, weary, heavy-laden, and hopeless, to Christ. What can be a more blessed, or more benevolent, or more divine desire? But do we mean that we merely wish to bring the sinner to know what Christ did and spoke, in those thirty-three years between his birth and his resurrection? I fear we shall never understand the infinite significance of those years, or be able to take the Gospel narratives of them simply as they stand, if we have no other thought than this, or if there is no other which we dare proclaim to our fellow-men. Do we not really believe that Christ was, before He took human flesh and dwelt among us? Do we not suppose that He actually conversed with prophets and patriarchs, and made them aware of His presence? Or is this a mere arid dogma, which we prove out of Pearson, and which has nothing to do with our inmost convictions, with our very life? How has it become so? Is it not because we do not accept the New Testament explanation of these appearances and manifestations; because we do not believe that Christ is in every man, the source of all light that ever visits him, the root of all the righteous thoughts and acts that he is ever able to conceive or do?

I am afraid, not only that we are letting this truth go, but that we are actually disbelieving it, and that we shall therefore fall not into the doctrine about Christ which prevailed in the last century, not into a belief of Him as a man and nothing more than a man,—various experiences have been making it difficult, almost impossible, for us to acquiesce in such a theory,—but into the notion of Him as a shadow-personage, whom the imagination has clothed, as it does all its heroes, with a certain divinity, really belonging to and derived from itself. That notion, when it is presented to our divines, strikes them at first with amazement, as an hypothesis which cannot by possibility gain acceptance with reasonable people. Then they discover how much acceptance it has gained; how naturally men in our day fall into it; how many of them seem to receive it as if it was that which they had always been holding, only they had not courage to tell themselves so, or skill to put their thoughts into words.

The next step is to look about for some method of confuting the theory; to see whether we can prove that Strauss and his disciples have misquoted the New Testament or abused ancient authorities. Perhaps, if we cannot establish these points sufficiently by our learning, our German friends, who have been more closely engaged in the battle, may help us. I dare say they can, and that we also may do something for ourselves in that line, if we try. But I am convinced, also, that the effort will be worth next to nothing, if it is made ever so skilfully, if our blows are ever so straight and well directed. That which is a tendency and habit of the heart, is not cured by detecting fallacies in the mode in which it is embodied and presented to the intellect. If you have no other way of showing Christ not to be a mythical being, or a man elevated into a God by the same process which has deified thousands before and since, except by convicting the propounder of the hypothesis of some philological and historical blunders, you may be quite sure that he will prevail, though those blunders were multiplied a thousand-fold.

I would earnestly entreat our divines to think well whether they are not to blame for the prevalence of this theory; and whether, if they would eradicate it, they must not, in the first place, deal much more honestly with the facts of human experience, and secondly, connect those facts with principles which they admit to a certain extent, when they are arguing with those who deny them, but which they seldom fairly present to themselves, and still more rarely bring home to the consciences of their suffering fellow-men. The facts I have tried to present in the light in which Scripture exhibits them to us,—Scripture abundantly confirmed by daily observation. We apply the principle to those facts, when we say boldly to the man who declares that he has a righteousness which no one shall remove from him—'That is true. You have such a righteousness. 'It is deeper than all the iniquity which is in you. It 'lies at the very ground of your existence. And this 'righteousness dwells not merely in a law which is 'condemning you, it dwells in a Person in whom you 'may trust. The righteous Lord of man is with you, not 'in some heaven to which you must ascend that you 'may bring Him down, in some hell to which you must 'dive that you may raise Him up, but nigh you, at 'your heart.'

The principle is expressed again when we say, 'You 'maintain that the pain you are suffering is not good 'but ill,—a sign of wrong and disorder. You say that 'it is a bondage, from which you must seek deliverance. 'You say that you cannot stop to settle in what part 'of you it is, that it is throughout you, that it affects 'you altogether, that you want a complete emancipation 'from it. Even so. Hold fast that conviction. Let 'no man, divine or layman, rob you of it. Pain is 'a sign and witness of disorder, the consequence 'of disorder. It is mockery to say otherwise. You 'describe it rightly; it is a bondage, the sign that 'a tyrant has in some way intruded himself into this 'earth of our's. But you are permitted to suffer the 'consequence of that intrusion, just that you may attain 'to the knowledge of another fact,—that there is a Re- 'deemer, that He lives, that He is the stronger. That 'righteous King of your heart whom you have felt to be 'so near you, so one with you, that you could hardly 'help identifying Him with yourself, even while you 'confessed that you were so evil, He is the Redeemer as 'well as the Lord of you and of man. Believe that He 'is so. Ask to understand the way in which He has 'proved Himself so. You will find that God, not we, 'has been teaching you of Him, that He has been 'talking with you in the whirlwind, while we were 'darkening counsel with words without knowledge; 'leading you to the sight of His glory, that He might 'make you willing to confess your own baseness. He 'has taught you that you have been in chains, but that 'you have been a willing wearer of the chains. To 'break them He must set you free. Self is your great 'prison-house. The strong man armed, who keeps that 'prison in safety, must be bound. The rod of the 'enchanter, who holds your will in bondage, must be 'broken by some diviner spell before the arms can be 'loosed, and the captive rise and move again.

'If you have carried away this lesson from your hours 'of suffering, and resolve to keep it, your latter days will 'be better than the beginning. The grey hairs of the 'stricken, worn out, desolate man, though no new chil-'dren should crowd his hearth in place of those that are 'departed, though no flocks and herds should be restored 'to him for those which the robbers have taken away, 'will be fresher, freer, more hopeful than the untaught 'innocence of his childhood. But you have had, in 'those hours, a glimpse into the deep mystery, how God 'may use the consequences of the evil to which you 'have yielded,—and can make also the deliverance, if 'it be at present only a partial one, from those conse-'quences,—instruments in your emancipation from the 'evil itself; because, through His discipline, these 'have become the means of leading you to the appre-'hension of Himself, and of that Daysman, between us 'and Him, whom Job saw that he needed, and who 'must be as much yours as He was his.'

The remarks I made in my last Essay show that I do not undervalue the testimony which the elder Unitarians bore against some of the phrases and opinions respecting human nature and human corruption, into which our popular religious teachers have fallen. They maintained stoutly, that ordinary men do good acts, and that we have no business to call such acts splendid sins. 'Either,' they said, 'words mean nothing, and human language, 'when it is turned to religious purposes, is used to con-'ceal not to express our thoughts, or else the epithets, '*gentle, brave, just,* to whomsoever they are applied, 'must be taken as expressing sincere moral commen-'dation, and must not be explained away because we 'have some mental reservation about the religion or 'irreligion of the person to whom we apply them.' All such protests seem to me honest appeals to the conscience, and to the truth of God,—denunciations of a style of thinking and judging which leads to the most fatal moral confusions.

But the Unitarians, I think, were very little able to sustain these useful assertions of theirs against an earnest and thoughtful man, who had known what evil was in himself, and who had adopted St. Paul's language, not only because it was St. Paul's, but because it expressed the deepest thoughts of his own heart, *In me, that is, in my flesh, dwelleth no good thing.* Such expressions seemed to them merely extravagant and foolish; indications of a temporary insanity in the person who resorted to them, which time or change of air would probably cure. Sometimes they saw that these remedies were effectual. The man's judgment of himself was connected with much that was morbid; his judgments of others, and the theories which he deduced from his experience, he gradually perceived to be uncharitable and untenable; his vivid impressions yielded to such discoveries and passed away. There were others whom neither time nor change of air, nor the observation of their own rashness, nor repentance for it, at all shook in this strong and solid conviction. They had found the Apostle's assertion to be true. They could abandon it for no Pelagian refinements. With them, these Unitarians felt themselves utterly at a loss. They could only talk to them about an external morality, of which the hearers made no account. The disputants were speaking of different subjects; but subjects between which there existed a close connexion; one of which, if rightly understood, would have been of the greatest help in explaining the other. The Unitarians discoursed concerning the *doings* of a man, those they called enthusiasts concerning his *being*. But how poor are his doings if they do not draw life from his being; how much he will deceive himself about his being, if it does not make itself manifest in doings! How soon will even commercial honesty perish, if you have not found out the secret of making the man honest! But how easy is it for a man to frame for himself a certain internal standard, which shall be compatible with the greatest external fraud and wrong!

I am sure people are coming to some discoveries of this kind; and that they are almost equally dissatisfied with that flimsy doctrine about behaviour, which was all that the religion of rewards and punishments could produce, and with that assertion of truths as belonging to the believer and not to other men, which is its antagonist. Both systems are falling by their own weight. The external moralist fails to produce the results he says are all-important; the exclusive religionist shows himself more worldly than his neighbours. But while each is separately perishing, was there no truth in each which cannot perish? What is it? How shall we find it out?

I have been led in this Essay to seek for this reconciliation, by a method which will seem to the Unitarian to the last degree strange and monstrous. What infinite pains Priestley and his school took to disprove the pre-existence of our Lord! How satisfactorily they showed that that pre-existence must imply something more than the Arians said it implied; that there was no resting in their half-conclusion! How indefatigably they strove to exhaust Scripture of all expressions which savoured of this mystical imagination! With what rapture they hailed a bad translation, or a doubtful reading! How resolved they were that even the early Church and the early heretics should not mean what all previous students of their language thought they must mean! They exhibited great diligence, undoubtedly, and diligence not without its reward. For their orthodox antagonists, eager to confute these statements, made a concession which, for their purposes, was quite invaluable. They argued as if you might start from the Unitarian hypothesis of our Lord's nature, and *then* prove Him to be something more than that hypothesis affirmed Him to be. It was to be taken for granted that the new Testament spoke of Jesus of Nazareth first as a good man and a great prophet; it was to be contended that it also spoke of Him as divine.

To be involved in such a controversy is to be involved in the necessity of arguing, refining, special-pleading for a principle which, at the same time, we affirm to be the substance of the Gospel, to be connected with the very life of man. What an utterly false position for men to be thrown into! How could the spectators help thinking that it was a fencing-match, the interest of which depended upon successful parries and thrusts; unless, as was too often the case, the combat acquired a deadly interest when one of the combatants was persuaded into the crime of Laertes, when, changing their rapiers, they struck each other with the poisoned instrument? And where there was on the one side the advantage of academical fame, of ecclesiastical dignity, the shouts of the crowd, the patronage of the state, the sympathies of the lovers of fair play would of course be bestowed on the opposite.

It was not exactly that the supporter of the orthodox side *chose* a bad standing-ground. In the last age this was felt to be the natural standing-ground. Some men were driven from it by spiritual convictions; some found it inconsistent with a scholarlike study of the Bible; but most spoke as if it were the *reasonable* position.

You yielded it up in deference to an invincible array of texts or authorities, or to some power which directly bore upon your own spirit. Those who maintained it were supposed to be adopting the faith which every philosopher and every simple man would adopt, unless he were prepared for a very bold infidelity, or unless, in deference to Scripture and tradition, he gave up his *common* sense.

In what I have said of Strauss, I have hinted how much the case is altered now in this respect. The habit of thought which made the arguments of the Humanitarians seem so strong and decisive, which was always ready to supply any gaps in their reasoning, is subverted. Through whatever influence the change has come to pass, philosophers recognise it; all feel it. There is no eagerness now to show that the disciples of Jesus did *not* attach a mysterious and supernatural dignity to His character; the labour is to prove that they did. Philology is discovered to have been in favour of the older notion of their opinions; only philosophy failed in accounting for them. The modern Unitarian has strong motives for looking favourably upon statements of this kind. They meet the discontent with which he has learnt to regard the dryness of his own creed. They justify his traditional dislike of the orthodox creed. They gratify his desire for a religion which shall point less to external conduct, more to internal life. If he can look upon Jesus as connected *in some way* with the experiences of his own heart, with those spiritual conflicts of which he has learnt to see the significance, what an emancipation it will be from the formalism which he hates, in his own school and ours! How much more easily than Priestley or Belsham, with how much less of outrage upon scholarship, he can get rid of mere texts and narratives; with how much more of delight than they ever betrayed, can he recognise all that was divinest in the life of him who is called the Son of Man; with how much more of freedom and less of exclusiveness can he connect him with all the other great champions of the race!

Yes; these are great temptations, irresistible temptations to one who, as Bunyan says, 'has not a burthen on his back.' I may easily persuade myself that the Christ I was taught to believe in, is a creation of the human intellect or imagination. That hypothesis will come to me clothed with a wonderful plausibility, when I stumble all at once, in my walks through this common world, upon mines of which I had not suspected the existence,—mines in which the most busy processes are going on, and must have been going on for generations. But if by chance while I am exploring these rich mines in myself, I am brought to a stand-still by the discovery that *I* am the worker of them; that I have worked them ill; that I am the steward of some one who is the possessor of them; that I am bankrupt, and guilty;—then it becomes a necessity—not of my traditional faith, or of my fears, but—of my inmost spirit, that I should find some One whom I did not create, some One who is not subject to my accidents and changes, some One in whom I may rest for life and death. Who is this? What name have you for Him? I say it is the Christ, whose name I was taught to pronounce in my childhood; the Righteous one, the Redeemer in whom Job, and David, and the Prophets trusted, the ground of all that is true, in you, and me, and every man; the Source of the good acts,—which are therefore not splendid sins,—of you, and me, and every man; the Light that lighteth every man who cometh into the world. Apart from Him, I feel that there dwells in me no good thing; but I am sure that I am not apart from Him, nor are you, nor is any man. I have a right to tell you this: if I have any work to do in the world it is to tell you this. And now I will tell you further why I hold that this righteous Being is the Son of God.

ESSAY V.

THE SON OF GOD.

"I BELIEVE in Jesus Christ, *the only Son of God*, our Lord," has been for eighteen centuries the creed of Christendom. The teachers to whom I alluded in my last Essay, are especially active in pointing out the delusion into which we have fallen upon this subject.

'All mythologies recognise Sons of God. Every 'legendary person in the Greek world was the offspring 'of some God; the most conspicuous, of Zeus the chief 'God. Where is your singularity? Where are the 'signs of some essential characteristic divinity in your 'faith? It bears about it the ordinary tokens of 'humanity. To these it owes its general acceptance. 'In this instance, as in all others, it has adopted into 'itself those human feelings and notions which had 'taken various forms in different ages and races; it has 'adopted them free from some adjuncts and accidents 'which were worn out and ready to perish. It has 'added to them accidents of its own, which will 'drop off in due time by a necessary law. It has 'especially connected a high ideal of humanity with 'a particular person. That ideal will be found to 'belong to the whole race, not to him. He will retain 'a high place among the asserters of human rights and 'duties, not that which the idolatry of his disciples has 'assigned him.'

I have admitted already that the ordinary methods of controversy are entirely out of place when statements of this kind are propounded. The question, whichever way it is decided, must concern the life and being of every one of us. It must affect the condition of mankind now, and the whole future history of the world. To argue and debate it as if it turned upon points of verbal criticism, as if the determination could be influenced by the greater or less skill in reasoning on either side, as if it could be settled by votes, must have the effect of darkening our consciences, of making us doubt inwardly whether the truth signifies anything to us, or whether we can arrive at it. To keep silence on these doubts, if this is the only mode of treating them, is not only a sign of religious reverence, but of common sense. But since there is, I believe, another way of dealing with them,—one which will be acknowledged as fairer by those who experience them, and yet one which does not require the heart and conscience to be asleep, but which asks all their help in determining whether we have received a fable, or are holding, all too weakly, an eternal verity,—I consider it much safer not to leave such a topic to the chances of ordinary conversation and popular literature, but to introduce it into solemn discourses as if we were aware of the number of human souls which it is tormenting.

Our first plain duty is to admit the fact as it is stated, not entering into particulars for the sake of showing whether there are any exceptions to it or limitations of it. For our purpose it is not necessary to inquire why the Oriental spoke more of emanations from God, and the Greeks, as well as our own Gothic ancestors, more of sons of God. The question is very interesting and even important. I may allude to it again at some other time, but it is enough here to admit the general proposition, that sons of God will be found occupying a conspicuous place in the mythology of every people which has left any strong impression of itself upon the history of the world. This being granted, the next point is to ascertain what are those general human feelings which this faith embodies. We cannot hesitate for a moment to allow that there are some; that it is very desirable to know what they are; and that they must be nearly related to Christianity.

First, then, it seems to be an instinct of men, so far as we may judge by these indications, that their helpers must come to them from some mysterious region; that they cannot be merely children of the earth, merely of their own race. If they belong to us,—so the conscience of man interpreted by history seems to bear witness,—they cannot understand our evils, or bring any power that is adequate to overcome them. Secondly, there seems to have been a strong persuasion among men that human relationships have something answering to them in that higher world from which they suppose their heroes to have descended. Thirdly, they seem to have been sure, that unless the superior beings were, not only related to each other, but, in some way related to *them*, their mere protection would be worth very little; they would not confer the kind of benefits which the inferior asks from them. These are the obvious common-place inferences from these stories, which suggest themselves to every one; they lie upon the surface of them.

And if so, it can hardly, I think, be *taken for granted* that we are showing our respect for the instincts and conscience of humanity, when we assume that all the beings who have done it good, have *not* come from any mysterious source, but have belonged to the common stock of human beings; that they have *not* been given to us, but, as to all their more transcendent qualities, created by us; that their relation to us was the ordinary one of flesh and blood; that we have glorified and deified them. These conclusions may be true, but they cannot follow from those facts to which our attention has been so eagerly directed; those facts would seem at first sight to contradict them. I am quite willing, however, to acknowledge that there is evidence, and very strong evidence, in favour of these opinions,—evidence which has made it most natural that serious thinkers should adopt them in this day and in other days. Notwithstanding that strong conviction in the minds of men, that their gods and heroes must be of a nature higher than their own, and that any sympathy with them must imply a condescension and stooping, it is quite manifest that they have imputed to the beings whom they reverenced, all the habits and peculiarities of the countries and races to which they belonged, all that was morbid in their own temperaments, much of the corruption and debasement to which they know themselves to be prone. About this point there is no dispute. It is no new discovery, but one which Greek sages made more than two thousand years ago, about their own countrymen. It was the secret of the unbelief of so many of them. It led a few into the strongest and most settled assurance, that there was that which man did not create, and to which he must be conformed. And there is no doubt that, from age to age, the tendency went on increasing, till the Gods became different from the mass of men only by being the models and ideals of a superhuman malice and cruelty.

But there is a chapter of human experience which we have not yet looked into. It is that of which I spoke in my last Essay. We found a man brought into a condition of physical and moral pain and weakness which deprived him of all advantages he might once have possessed, and confessing himself on a level with the most wretched of human creatures. There came to this man, so smitten, a consciousness of evil, which was perfectly new to him. This consciousness was strangely mixed with the assurance that there was a righteousness which he could actually claim as his. The righteousness was more deep than the evil. At times he felt that it was even more his own, though that seemed bone of his bone and flesh of his flesh. This conflict in his mind was connected with another. He could not deny that his suffering had come from God; but yet he felt it to be a plague, an evil, an enemy. It spoke to him of bondage and oppression. Could God be the oppressor? This man, we found, was gradually taught that God was not his oppressor, but the defender of his cause,—the asserter of his righteousness. How was this? Was he then righteous? Was he not the sinner he had believed himself to be? Yes; it was then first that he felt himself to be *wholly* a sinner,—that he became ashamed of all the pleas he had put forth on his own behalf. But there was, in some mysterious manner, a Redeemer,—an actual person connected with him,—one who he was sure lived,—one who was at the root of his being,—one in whom he *was* righteous.

I tried to show, not from a particular sentence, but from the context of the book, that this was Job's experience. I tried to show further, that Job was not a man unlike other men, placed under rare and peculiar conditions, which enabled him to ascertain certain facts as true for himself, which are not true for his race; but that by hard discipline, he was drawn out of that which was local and individual, brought to the apprehension of that which is human and universal. I tried to show that any other hypothesis is inconsistent with our reverence for the book of Job as part of the canon of Scripture, equally inconsistent with the testimonies which have been borne to its truthfulness by people of the most various characters, and in the most dissimilar circumstances. If so, the Avenger or Redeemer whom Job confessed was not *a* Redeemer, but *the* Redeemer; not one of those who came down from time to time, out of some unknown world of light, to scatter some portion of the world's darkness, but the actual source of light; not one of those who here and there puts down one of the earth's oppressors, but the asserter of *man's* right against the oppressor of *man*. He cannot be one of those whom men have called into existence, and invested with the qualities which belong to them as members of some particular race or locality. The sufferer has been compelled to feel himself simply a man. All accidents are nothing to him now. If he has not hold of a substance, he must perish in his despair.

Such are the results at which we have arrived already. But if that part of the story is true,—and no part of it can be true if that is not,—which represents God as Himself discovering to the innermost heart and spirit of the man his righteousness as well as his sin,—the Avenger as well as the oppressor,—the question must have forced itself upon Job, and forces itself upon us: Is this Redeemer, so closely connected with the human sufferer, not connected also with that divine Instructor who answered him out of the whirlwind? Was this righteousness which Job perceived, not the righteousness of God Himself? Was He as widely separated from His creature as ever? Was there no meaning in the assertion that one was the image of the other? What did all this history of a struggle signify, if that assertion was false? Why had Job cared to know the mind and purpose of his Maker? Why had he that sense of separation from Him—that longing to plead with Him? Whence came that cry for a Daysman between them?

If *the* Lord and Redeemer whom Job, and thousands besides Job, in that day and in all days, in that country and in all countries, felt after and found, explains to us those many lords and redeemers, whom men in different places and ages have dreamed of or hoped for, may not He also explain those many sons of God of whom I have been speaking here? May not this be the great radical experience which interprets those superficial experiences; the great universal experience which interprets those partial ones? Job could not think of this

Daysman, near as He was to his very being, except as one who had come to Him,—who had stooped to him,—who belonged to a world of mystery. Job could not think of Him, except as related to the Invisible Lord of all. Job's most intimate conviction was that He was related to himself. These are the conditions that meet in all those dreams of demigods and heroic men which mythology presents us with. But here are not the causes which make those dreams local, temporary, artificial. It is from the One Being, the Lord of the spirit of all flesh, that this Son of God must have come. He must be spiritual like that Being; for it is the spirit and not the sense of the sufferer, which confesses Him. And whatever righteousness and goodness are perceived by the erring, trusting, broken-hearted penitent to be in the One,—speaking to his sorrows and wants,—must be the image and reflex of an absolute righteousness and grace in the other, which he could only adore.

Many readers fancy that when we speak of a Person who is at once divine, and the ground of humanity, we must be assuming an Incarnation. I have not yet touched that doctrine; what I am saying here has no reference to it. Christian theology does not speak of an Incarnation, till it has spoken of 'an only-begotten 'Son, begotten of his Father before all worlds, of one 'substance with Him.' These words, though we unite so often in pronouncing them, and though in former times they were the strength and nourishment of confessors and martyrs, have come, in modern days, to be regarded as mere portions of a school divinity, which learned men must maintain by subtle arguments and an army of texts; which ordinary men are to receive implicitly, because it is dangerous to doubt them; but which have no hold upon our common daily life, which can be tested by no experience, which those who are busy with religious feelings and states of mind will pass by with indifference, as not concerning vital godliness. We owe it to those objectors of whom I have spoken, (and this surely ought to convince us how faithless and heartless our dread of any objections is, and how much we are fighting against God, when we try to suppress them),—we owe it to them that this delusion has been scattered, or must soon be scattered; and that these truths are compelled to come forth from amidst the cobwebs in which we have left them, to prove that they can bear the open day, and that they bring a more glorious sunlight with them, which may penetrate into all the obscurest caverns of human thoughts and fears. If we take the Apostle St. John as our guide, we shall find that those mysteries, from which we have shrunk back, as if they must rob us of all simple and child-like faith, are the preservers of simplicity in thought, in word, in act, from the innumerable temptations to artifice and falsehood which beset religious men, not less, but more, than others; that they can set us free from a host of vulgar earthborn notions and superstitions, which we have adopted from the cloister or the crowd into our Christian dialect and practice; that they can show how the one fundamental truth of God's love and charity makes all other facts,—those belonging to the most inward discipline of the heart, those concerning the most outward economy of the world,—sacred and luminous.

I can only see at a great distance, that this must be so and is so, and can hope and pray that God may raise up some in these latter days of the world who will help us to feel that it is so. The utmost I shall attempt now is, to say a few words on one passage of St. John's Gospel, in which our Lord points out, as it seem to me, in a wonderful manner, the relation in which a belief in the Son of God stands to that consciousness of bondage which is inseparable from the consciousness of sin.

If I traced in this passage any allusion to a belief in His Incarnation or to that Passion which had not yet taken place, I should not quote it. But the only way in which the words bear upon the first of these subjects is this: they were addressed to certain Jews who had believed on Christ as a teacher, as a man standing visibly before them. He desired to lead them into a higher and better faith, the one which true men had held before He was born into the world, the only one which could sustain any after He had left it. He had said to those Jews who believed on Him, '*If ye continue in my word, then are ye my disciples indeed, and ye shall know the truth, and the truth shall make you free.*' They answered, '*We are Abraham's children; we were never in bondage to any man. How sayest thou then, Ye shall be made free?*' A strange question for men who were looking so earnestly for a deliverer from the Roman yoke, and yet one which had a good meaning in it. They were certain that in some way or other the privilege of being Abraham's children was the gift of a higher freedom, a nobler citizenship, which the Cæsars could not take from them. Perhaps it *was* this. Perhaps our Lord came to show them *how* it was this. But in the mean time, there was a plain staring fact which they must admit. Whether they were Abraham's children or not, they had committed sin; they felt and knew that they had. And that sin did make them bondsmen. They were under a yoke, a heavy one to each of them, however he might slight his subjection to the emperor, however little that might practically or individually gall him. His will had a master; he confessed it in a thousand ways; he continually pleaded its subjection as an excuse for doing wrong acts, for not doing right ones. It was better simply to own the fact than to dissemble it. To own it was the beginning of emancipation. '*For the servant abideth not in the house for ever, but the Son abideth ever.*' Over that house of theirs, not made with hands, there was a Son actually ruling, a Son of God. To Him the house belonged, not to the poor slave who fancied it was his. Let him once confess the true Lord of it, let him once give up his own imaginary claim of dominion, which was submission to a real servitude, and his chains would drop off. '*For if the Son shall make you free, then are ye free indeed.*' All other attempts to shake off the yoke from your wills, make it harder and heavier. In the confession that a Son, an actual Son of God is your Lord, lies the secret of freedom. This is the true Hercules who takes Prometheus from his rock, and slays the vulture that is preying upon him. This is the deliverer of each man, because He is the deliverer of mankind.

I believe there never has been, is not, nor will be, any other way of asserting freedom or of preserving it than this. And I do believe that God is leading us by strange and hidden paths, to seek for this freedom and to find it. Many a heart, I trust, which shrinks back from our teaching, and perhaps thinks that we are binding grievous chains on men's necks, is yet praying this prayer;

"Strong Son of God, Immortal Love,
Whom we, that have not seen thy face,
By faith, and faith alone, embrace,
Believing where we cannot prove;
* * * * * *
"Thou wilt not leave us in the dust:
Thou madest man, he knows not why;
He thinks he was not made to die;
And Thou hast made him: Thou art just.

"Thou seemest human and divine,
The highest, holiest manhood, Thou:
Our wills are ours, we know not how;
Our wills are ours, to make them Thine.

"Our little systems have their day;
They have their day and cease to be:
They are but broken lights of Thee,
And Thou, O Lord, art more than they."[1]

Yes! it is deeply and eternally true that 'Thou, O Lord, art more than they.' And therefore it becomes us most earnestly, for the sake of our fellow-men and of all the thoughts and doubts which are stirring in them so mightily at this time, not to let the faith in an actual Son of God be absorbed into any religious or philosophical theories or abstractions. When we lose that, we lose all hope of freedom: our own conceits become our masters, and we are at the mercy of any ingenious and skilful combiner, who can put those conceits into a system; we become liable for a time to all the caprices and fantasies of the age in which we live; we shall probably sink at last into the implicit credence which we suppose to be the characteristic of ages that are past. Let us look, therefore, courageously at the popular dogma, that there are certain great ideas floating in the vast ocean of traditions which the old world exhibits to us, that the Gospel appropriated some of these, and that we are to detect them and eliminate them from its own traditions. We have found *these* great ideas floating in that vast sea;—the idea of an Absolute God, the idea of a Son of God, who has close and intimate relations with men as their Lord and their Deliverer. We have found that these ideas demand to be substantiated; that

[1] "In Memoriam," opening verses.

all mischief, confusion, materialism, surrounded them when they became the creatures of men's fancy, liable to be altered, disturbed, divided, at their pleasure. What we ask for, is—not a System that shall put these ideas into their proper places, and so make them the subjects of our partial intellects, but—a Revelation which shall show us what they are, why we have had these hints and intimations of them, what the eternal substances are which correspond to them. We want such a Revelation for philosophers and common men, for the prince and the serf: we ask if there is such a one or no: we beseech the Father of Lights, if He is the God of infinite Charity we proclaim Him to be, to tell us whether all our thoughts of Freedom and Truth have proceeded from the Father of Lies; whether for eighteen centuries we have been propagating a mockery when we have said that there is a Son of God, who is Truth, and who can make us free indeed.

'And is this all you have to say,' asks a grave Unitarian of the older school, 'to convince me that 'I must believe those mysteries, so outrageous to my 'reason, which you confess that even persons proud of 'their orthodoxy are rather eager to dismiss from their 'thoughts? That is really, as the lawyers say, your 'case?' I will tell you, friend, why I have said thus much, and why, on this topic, I mean to say no more. It is because I know that I have you on my side; because you are the principal evidence for what I have been maintaining. You never have made up your minds to abandon the name, 'Son of God.' You find it in the Gospels. Your desire to assert the letter of them, against what you suppose our figurative and mystical interpretations, forces you to admit the phrase. You not only do so, but you make the most of it. You quote all the passages in which Christ declares that the Son can do nothing of Himself, that the Father is greater than He, as decisive against the doctrine of our creeds. You do a vast service by insisting upon them, by compelling us to take notice of them. They are not merely chance sentences carelessly thrown out, inconsistent with others which occur in the same books. You are right in affirming that they contain the key to the life of Christ on earth. You have suggested the thought to us,—you could not, consistently with your scheme, bring it forward, but it was latent in your argument,—that what He was on earth must be the explanation of what He is. Never can I thank you enough for these hints, for the help they have been to me in apprehending the sense and connexion of those words which you cast aside. If the idea of subordination in the Son to the Father, which you so strongly urge, is once lost sight of, or considered an idle and unimportant school tenet, the morality of the Gospel and its divinity disappear together. You have helped to keep alive in our minds the distinction of the Persons, and that I believe is absolutely necessary that we may confess the unity of Substance.

But, moreover, you have borne a very strong and earnest protest against Idolatry. You have said that the Christian Church is just as liable to idolatry as the Heathen world was, and that its idolatry may be, probably will be, of the same kind, one adopted from the other. Truths most needful to be uttered, which Christian men refuse to heed at their peril! We Protestants require them as much as Roman Catholics; we Englishmen, as much as Spaniards or Italians. May I venture to add, You need them also? In so far as you feel,—and I am sure many of you do feel,—a sincere, fervent admiration and love for the character of Jesus Christ, in so far as you believe him to be the wisest, holiest, most benignant Teacher the world ever had, are you not in danger of setting a man above God? For I think the dim and distant vision of a Being nowise related to you, as far as your theory is concerned,—though by a happy and noble inconsistency you delight to call Him, Father,—cannot, by any possibility, be so satisfactory as the thought of one who has actually done good and wrestled *with* evil, and, in some sense, *for* you. When you can fairly say, we are contemplating either, *that* is the fairer object, is it not?—the one upon which you would rather dwell, even, if it must be so, to the exclusion of the other? Well! but surely here is the commencement and germ of all idolatry. For you do not mean by idolatry, plain and practical people as you are, the mere outward service of the temple, the bowing the knee to a certain name; you mean the deliberate preference of the judgment and the affections. And that, it seems to me, you will and must bestow upon Christ rather than upon God, if you do not accept the doctrine, that He is God of God, Light of Light.

And do not think that it is possible for you, or for any man, to stop short at this point of idolatry. I think I could show from the history of the Christian no less than of the ancient world, that where a Son of Man, simply in *that* character, has attracted to himself the reverence, affection, gratitude, homage, which are not paid to God, those sons of men and daughters of men, who are felt to be less removed from the sins and impurities of ordinary creatures than He is, practically overshadow him. I intreat you, as resolute asserters of the worship due to the One God, seriously to consider this evidence, as history presents it to us, and then seriously to compare it with the evidence which your own hearts present to you. By utter coldness, by becoming merely men of the world, by forgetting Christ habitually, and using the name of God merely as the symbol of a formal worship, you or we may contrive to escape any fervent idolatry either of natural or human objects, because the sleepy, habitual, unconscious, all-pervading idolatry of Mammon in his grossest form takes its place. But let any earnest sympathy or affection be awakened in us, and does not the clear, definite creature supplant the dim vision of the Creator, unless, in some way or other, it suggests Him? If it suggests Him, how and why? What link is there between the human love and the divine? What and where is the Daysman? Who can it be—must there not be some one?—in whom the human love entirely represents and images the divine?

I do not wish to press this argument further, lest it should become *too* satisfactory to your reason, before it has satisfied your conscience. There is an ascent by another and more rugged road, which is, I believe, generally safer. In the sad hours of your life, the recollection of that Man you read of in your childhood, the Man of Sorrows, the great sympathiser with human woes and sufferings, rises up before you, I know; it has a reality for you, then; you feel it to be not only beautiful, but true. In such moments, does it seem to you as if Christ were merely a person who, eighteen hundred years ago, made certain journeyings between Judea and Galilee? Can such a recollection fill up the blank which some present grief, the loss of some actual friend, has made in your hearts? It does not, it never did this for you, or for any one! Yet I do not doubt for a single instant, that a comfort has come to you from that contemplation. So far from denying your right to it, I would wish you and all earnestly to believe how strong and assured our right to it is. In Him, and for Him, we were created; this is our doctrine, or rather the doctrine of St. Paul; for *we* have said little enough about it. If so, is it wonderful that He should speak to you, and tell you of Himself? And Oh! if that voice says, 'You may trust me, you may lean 'upon me, for I know all things in heaven and earth— '*I and my Father are one;*' is the whisper too good to be true, too much in accordance with the timid anticipations and longings of our spirits *not* to be rejected?

In some of the younger Unitarians, I hope, these words, (or if not these, yet the thoughts which they try to express, in some other words or without any,) may find a response. I do not mean in those who have learnt to talk of the great defenders of humanity and human rights, the Moseses, the Zoroasters, the Jesus Christs, the Mahomets, the Robespierres. Men who put forth language of this kind to grieve their mothers and sisters, and insult those whom they pretend to call their brethren, are not in earnest. They use words to which they attach no meaning. They may be Unitarians or Emersonians to-day. After a little time they may become stiff Anglicans. Then they may take a turn with Cardinal Wiseman. One can only hope for them that in their final transmigration, after they have had a glimpse into the bottomless pit of Atheism, they may become little children again, eager to learn something, if it be but their alphabet. I do not speak of these. But there are many who are confounded with them,—who, in a kind of recklessness, adopt phrases nearly akin to theirs, or who take that course from disgust with our hard speeches and narrowness of heart,—between whom and the vain coxcombs with whom they are associated there is the breadth of a whole heaven. What I fear for them is a great and vehement reaction against the opinions which they have learnt, not in orthodox but, in liberal and Unitarian nurseries. Instead of recognising an impassable chasm between the human and the divine, these become in their minds utterly confounded. The distinction between them, they describe as impalpable, impossible to discover; the plague of orthodox divinity they say is, that it has made the attempt, that it has used hard and stiff words to define the boundary. 'Of course, Christ is divine. 'Why should he not be? How can so beautiful a conception as that which his character exhibits, be otherwise than divine?' But the vehement struggle against their earlier faith which this mode of speaking indicates, shows also how strong the impression of that early faith has been. They are working up from the earthly ground; they can recognise no basis except that; they conceive Divinity only as an apotheosis of humanity.

Now here is and must be the beginning of a very extensive and very frightful idolatry. The Straussians are perfectly right. There always have been sons of God; there always must be. We cannot contemplate the world without them. They always must stand in the most close relation to us; they must leave their footprints on every different soil. Buddhists, old Greeks, modern Romanists, we of this utilitarian time and country, have all traced them and confessed them. The temptation of one and all has been, by measuring and comparing these footprints, to form an abstraction which is called a God, and which may be anything, everything, nothing. The witness in all these hearts has been—It cannot be so that we arrive at Divinity. These must be the sons of a *God*. An abstraction, a generalization, cannot be their Father.

'The witness of all these hearts! Why that is your 'old orthodox dogma, against which we have been all 'our lives protesting!' I cannot help that. *You* can help embracing that dogma. You can continue your protest. But will you not think a little of the other alternative? Will you not ask yourselves seriously if you can escape the worship of ten thousand imaginary Buddhas and demigods? Have you courage to go with me into the yet further question, whether you can avoid the acknowledgment of *fleshly* beings made into gods, with all their infirmities and crimes, if you are not prepared to confess that there is an only-begotten Son of God, who has been made flesh?

ESSAY VI.

THE INCARNATION.

The Sons of the gods in Greek mythology can scarcely be separated from human forms, from actual flesh and blood. Those mysterious emanations from the Divinity which the Oriental spoke of, and which became closely connected with the later Greek philosophy, shrunk from this contact. But the hearts of the people, as much in the East as in the West, demanded Incarnations; no efforts of the more spiritual and abstracted priests could resist the demand. If you consider the passages in the Old Testament which speak of Angels or Sons of God, you will be struck with a resemblance to both these conceptions, and a difference from both. They are persons, not abstractions; they converse with human beings as if they were of the same kind; no clear or deep line is drawn between them. On the other hand, they are never spoken of as assuming flesh, as putting on any vesture of mortality. You know not how, but they leave on you an impression of spirituality all the more strong, because no pains are taken to produce it. Yet it is not an impression made at our cost; we feel ourselves to be raised by what is told us of them; if they are spiritual, we must be so likewise. For this reason, the Jew had no difficulty in acknowledging one higher Angel, one Son of God, above all the rest; who yet was in more direct and continued communication with human creatures than they were; a Word who spoke to prophets and holy men, drew them away from the phantoms of sense, taught them that they were spirits, inspired them with cravings for the knowledge of God. Such a Person they traced through their Scriptures. Those perceived Him most who entered into the Scriptures most, and whose own minds were most alive. The formal Scribes, who were busy in framing a religion about God from the Bible and the Elders, might never discern Him, though they might expect, some day or other, the coming of a great King and Messiah. But those who believed that God was speaking and ruling, who had some vision of His awfulness and absolute perfection, who yet felt that He had made men in His image, and meant them to know Him, could inquire earnestly how and in whom He governed and spake, how that awfulness and perfection could come into relation with creatures, and be apprehended by them. They did not confine the illuminations of this mysterious Teacher to the wise of their own land, but they believed that the Law and the Prophets interpreted

His relation to God and to the souls of men as no other books did, and that their nation was chosen to be an especial witness of His presence.

But when the voice went from a band of despised men, '*The Word, or the Son of God, has been made flesh, and has dwelt among us,*'—each of these classes, the Oriental, the Greek sage, the learned and devout Jew, as well as the popular idolater, had his own reason to be offended. Was not flesh the very seat of all evil, if not its cause? Was not the great effort of the wise man, to disengage himself from fleshly appetites and fleshly illusions? Had not the Divine Word especially chosen out a band of spiritual men to apprehend secrets, which the multitude, given up to the pursuits of the flesh and the world, must remain ignorant of? These were arguments of prodigious weight for all who had pursued the deeper wisdom. The traditional worshippers, Jew or Gentile, did not need arguments. The force of habit and prescription was strong enough without them. The love of what was fleshly and external was as mighty a motive with these for rejecting the new message, as the dread of it was with the others. They were told to turn from their dumb idols—and the Jew was given to understand that the rites in which he trusted had become his idols—to the Living God. The Son of God was said to have taken flesh that He might reclaim all for the servants of His invisible Father.

Accordingly, the chief struggle of all minds in the first centuries after the Church had established itself in the world, was against this belief. I say emphatically and deliberately, in *all* minds, for the conflict was just as apparent among those who had been baptized, as among their opponents. As they became less alive to their own personal necessities, they had leisure to contemplate the many sides which the Gospel presented to the student and to the world—the points of contact between it and surrounding opinions. Then this and that teacher arose to show how possible it was to regard Christ as one of the emanations from the unseen and absolute Essence, one of the stars which had penetrated from the world of light into a world of darkness, one of the agents of a good Being, who had come to recover elect souls from fleshly corruption, and to make them capable of the highest knowledge. Then more accomplished teachers traced an order and scheme of emanations; assigning to Christ a place amidst a multitude of qualities, energies, intellectual or physical principles. Then the modes of attaining the higher intuitions were duly set down and distinguished by each school for its own initiated disciples. But in every one, it was necessary to account for the appearance of our Lord in the world, without supposing Him to have been actually endowed with a human body. The connexion, it was said, was not real but fantastic; the Christ or the Son of God had descended for a while into the body of Jesus at His baptism, leaving it before His passion, not actually participating in any of its infirmities. By some means or other, it must be explained how a deliverer could come among men without being one of themselves, without being associated with that in which lay, as these teachers held, all defilement.

I have expressed what I believe were the three maxims common to these various and dissentient schools. They held, first, that it was possible to know God without an Incarnation; secondly, that it is not right or possible, that a perfectly good Being should be tempted as men are tempted; thirdly, that all we have to look for, is a deliverer of some choice spirits out of the corruption and ruin of humanity, not a deliverer of man himself, of his spirit, his soul, and his body.

These being the three cardinal dogmas of the teachers who departed from the general creed of the Church, the convictions which have sustained that creed cannot, perhaps, be expressed better than by reversing these propositions. First, We accept the fact of the Incarnation, because we feel that it is impossible to know the Absolute and Invisible God as man needs to know Him, and craves to know Him, without an Incarnation. Secondly, We receive the fact of an Incarnation, not perceiving how we can recognise a perfect Son of God, and Son of Man, such as man needs and craves for, unless He were, in all points, tempted like as we are. Thirdly, We receive the fact of an Incarnation, because we ask of God a Redemption, not for a few persons, from certain evil tendencies, but for humanity from all the plagues by which it is tormented. I will take these points in their order.

1. Rapt devotees who have lived in perfect abstraction, have obtained a vision of a cloudless essence, of that which they felt was awful and infinite, and which they could adore in silence. Thoughtful and earnest seekers after wisdom, by careful study of all common things which are presented to them, by honest meditation upon the words which they use, by diligent efforts to escape from the appearances of the senses and the prejudices of the intellect, have been enabled to confess, and confidently to believe, that there is an Absolute and Eternal substance at the ground of all things. Suffering men, tormented by pain of body and anguish of spirit, have perceived that there must be a health deeper than their sickness, a righteousness beneath their evil. Are we to slight any of these discoveries, or not to reckon them true and divine? Certainly not. Their worth is, I believe, unspeakable. But why were not those who obtained them satisfied with them? Why did Heathen sages turn back with a look half of longing, half of loathing, to the popular legends? They saw that there was in them a witness of the presence of Guardians, Brothers, Fathers, which they could not part with. To accept these, clothed in all the tempers and tendencies which they felt to be imperfect and distorted in them-

selves, was impossible for their reason. But their reason *demanded* a standard for acts; *the* grace and righteousness which they saw in different divided human images; a foundation for the relations upon the preservation and purity of which society depends; an absolute Truth, which should not be merely dry existence, merely an ultimate Hercules' Pillar of the Universe, but living; such as truth is when it comes forth in a guileless person.

St. John says, '*We beheld His glory as of the only-begotten of the Father, full of grace and truth.*' Am I to believe this, asks the objector, on the testimony of a Galilean fisherman, or, for aught we know, of some later doctor assuming that guise? I answer, You are not to believe—you cannot believe—either fisherman or doctor, if the assertion itself is contrary to truth, to the laws of your being, to the order and constitution of the Universe in which you are living. They may repeat it till doomsday. It may come, as it did, with no authority, against the weight of all opinion, breaking through the customs and prescriptions of centuries, defying the rulers of the world; or it may come clad with authority, with the prescriptions of centuries, with the help of rulers and public opinion; it is all the same; you cannot believe the words, however habitual and familiar they may be to you, if there is that in them which contradicts the spirit of a man that is in you, which does not address that with demonstration and power. What we say is, that these words have not contradicted that spirit, but have entered it with the demonstration of the spirit and of power. Men have declared, 'The actual creatures of our race do 'tell us of something which must belong to us, must 'be most needful for us. A gentle human being does 'give us the hint of a higher gentleness; a brave man 'makes us think of a courage far greater than he can 'exhibit. Friendships, sadly and continually inter-'rupted, suggest the belief of an unalterable friendship. 'Every brother awakens the hope of a love stronger than 'any affinity in nature; and disappoints it. Every 'father demands a love, and reverence, and obedience, 'which we know is his due, and which something in 'him as well as in us hinders us from paying. Every 'man who suffers and dies rather than lie, bears witness 'of a truth beyond his life and death, of which he has 'a glimpse.' Men have asked, 'Are all these delusions? 'Is this goodness we have dreamed of all a dream? this 'Truth a fiction of ours? Is there no Brother, no Father 'beneath those, who have taught us to believe there must 'be such? Who will tell us?'

What St. John answers is this: 'No, they are not 'delusions. It has pleased the Father to show us what 'He is. A man did dwell among us—an actual man 'like ourselves, who told us that He had come from 'this Father, that he knew Him. And we believed 'Him. We could not help believing Him. There did 'shine forth in His words, looks, acts, that which we 'felt to be the grace and the truth we were wanting to 'see. We were sure they were not of this earth; that 'they did not spring from that body which was such as 'ours is. We should have been ready enough to call 'them His. But *He* did not—He said they were His 'Father's, that He could do nothing of Himself, only 'what He saw His Father do. That was the most 'wonderful token to us of all. We never saw any man 'before who took nothing to Himself, who would glorify 'Himself in nothing. Therefore, when we beheld Him, 'we felt that He was a Son, an Only-Begotten Son, and 'that the glory of One whom no man had seen or could 'see was shining forth in Him, and through Him upon us.'

But why must we think that this person was more than *a* shrine of the Holiest? why should we speak of Him as *the* One? why should this name of 'the Only-Begotten' be bestowed upon Him? Again I say, Withhold it if your heart and conscience bid you do so. But do not deceive yourselves. The question is not any longer, whether there should be an Incarnation, whether God can manifest Himself in human flesh; but *what* the Incarnation should be, in what kind of person we are to expect such a manifestation; or whether He will diffuse His glory through many persons, never gathering it into one. With respect to the former question, the Church has always admitted, the Apostles eagerly asserted, that the demand which they made upon human faith was enormous. The glory of God revealing itself, not in a leader of armies, a philosopher, a poet, but in a carpenter,—could anything be more revolting? There was no shrinking from the shameful confession. It was put forward prominently; it was part of the Gospel which was preached to Jews, Greeks, Romans. And it was received as a Gospel, a message of good, not of ill, because the heart of man answered, 'We want to 'see, not some side of earthly power elevated till it 'becomes celestial; we want not to see the qualities 'which distinguish one man from another, dressed out 'and expanded till they become utterly unlike anything 'which we can apprehend or attain to. We want to 'see absolute Goodness and Truth. We want to know 'whether they can bend to meet us. That which can-'not do this is not what we mean by Goodness. It 'is not what we should call goodness in any man. 'That truth which belongs to a few and not to all, is 'not what we mean by Truth. The truest man we know, 'has a voice which commends itself to all, which 'reaches even the untrue, if it be but to frighten and 'incense him. The goodness which can stoop most, 'which becomes, in the largest sense, grace,—the truth 'which can speak to the inmost heart of the dullest 'human creature, is that which has for us the surest 'stamp of divinity.'

And here lies also the answer to the other question,

'Why should not the Glory of God be diffused 'through many images? why must it be concentrated 'in one?' The practical reply which Christendom has made is: 'That it may be diffused through many, it 'must be concentrated in One. That there may be sons 'of God in human flesh; men shining with the glory 'of God, reflecting His grace and truth; there must be 'One Son who has taken human flesh, in whom that 'full glory dwelt, who was full of grace and truth.' He, so we have proclaimed, who could say, *My Father*, could say, *Your Father;* he who could say, *He has sent Me*, could say, *So send I you.* And Christendom has not merely put this doctrine forth in a proposition. She has been able to establish it by the experience of other men's truths; still more by the experience of her own errors. She can say, 'Take away the belief of the 'one incarnate Son of God and Son of Man, and all the 'heroes of the old world and of the new become merely 'so many men who have earned a right, by their supe-'riority to the mass of their fellow-creatures, to despise 'them and trample upon them. Admit Him to be the 'centre of them, and they all fall into their places; 'each has had his separate protest to bear, his appointed 'work to do. Though he may not have known in 'whose name he was ministering, his ministry, so far as 'it was one of help and blessing to mankind, so far as 'it implied any surrender of self-glory, may be referred 'to THE man, may be hailed as proceeding from Him 'who took upon Him the form of a servant.' On the other hand, the Church can say, and should say, with the deepest humiliation, 'Look what miserable creatures 'the saints whom I have boasted of have become, when, 'through their own crime, or the crime of those who 'have magnified them, it has been supposed that they 'had some independent merits, that their souls or their 'flesh had some sacredness of their own. Look through 'my whole history, and see whether the greatest con- 'fusions I have wrought in the world, the cruellest 'oppressions of which I have been guilty, have not been 'caused by my desire to exalt individual men into the 'place of the Christ; by my efforts to accomplish the 'very object which you hope to attain, when you have 'emancipated yourselves from my Creed.'

2. But I pass to the second point, upon which the teachers who deny an Incarnation are at variance with the Apostles, and, I think, with the conscience of mankind. They say, 'It destroys the idea of a Son of God, 'to suppose him in contact with the temptations of ordi- 'nary men.' We say, 'We cannot know Him to be 'the sinless Son of God, except He was in all points 'tempted like as we are.' This is that side of Christian divinity which presented itself in all its power to Milton; Paradise was, according to him, regained by the endurance of temptation. His strict adherence to that one idea has given a unity to his second poem, as a work of art, which is wanting to its more magnifi-

cent predecessor. And this unity it would not have received, if the soul of the writer had not been penetrated and absorbed by the principle which it embodies. In it lay the strength and vitality of the age which he represented; especially of the Puritan part of it. Men felt then that they had a battle with principalities and powers; the test of the Son of God was, that he had entered into that battle, and had overcome in it. This thought might become too exclusive in their minds; when it was separated from the one we have just been considering, it was liable to various perversions; but I can scarcely conceive of any which has stood men in greater stead, or which we can less afford to dispense with. In fact, as I said in a former Essay, it seems to me that our actual forgetfulness of it, our effeminate timidity in acknowledging the existence of an Evil Spirit, our desire to represent all temptations as arising out of our nature, has been the cause of more superstitions, and more dishonourable thoughts of ourselves and of God, than any other of our popular religious habits. But it is inevitable while there is the least reluctance to adopt the language of the New Testament respecting our Lord's temptation. We cannot and dare not think that there is an actual spirit striking at the deepest root of our being, striving to separate us from what is good and true, if we do not believe that righteousness is mightier, or if we suppose it has only a distant abstract superiority; not one which has been ascertained in an actual trial. If we suppose that the Son of God had any advantage in that trial, any power save that which came from simple trust in His Father, from the refusal to make or prove Himself His Son instead of depending on His word and pledge, we shall not feel that a real victory has been won. And thence will come, (alas! have come,) the consequences of supposing our flesh to be accursed in itself, our bodies or our souls to be subject to a necessary evil, and not to be holy creatures of God, made for all good. It is needful to repeat these maxims often; for the habits and maxims which contradict them, are presenting themselves in every variety of form and application, and are, I think, disturbing all our lives. I recur to them now, because I wish to put that doctrine of the Incarnation, which is so often denounced as an outrage upon reason, conscience, and experience, to every possible test of reason, conscience, and experience. If there are any tests besides these, I do not ask that it should be tried by them; these should not be declined by those who are continually appealing to them. Let them fairly and manfully ask themselves whether they do not evade either some great fact of daily experience, some evidence of actual misery and evil, or else some sure and authentic testimony of the heart that nothing in its principle and constitution can be evil, if they deny that there has been One, who, in our condition, was tempted by the Devil; and that it was no imaginary temptation, but the real one, that which makes others real. Either I shall resort to some subterfuge to conceal my own evil, or I shall shrink from acknowledging my relation in hope and in sorrow to all human beings, or I shall invent some wretched substitute for the Friend whom I have lost, if I am too refined to believe that there is one who showed himself in my flesh, to be a sharer of all God's truth and of all my danger.

3. This refinement in the Gnostical teachers had the closest connexion with that third characteristic of theirs to which I alluded,—their belief that Christ descended from some pure and ethereal world, to save certain elect souls from the pollutions of the flesh and the death which was consequent upon them; not to save the human race; above all, not to save that which was designated as the poor, ignoble, accursed body.

The whole Gospel history was a most cruel insult to the feelings which this opinion denoted. Christ is represented as addressing himself to multitudes. Those selected out of these multitudes to be His disciples, are ignorant men, not better, not more spiritual, than their fellows. Those who gather about Him are publicans and sinners. He heals their *bodies*. He speaks of their bodies as bound by Satan. Pain, disease, death, are treated not as portions of a divine scheme, but as proofs that it has been violated; as witnesses of the presence of a destroyer, who is to be resisted and cast out. These are the startling phenomena of the Gospels, subversive of their credit and character with all persons who, on any grounds whatever, religious or philosophical, are maintaining an exclusive position, striving to separate themselves from other human beings, or wishing to disparage animal existence as the only way of exalting that which is intellectual or spiritual. The traditions of their country may induce some of these to suspend their condemnation of the documents,—nay, even to express unlimited belief in them. Some may hesitate, from sympathy with that in them which their hearts acknowledge as beautiful and divine. But when the chain of authority is broken for the one, when the other find books appealing more directly to their tastes and temper, as being dressed in the fashion of their own time, it will be seen how gladly they will welcome any mode of accounting for the Gospel narratives, which shall not compel them to accept what they do not like to think divine because it is so human. And here again it is to the great human heart that theology must make its appeal. That has found a witness for the Gospels and for the fact of an Incarnation in these offensive passages. That has clung to them because it demands one who comes into contact with its actual condition; who relieves it of its actual woes; who recognises not the exceptions from the race, but the lowest types of it, as brethren with Himself, and as the children of His Father; who proves man to be a spiritual being, not by scorning his animal nature and his animal wants, but by entering into them, bearing them, suffering from them, and then showing how all the evils which affect man as an animal have a spiritual ground, how he must become a citizen of the kingdom of heaven, that everything on earth may be pure and blessed to him. '*The Son of God was manifested that He might destroy the works of the devil;*' this is St. John's summary of the whole matter. He revealed the Father, and so in human flesh He destroyed the great calumny of the devil, that man has not a Father in heaven, that He is not altogether good, that He does not care for His creatures: He submits to all temptations in human flesh, and so proves that man is not the subject and thrall of the tempter. He in human flesh delivered spirits, souls, and bodies out of bondage, so affirming that the state into which the devil would draw them is not the state which is meant for them, that His own humanity is the standard of that which each man bears, and is that to which man shall be raised.

The evangelists say that when the Son of God was to be manifested to men, there did not come a great prophet to argue and prove the probability of an Incarnation; but there came a prophet preaching in the wilderness, and saying, '*Repent, for the kingdom of Heaven is at hand.*' I have said already that I believe such a call to repentance is the true way of bringing evidence for any one of the articles of Christian theology. When the hearts of the fathers are turned to the children, when the doctor or pharisee feels himself on the level of the publican and the harlot, then these articles come forth in their own native and divine might; then the objections, which are merely the creatures of fancy or of pride, are scattered as chaff before the wind; then those deeper objections, which touch the heart and reason, are seen to affect not the principles themselves, but only some earthly additions to them, which have weakened and subverted them. While we are frivolous, exclusive, heartless, no arguments ought to convince us of Christ's Incarnation; they would carry their own condemnation with them, if they did. When we are aroused to think earnestly what we are, what our relation to our fellow-men is, what God is,—the voice which says, '*The Word was m de flesh and dwelt among us,*' '*The Son of God was manifested that He might destroy the works of the devil.* will no more be thought of as the voice of an apostle. We shall know that He is speaking to us Himself, and that He is the Christ that should come into the world.

Let no Unitarian suppose that these last words are pointed at *him*,—that I suppose *he* has greater need of repentance than we have, because some special moral obliquity has prevented him from recognising the truth of the Incarnation. I had no such meaning; I was thinking much more of the orthodox. I was considering how many causes hinder *us* from confessing with our hearts as well as our lips, that Christ has come in the flesh. The conceit of our orthodoxy is one cause. Whatever sets us in any wise above our fellow-men, is an obstacle to a hearty belief in *the* Man; it must be taken from us before we shall really bow our knees to Him. I know not that if He were now walking visibly among us, He might not say that many a Unitarian was far nearer the kingdom of heaven than many of us; less choked with prejudice, less self-confident, more capable of recognising the great helper of the wounded man who has fallen among thieves, than we priests or Levites are, because more ready to go and do likewise. I cannot say that this might not be so; I often suspect that it would be so; and therefore I certainly did not intend to convey the impression that the moral disease at the root of their most vehement intellectual denials, is, necessarily, a malignant one.

But though I do not think that such a call as we are told went forth from the lips of John the Baptist, to prepare the way for Christ, is less needful for us than for them, I should be far indeed from wishing to shut them out from so great a benefit. We all want it, I think, for the same reason. When St. John explains the object of the Baptist's mission, he does not use the language of the other evangelists. He says, '*He came to bear witness of the LIGHT, that all men through Him might believe.*' This is not a mere equivalent for the words, '*Repent, for the kingdom of heaven is at hand;*' but it gives us the innermost force of those words; it takes away their vagueness; it shows why one person, as much as another, had need to hear them. 'There is a light within you, 'close to you. Do you know it? Are you coming to it? 'Are you desiring that it should penetrate you through 'and through? Oh, turn to it! Turn from these idols 'that are surrounding you,—from the confused, dark 'world of thoughts within you! It will reveal yourself 'to you! It will reveal the world to you!' 'What do you mean?' asks the well-instructed, formally, habitually religious man: 'my conscience, I suppose.' 'Call 'it that, or what you please; but in God's name, my 'friend, do not cheat yourself with a phrase. I mean a 'reality; I mean that which has to do with your inner-'most being; I mean something which does not proceed 'from you or belong to you; but which is there, searching 'you and judging you. Nay! stay a moment. I mean 'that this light comes from a Person,—from the King and 'Lord of your heart and spirit,—from the Word,—the 'Son of God. When I say, Repent; I say, Turn and 'confess His presence. You have always had it with 'you. You have been unmindful of it.'

Such words would startle some Unitarians, but not more than they would startle those who are settled on the lees of a comfortable orthodoxy. The cries of 'Mysticism,' 'Lore imported from the Alexandrian fathers,' 'Utterly 'inconsistent with all sound modern philosophy,' 'Derived from our own conceits, not from the Bible,'

'Fénélon, Madame Guion, Jacob Böhme,' &c., would rise just as loudly from one as from the other. The teacher, if he happens to know anything of the persons he is accused of copying, may tell what he knows; but he will do better if he delivers his message simply to those who have need of it. They will discover in themselves whether it is a poor plagiarism; they will know whether it fills them with mystical conceits, or scatters those conceits. If he has courage to go on, he will find a response, not only in those who have been told, from their youth upward, that the voice of conscience is Christ's voice, but from a number who are nominally and in profession materialists; who cannot conceive of any spiritual communication whatsoever, who think that the testimonies of conscience are the echoes of words addressed to the ear. For theories signify little when the question is one of fact and moral demonstration. They disappear, as they do before any great and decisive experiment in physics, and adjust themselves, not at once but gradually, to the law which has been brought to light. And a materialist who has been honest with himself, has sought to do right, and has not used phrases which for him had no meaning, is quite as likely as another man to yield to such evidence.

It is necessary for my present purpose to make this statement; for I cannot disguise from myself the truth that there are many, not only among Unitarians, but among us, who would be simply bewildered by the proposition, '*Christ took flesh.*' What Christ? they would ask, if they were not withheld by some fear. 'Is 'not Jesus of Nazareth the Christ?' And this difficulty is not relieved, but increased, by the emphasis with which the ablest, most devout, and most learned divines, both here and in Germany, are dwelling on the words, '*God manifest in the flesh.*' I do not mean that these divines care whether or not that precise expression occurs in the Epistle to Timothy; whether the line in the O can be detected with the aid of spectacles or not; they are far too manly and too well grounded in their faith, to make it depend upon this or any other philological *crux.* They take these words as expressing the very sense of the Gospel and of the New Testament. I do not think they can be stronger in that persuasion than I am; but I cannot help perceiving,—and a consideration of Unitarian difficulties has especially led me to this conclusion,—that if, in their eagerness to set forth the manifestation, they take no pains to declare who is the manifester, they will leave an impression on a number of minds, the very opposite to that which they seek to produce. They will lead people to suppose that the Image of the Holy One had no reality till it was presented through a human body to men, or at least, that till then, this Image had no relation to the creature who is said in Scripture to be formed in it. By this means the whole of the Old Testament economy, instead of being fulfilled in the revelation of the Son of God, becomes hopelessly divided from it. But, what is worse still, by this means the heart and conscience of human beings become separated from that revelation. It stands outside, as if it were presented to the eye, not to them; as if those who saw Christ in the flesh must really have known Him for that reason, whereas every sentence of the Gospels is telling us that they did not.

I conceive the method of St. John is far more scientific, and also far more human and practical. He declares to us the Word as God, and also as with God; as Him by whom all things were created; as Him whose Life was the Light of men; whose light was shining in the darkness, and the darkness did not take it down into itself; whose Light was witnessed by the visible teacher, that all men might believe; Who was in the world, though the world knew Him not; Who came to his own house, and its inmates did not receive Him; Who gave those who did receive him power to become sons of God, being born not of flesh nor of blood, nor of the will of man, but of God; Who at last was made flesh and dwelt among men, and in Whom the glory of the Only-begotten of the Father, full of grace and truth, was seen. Quite aware how strange this method must seem to many of ourselves, still stranger to the Unitarian, I have yet tried to follow it, because it appeals, I think, both to the reason and to the conscience, and because I should be very inconsistent if I supposed that the Light which lighteth every man did not light the

Unitarian, or that he may not come to it and discover whence it flows. Nor do I think that any one of the grounds upon which I have rested my defence of our creed concerning the Incarnation, will be entirely unintelligible to him.

1. I have told him before, that I think he is exposed to a danger, of which he least dreams,—that of honouring the Son, not *as* he honours the Father, but *above* Him. I would now ask him seriously to consider, whether the best part of the honour he ever *has* paid to the Father, that which has been most real and akin to his heart, has not been derived from the image which was presented to him in Christ? He may have used some large phrases about Omnipotence, or Omnipresence. I do not say that they conveyed no meaning to his mind. But was it such a meaning,—so deep, so penetrating, so satisfactory to his moral instincts,—as that which was brought to him by the story of a person actually, thoroughly, inwardly and outwardly, righteous? If the quality of mere power became more sacred and venerable in his mind than that of righteousness, or mercy, or truth, will he not have suspected himself? will he not have said, 'I am 'yielding to a disease, I am borrowing my notions from 'the phantoms of greatness and glory, which the world 'worships; I am forgetting the moral standard which 'I profess to set up?' And if, (as I think,) power *is* intended to command a reverence, and must always

command it, though in subordination to that which determines its ends, have not the instances of calm power, recorded in the Gospel,—of Christ ruling the waves, for instance, or feeding the multitude,—appealed more directly to the faculty which receives that impression, and bows to it, than any such mere abstraction as this of Omnipotence? These are hints which I should like any Unitarian who wishes to give a fair account to himself of his own emotions and convictions, steadily to follow out, not minding whither they lead him. They may not lead him at once, or for a long time, to accept our language, 'of one substance with the Father;' he may make a great many attempts to avoid it, by speaking of a Unity of purpose or of will. But if he once comes to understand himself about Unity of purpose and will, and carefully to consider what that involves, I have no fear but that he will by degrees understand thoroughly what the Church intends by Unity of Substance.

2. Nor do I fear that the younger Unitarian, especially, will discard what I have said of Christ entering into our temptations, as worthless and unmeaning. What I do fear for him, as I have told him already, is, that he may adopt a kind of sentimental talk, very prevalent in our day, about struggles and conflicts of the spirit,—as if these were striking phenomena to observe in men of other ages, who are entitled to our patronage, and in a qualified sense to our admiration, for

having passed through tempests, which we can contemplate and criticise from a calm and secure height. I know *this* temptation; I do not warn them of it as if *I* were on a calm height out of its reach. It assaults us all continually; I cannot tell how often I may have yielded to it while writing this book. But I can testify that the only escape I have ever found from it, is in the belief that a real and 'strong' Son of God encountered the enemy of me, and of all the men who are living now, or ever have lived. While I hold fast that confidence, I cannot suppose that the fight which our fathers had to fight is a different one from ours. I cannot fancy that I have acquired any position or any skill, which gives me the slightest advantage over them, or on the other hand, that our circumstances are the least to be deplored; that the former days were better than these. I must believe that the struggle becomes intenser as it approaches nearer to the final decision; but the thought of that decision, and that it will be for, not against, the race whose nature Christ took, ought to make us more trusting, not more self-confident, than those were who have finished their course.

3. If I dared to indulge in a mere *argumentum ad hominem*, I might hope to make much of my third proposition in discoursing with a Unitarian. He is pledged to hostility against the Calvinistical theory of election; he has often fraternised with Churchmen on that ground. But I think that he and the Arminians of my own com-

munion, have been equally to blame, for the course which they have taken in this controversy. They have complained of the Calvinist partly for his exclusions, partly for his zeal in proclaiming the will of God as the sole cause of man's redemption and salvation. Because I dislike and repudiate his exclusions, I would follow him with all my heart and soul in that proclamation. If man is held to choose God, and not God to choose man, I see no deliverance from the darkest views of His character and of our destiny. Some of the Unitarians appear to be making this discovery; at least I judge so, from a very impressive sermon by Mr. Martineau, on the words: '*Ye have not chosen me, but I have chosen you.*'

Before, then, we enter into any alliance, offensive or defensive, against Calvinism, it must be clearly understood that we do not mean this side of Calvinism; for that is as much presumed in the doctrine that God redeems mankind, as in the doctrine that He redeems certain elect souls out of mankind. Every redeemed person must, according to me as much as according to the Calvinist, refer every good that is in him, that he does, that befals him, to the Father of Lights,—must consider his will as freed by Him from a bondage, and as freed, that it may become truly a servant. Nay, so strongly do I feel this, that I see no refuge from the exclusiveness of some of those who consider themselves very moderate Calvinists, especially from those favourite divisions of theirs which seem to make the 'believer' something different from a man, and so to take from him the very truth, which he has to believe,—but by recalling the strong and energetic statements of the earlier Calvinists, respecting the one root and origin of faith, as well as of right acts. But this is not all. I have no right to denounce the exclusiveness of the Calvinists, unless I am willing to renounce all that may cleave to myself. The Unitarian may fairly say to me, 'Give up your Anglican exclusiveness if you 'wish me to think you sincere in your complaints of 'them.' And I, if I am striving to do so, may turn upon him and say, 'Give up your Gnostical 'exclusiveness, your Emersonian exclusiveness, your 'notions of a high intellectual election, if you wish me 'to think you sincere in your complaints of Calvinists 'or of Anglicans.' I do not believe that we shall any of us comply with these demands, each of which is perfectly reasonable and righteous, unless we heartily and unfeignedly acknowledge that Christ, the Son of God, has taken the nature of every man. With that faith, when it has possessed our whole being, exclusiveness of any kind cannot dwell.

To conclude. I should be content to put the whole cause on this issue. Let it be considered earnestly what has made the difference between the belief concerning God and concerning Man, which has prevailed in Christendom, and that which exists in any part of heathendom. To understand the difference, study as carefully the resemblances,—all the dark and horrible thoughts respecting our Father in heaven, and our fellow-creatures on earth, which exist among us, and which we have adopted from Heathenism. Let all allowance you please be made for varieties of races, and for progress of civilization, on condition that you are not satisfied with these formulas, but are willing to regard them as indications of facts, which need to be explained. And then let it be seen whether the belief that the Jesus Christ set forth in the Gospels is the express Image of God, and the image after which man is formed, has not been the secret of all that is confessedly high, pure, moral in our convictions; the departure from that belief, and the attempt to deduce the nature of God from some philosophical generalization, or from some heroical man, or from a number of men, or from ourselves, has not been at the root of all that is cruel in our doctrine, as well as of that which is most feeble and base in our practice.

ESSAY VII.

ON THE ATONEMENT.

It will be evident, I hope, by this time, on what grounds I object to the so-called Theology of Consciousness. Not, surely, because I am not anxious to observe all the experiences and consciousnesses which the history of the world bears witness of. Not because I do not desire that all these should be understood, as they can only be understood, through the conscience of each man. Not that I do not ask of theology that it should explain these consciousnesses, and clear and satisfy that individual conscience.

But I find that a theology which is based upon consciousness, which is derived out of it, never can fulfil these conditions. In former Essays, I have tried to indicate the feelings and demands of a man who has been awakened to know sin in himself. He asks for deliverance from a plague, which seems part of his own existence. He asks that some power, which is crushing him and vanquishing him, and making free thought and action impossible, may be put down. He is in despair, because he is sure that he is at war, not merely with a Sovereign Will, but with a perfectly good will. He is convinced that, in some way or other, he has a righteous cause, though he is so deeply and inwardly evil. He thinks a righteous Being must be on his side, though he has grieved Him, and been unrighteous. He thinks he has an Advocate, and that the mind of this Advocate cannot be opposed to the mind of the Lord of all, the Creator of the universe, but must be the counterpart of it. He thinks that the true Son of God must be his Redeemer. He thinks He must stand at some day on the earth, to assert His Father's righteous dominion over it, and to redeem it from its enemies.

Here are strange, conflicting, 'consciousnesses,' all of which are actually found in human beings, all of which must be heeded, which will make themselves manifest in strange ways if they are not. The consciousness of sin will lead to a consciousness of consequences flowing from sin, stretching into the furthest future. And when this consciousness tries to construct a theology for itself, those consequences, apprehensible, tangible, material, will determine the character of the theology. How can I escape from these? will be the question. Who shall sever the consequences from the cause? The consciousness that the Creator has linked the one to the other, suggests the thought that pain, suffering, misery, are especially His work, the signs which denote His feelings towards His creatures. The consciousness of a tyrant and oppressor leads to the supposition that He is that tyrant and oppressor. The consciousness of an Advocate, leads to the supposition that He may be the instrument of delivering us out of the hand of the Creator, of saving us from the punishment which the Creator has appointed for transgression. The consciousness that we share our sin with our fellow-creatures, and that we are obnoxious to a punishment which belongs equally to them, leads to the reflection, 'How 'can we put ourselves into a different position from 'theirs? how can we escape from the calamities with 'which God has threatened them?'

What I wish the reader to observe is, that in each of these cases a notion or maxim respecting theology is likely to be generalized from the *consciousness*, which will oppose and outrage the *conscience.* Building on his own ground, assuming all his own vague and contradictory impressions as data, the man of necessity works out a system, on which he afterwards gazes with horror, from which he longs to break loose, which he charges priests and doctors with having created. No doubt they have contributed their wicked aid to the fabric; their guilt is heavier than that of the poor bewildered creatures who have consulted them. But their guilt has consisted in the willingness which they have shown to create a religion out of consciousnesses; to endorse all the conceptions and conclusions about God which the diseased heart fashions for itself, while they have a witness within them of truths which contradict these conceptions and conclusions; to supply intellectual links which may fasten together what would be loose, incoherent, fragmentary fancies; to devise rules, and ethical practices, which may meet the morbid and selfish cravings of the heart, and be justified by the theory the understanding has moulded from them; finally, to stamp with the name, dignity, and sacredness of faith, that which is grounded, in great part, upon fear and distrust.

I believe that priests, in all lands, have been chargeable with this great crime of accommodating themselves to the carnal notions and tendencies of those whom they might have raised and educated. For I believe they have had an intuition of a higher truth, which it was their calling to proclaim, and which alone gave substance to the opinions with which they and their disciples disfigured it. I dare not deny that this crime has been greatest in the priests of Christendom, precisely because I hold that they have a theology revealed from Heaven, which perfectly satisfies the demands of the human heart; which explains to men the contradictions in their own impressions and experiences; which presents such a God as the conscience witnesses there must be and is, not such a one as the understanding tries to shape out from its own reflections on the testimony of the conscience; which shows what the relation between Him and men is, what the cause of the separation between Him and men is, what He has done to establish the relation, to destroy the separation.

I have now reached the subject which is the test of all that I have been saying hitherto. Those who cry for a theology based upon consciousness, which shall supersede the theology of Christendom, say that the doctrines respecting sacrifice and atonement which prevail in Christendom, among Protestants as well as Romanists, prove more clearly than anything else what need there is of the reform which they seek. 'These doctrines,' they say, 'darken the sense of right and wrong in the minds of 'Christians; bewilder their understandings; sanction 'the most false conceptions concerning sin, the most 'cruel conceptions concerning God. The conscience of 'human beings is in revolt against them. Civil authority 'owns that it can defend them no longer. Ecclesiastical 'authority tries to defend them. They have a certain 'public opinion on their side;—that which has resisted 'in every age every great moral improvement, that 'which has sustained every false religion. They derive 'a support from those who half believe them, who dare 'not say how much of them they do not believe. But 'they are doomed; texts of Scripture will not preserve 'from burial that which is already dead. No appeal to 'the verdict of centuries will galvanise doctrines which 'do not represent our convictions. We must have a 'theology which embodies *them*, or none.'

On this point I join issue with them. I say that they are right in imputing to Romanists and Protestants a set of notions,—some of them common to both, some peculiar to each,—which deserve the epithets they bestow on it; which outrage the conscience, which misrepresent the character of God, which generate a fearful amount of insincere belief, of positive infidelity,—also, I think, of immorality. I see, with them, that these notions are becoming more and more intolerable to thoughtful and earnest men; that those who are neither, often maintain them merely because they do not care to look at them, or to question themselves about them. I cannot conceal from myself that our want of courage in saying whether we regard these as parts of our creed, or not, is leading thousands to identify them with it, and to reject it as well as them. But I maintain that these notions are not parts of God's Revelation, or of the old Creeds, but belong to that Theology of Consciousness which modern enlightenment would substitute for the Theology of the Bible and of the Church; that their rise can be distinctly and historically traced to this source; that the protest on the part of the conscience against them in other days, has been a confession of its own inability to construct a Theodicæa, a claim that God should remove its confusions by revealing Himself; that the protest of the conscience against them in our day is of the same kind, and must have the same issue, if it is not unnaturally silenced; that Christian theology, as expressed in the language of the Bible and of the Creeds, construed most simply, is a deliverance from these oppressive notions, and is the only one which has yet been or ever will be found.

1. The account which I have given of the way in which different consciousnesses, beginning with the consciousness of sin, have worked themselves out into a scheme, is precisely that which has been given over and over again by liberal historians, who have wished to describe the growth of the Romish system. 'Men,' they have said, 'who were stung with the recollection of evil 'acts, thought they might do something to win the 'favour or avert the wrath of the Divine Being. They 'must make sacrifices, the greatest they could think of, 'or which any could suggest to them, that their sins 'might be forgiven. What sacrifices these should be, 'they could very imperfectly guess; they must ask 'wiser people to tell them. They found an organized 'hierarchy established for the very purpose of explain-'ing the relations between the visible and the invisible 'world, and of maintaining the intercourse between 'them. Those who composed it ought to know what 'they should do. And these devised indulgences to 'soothe the pains of the diseased patients, penances that 'irritated them. At first, the suggestion might be merely 'benevolent, even suitable to the case, grounded on a 'knowledge of the symptoms. Then came in the love

'of power, with the discovery how much of that (which 'presented itself to the vulgar priest in the form of ma-'terial riches) might be obtained by catering to the 'cravings of a morbid appetite. If the regular prac-'titioner did not meet them, popular confessors appear-'ing in new orders supplied the defects of the original 'system. But neither one nor the other were sufficient. 'The poor offender felt, all confused as he was, that his 'sacrifices could never of themselves move the mind of 'God. He must ask the aid of those who had prevailed 'in the fight, in which he seemed likely to be worsted. 'Saints must be invoked, who would themselves invoke 'the Highest of all, to be merciful. A number of acci-'dents of time, place, occupation, education, would dic-'tate which should be besought by any particular person. 'The Virgin Mother would be a more general pleader, 'especially for the female suppliants. Those who 'habitually sought her intercession with the Divine 'Son, might hope that His infinite sacrifice would 'remove the sins which they had contracted, after 'the great original sin had been purged away in 'baptism.'

Something like this is the natural history of Romanism, past and present, which we find in books not pretending to be specially theological, but trying to look at the subject fairly, from an ordinary human point of view. To make the statement quite fair, I suppose most persons would admit,—I, at least, as a very vehement

Protestant, should,—that there is an immense amount of moral and spiritual influences acting upon those who are tied and bound in this system, which does not proceed from it, and is not expressed by it. Romanists will be found in no ambiguous phrases acknowledging the love of God and His free grace as the only source of good human acts, submission to His will as the only acceptable sacrifice. They will make these confessions, not as if they were conceding something to us, but as the proper expression of their own faith, as implied in the very nature of a Catholic church; they will prove the sincerity of them by their lives. All such facts are to be admitted, not reluctantly, not as if it was a shock to our belief that we were obliged to make them, but with the most unspeakable delight; as well for the sake of those to whom they apply, as because they prove how utterly the notions which oppose these confessions are at war with the deepest and truest convictions of men, how unnatural it is to associate them with any faith. Multiply proofs of this kind a thousandfold, you increase the evidence that it is a duty to labour continually that a cancer may be extirpated, which is eating out the heart of Christendom, the poisonous quality and deadly effects of which our most vehement Protestant declaimers do not exaggerate, but underrate.

2. Nor can I discover that those declaimers are the least mistaken in the explanation which they commonly give of the means whereby this mischief was detected, and by

which some were enabled to escape it. They say that when Luther found out that he was a sinner, when he knew that fact in the length and breadth of it,—not by the hearing of the ear, but by his own tremendous experience,—he could no longer be content with any of the priestly inventions for putting away sin; that he then knew that he could only be delivered from it if God delivered him; that he demanded to know whether He had proclaimed forgiveness of sin; whether there was any sacrifice which He had appointed and accepted? They say that Luther found the answers to these questions in the Bible: that he was content when he was told, on its authority, that the Son of God had taken away sin; that this might be received and preached to all men as His Gospel. The person who differs most with Luther, must accept this as a statement of notorious facts; it is as much acknowledged by Michelet as by Marheineke, or Merle d'Aubigné. I accept it also as being entirely in accordance with internal evidence,—with the law which I am endeavouring to establish. Luther's conscience did not make a system. It protested against one which had been made in compliance with apparent necessities of the conscience. It said that the real necessity of the conscience was, that God should speak to it, declare Himself to it,—should proclaim Himself as its reconciler, should show how and in whom He had accomplished that work on its behalf.

3. But I admitted that there were grave and earnest

protests against much of what is called *our* doctrine of the Atonement. 'You hold,' it is said, 'that God had 'condemned all His creatures to perish, because they 'had broken His law; that His justice could not be 'satisfied without an infinite punishment; that that in- 'finite punishment would have visited all men, if Christ 'in His mercy to men had not interposed and offered 'Himself as the substitute for them; that by enduring 'an inconceivable amount of anguish, He reconciled the 'Father, and made it possible for Him to forgive those 'who would believe. This whole statement,' the objector continues, 'is based on a certain notion of justice. 'It professes to explain, on certain principles of justice, 'what God ought to have done, and what He actually 'has done. And this notion of justice outrages the con- 'science to which you seem to offer your explanation. 'You often feel that it does. You admit that it is not 'the kind of justice which would be expected of men. 'And then you turn round and ask us what we can know 'of God's justice; how we can tell that it is of the same 'kind with ours? After arguing with us, to show the 'necessity of a certain course, you say that the argu- 'ment is good for nothing; we are not capable of taking 'it in! Or else you say that the carnal mind cannot 'understand spiritual ideas. We can only answer, We 'prefer our carnal notion of justice to your spiritual one. 'We can forgive a fellow-creature a wrong done to us, 'without exacting an equivalent for it; we blame our-

'selves if we do not; we think we are offending against 'Christ's command, who said, "*Be ye merciful as your 'Father in Heaven is merciful,*" if we do not. We do not 'feel that punishment is a satisfaction to our minds; we 'are ashamed of ourselves when we consider it is. We 'may suffer a criminal to be punished, but it is that we 'may do him good, or assert a principle. And if that 'is our object, we do not suffer an innocent person to 'prevent the guilty from enduring the consequences of 'his guilt, by taking them upon himself. Are these 'maxims moral, or are the opposing maxims moral? If 'they are moral, should we, because God is much more 'righteous than we can imagine or understand, suppose 'that His acts are at variance with them? Should we 'attribute to Him what would be unrighteousness 'in us?'

These questions are asked on all sides of us. Clergymen are exceedingly anxious to stifle them. 'We 'know,' they say, 'by experience whither such doubts 'are leading. The objector begins with disputing 'some views of the Atonement, which may perhaps be 'extreme. He goes on to deny the doctrine itself; to 'say that it has no place in the scheme of Christianity. 'He knows, however, that his fathers held it to be a 'vital doctrine. He suspects that it is in the Bible. 'The end is, that he denies the Bible itself.' Such a conclusion may well startle a good man. He feels that principles which his experience has proved to be infinitely precious are in hazard. He has never visited the dying bed of a humble penitent who did not cling to the cross of Christ as her dearest hope, who did not feel that without His sacrifice and death she could have no peace. He asks whether he is to rob the poor and meek of these jewels because certain proud men do not like the casket which contains them, because they cannot bring the teachings of the Bible to the level of their understandings?

Debates are going on in every corner of our land suggested by these difficulties. What misery, what alienation of heart arises from them no one can tell! On the one side, the consequence of the strife is an ever increasing hardness and dogmatism blighting all the fruits of the Spirit; on the other, a barren hopeless infidelity. It must then be the most serious of all duties to labour so far as in us lies that the sound and deep convictions which evidently are in the heart of the divine and the moralist may not become utterly destroyed through their separation, that each should confess the error which was mingled with that truth in his mind and is threatening to make it inoperative.

The statement of the clergyman is certainly not exaggerated, that the best, the humblest, truest hearts are those which rest with most childlike faith upon the belief that '*God has reconciled the world unto Himself, not imputing their trespasses unto them;*' that the death of Christ is the death of that '*Lamb of God who taketh away the sins of the world.*' To tell such persons that no atonement has been made between man and God, would be to tell them that the future is only a perpetual lengthening out of the anguish of conscience which is and must be bitterer to them than all other anguish; that there is an impassable gulf between them and all truth and righteousness. What is it to assure them that transgressions are forgiven by a bare act of amnesty, unless the sin of the heart and will, the separation from God, which is the root of these transgressions, is at an end? How can you ever persuade them that it is at an end unless God Himself has removed it? How can God have removed a separation unless there is some One in whom we are bound more closely to Him than our evils have put us asunder?

The broad simple Gospel, that God has set forth His Son as the propitiation for sin, that He has offered Himself for the sins of the world, meets all the desires of these heart-stricken sinners. It declares to them the fulness of God's love, sets forth the Mediator in whom they are at one with the Father. It brings divine Love and human suffering into direct and actual union. It shows Him who is one with God and one with man, perfectly giving up that self-will which had been the cause of all men's crimes and all their misery. Here is indeed a brazen serpent to which one dying from the bite of the old serpent can look and be healed. The more that brazen serpent is lifted up, the more may we look for health and renovation to the whole of humanity, and to every one of its palsied and withered limbs.

I do not deny, that besides these leading convictions which take possession of the heart as it contemplates the Cross of Christ, there are others apparently of a different kind. Since nowhere is the contrast between infinite Love and infinite Evil brought before us as it is there, we have the fullest right to affirm that the Cross exhibits the wrath of God against sin, and the endurance of that wrath by the well-beloved Son. For wrath against that which is unlovely, is not the counteracting force to love, but the attribute of it. Without it love would be a name, and not a reality. And the endurance of that wrath or punishment by Christ came from His acknowledging that it proceeded from love, and His willingness that it should not be quenched till it had effected its full loving purpose. The endurance of that wrath was the proof that He bore in the truest and strictest sense the sins of the world, feeling them with that anguish with which only a perfectly pure and holy Being, who is also a perfectly sympathising and gracious Being, can feel the sins of others. Whatever diminished his purity, must have diminished his sympathy. Complete suffering with sin and for sin is only possible in one who is completely free from it.

But is the clergyman who preaches this gospel, and sees the effect of it upon some of his flock, therefore bound to adopt those conclusions respecting the reasons of Christ's death, which have so shocked the conscience of the sceptic whom he is condemning? Properly speaking, his business is simply to proclaim the good news of reconciliation. Reasons may occur to him besides those which the Bible gives us. Some may be plausible, some may be tolerable. But they do not belong to the essence of his commission. Woe be to him, if he mistakes the best of them for that which it tries to account for. Since, however, it is inevitable that his understanding and imagination will be busy with this and every other subject divine or human that he handles, it is very necessary that he should perceive what conclusions of theirs may contradict the truth which God has committed to him. For this purpose, I would beseech him to observe carefully which portions of his statements come home to the hearts of the really humble and contrite—which afford delight and satisfaction to the conceited, self-righteous, self-exalting men and women of his flock, who in ease and health think that they are safe, because they are condemning others, who in sickness and on a death-bed discover that in seeming to believe everything, they have actually believed nothing. This comparison, if it is faithfully pursued, and never separated from self-examination, will lead him I believe, to precisely the same result at which he would arrive by the other method of considering what is demanded by the principles which Protestants and Romanists recognise in common. On this last subject, I wish to speak a little more at large. I wish to show that the orthodox faith as it is expressed in the Bible and the Creeds, absolutely prevents us from acquiescing in some of those explanations of the Atonement, which both in popular and scholastic teachings have been identified with it.

1. It is involved in the very method of theology, as the Bible and the creeds set it forth to us, that the Will of God should be asserted as the ground of all that is right, true, just, gracious. There is no acknowledged difference of opinion on this point. It would be accounted heresy in all orthodox schools to deny that the Father sent the Son to be the Saviour of men; that the Father set forth the Son to be the propitiation for our sins; that Christ, by his life, proved that God is light, and that in Him is no darkness at all. These declarations of St. John are admitted as fundamental truths, to which all others must do homage, which no other passages can contradict. All I ask is, that we may hold fast this profession without wavering; that no feeble compromiser may be suffered to come in and say, 'All this is true in a sense,' without telling us in what sense; and if it is such a sense as clearly is not meant to govern all our thoughts, determinations, conclusions, he may be dismissed as one who has no business to call himself an orthodox man.

2. It is admitted in all schools, Romanist and Pro-

testant, which do not dissent from the Creed, that Christ the Son of God was in heaven and earth, one with the Father, one in will, purpose, substance; and that on earth His whole life was nothing else than an exhibition of this Will, an entire submission to it. There is no dispute among orthodox people about this point, more than about the other. And there is no dispute as to the principle being a fundamental one, that on which the very nature of Christ's sacrifice must depend, as the writer of the Epistle to the Hebrews declares that it does. What we have a right to insist on is, that no notion or theory shall be allowed to interfere with this fundamental maxim. If we would adhere to the faith once delivered to the Saints, we must not dare to speak of Christ as changing that Will which He took flesh and died to fulfil.

3. It is confessed by all orthodox schools, that Christ was actually the Lord of men, the King of their spirits, the Source of all the light which ever visited them, the Person for whom all nations longed as their Head and Deliverer, the root of righteousness in each man. The Bible speaks of His being revealed in this character; of the mystery which had been hid from ages and generations being made known by His Incarnation. If we speak of Christ as taking upon Himself the sins of men by some artificial substitution, we deny that He is their actual Representative.

4. The Scripture says, Because the children were

'*partakers of flesh and blood He also Himself took part of the same.*' He became subject to death, '*that He might destroy him who had the power of death, that is, the Devil.*' Here are reasons assigned for the Incarnation and the death of Christ. He shared the sufferings of those whose head He is. He overcame death, their common enemy, by submitting to it. He delivered them from the power of the Devil. All orthodox schools, in formal language,—tens of thousands of suffering people, in ordinary human language,—have confessed the force of the words. Instead of seeking to put Christ at a distance from themselves, by tasking their fancy to conceive of sufferings which, at the same moment, are pronounced inconceivable, they have claimed Him as entering into their actual miseries, as bearing their griefs. They have believed that He endured death, because it was theirs, and rose to set them free from it, because it was an evil accident of their condition, an effect of disorder, not of God's original order. They have believed that He rescued them out of the power of an enemy, by yielding to his power, not that He rescued them out of the hand of God by paying a penalty to Him. Any notion whatever which interferes with this faith; any explanation of Christ's sufferings which is put in the place of the Apostle's explanation, or does not strictly harmonize with it; far more any that contradicts it, and leaves us open to the awful danger of confounding the Evil Spirit with God,—

we have a right to repudiate as unorthodox, unscriptural, and audacious.

5. The Scripture says, '*The Lamb of God taketh away the Sin of the world.*' All orthodox teachers repeat the lesson. They say Christ came to deliver sinners from sin. This is what the sinner asks for. Have we a right to call ourselves scriptural or orthodox, if we change the words, and put 'penalty of sin' for 'sin;' if we suppose that Christ destroyed the connexion between sin and death,—the one being the necessary wages of the other, —for the sake of benefiting any individual man whatever? If He had, would He have magnified the Law and made it honourable? Would He not have destroyed that which He came to fulfil? Those who say the law must execute itself, must have its penalty, should remember their own words. How does it execute itself if a person, against whom it is not directed, interposes to bear its punishment?

6. The voice at Christ's baptism said, '*This is my beloved Son, in whom I am well pleased.*' Christ said, '*Therefore doth my Father love me, because I lay down my life for the sheep.*' All orthodox schools have said, that a perfectly holy and loving Being can be satisfied only with a holiness and love corresponding to His own; that Christ satisfied the Father by presenting the image of His own holiness and love, that in His sacrifice and death, all that holiness and love came forth completely. There is no dissent upon this point, among those

who adhere to the Creed. But it cannot be an accidental point; it must belong to the root and essence of divinity. How, then, can we tolerate for an instant that notion of God which would represent Him as satisfied by the punishment of sin, not by the purity and graciousness of the Son?

7. Supposing all these principles gathered together; supposing the Father's will to be a will to all good;—supposing the Son of God, being one with Him, and Lord of man, to obey and fulfil in our flesh that will by entering into the lowest condition into which men had fallen through their sin;—supposing this Man to be, for this reason, an object of continual complacency to His Father, and that complacency to be fully drawn out by the Death of the Cross;—supposing His Death to be a Sacrifice, the only complete sacrifice ever offered, the entire surrender of the whole spirit and body to God; is not this, in the highest sense, Atonement? Is not the true, sinless root of Humanity revealed; is not God in Him reconciled to man? Is not the Cross the meeting point between man and man, between man and God? Is not this meeting point what men, in all times and places, have been seeking for? Did any find it till God declared it? And are not we bringing our understandings to the foot of this Cross, when we solemnly abjure all schemes and statements, however sanctioned by the arguments of divines, however plausible as implements of declamation, which prevent us from believing

and proclaiming that in it all the wisdom and truth and glory of God were manifested to the creature; that in it man is presented as a holy and acceptable sacrifice to the Creator?

'I am not nearer, then, to Unitarians, because I have 'joined them in repudiating certain opinions which they, 'and many of us, have supposed inseparable from the 'doctrine of the Atonement?' Not nearer to them, certainly, in any one of their negative conclusions. On the contrary, I have used the articles in the Creed which they most dissent from, as my weapons against the representations of God, which we agree in thinking horrible. I have appealed to the Creed, as my protection from dogmas which I have attributed to the active workings of the consciousness and the intellect; one or other of which they are generally inclined to deify. Nor can I help further offending them by saying, that the tenacity with which my orthodox brethren have maintained notions, at variance, as I think, with their inmost faith, has been owing in great measure to their Unitarian opponents. They have heard the faith and the opinions assailed together; they have supposed that there must be an intimate connexion between them; they have feared to ask whether there is or not. Men of the Evangelical school, who did not like Archbishop Magee's book, because they found nothing in it which responded to the witness of their hearts, yet accepted it on the poor calculation that it was a learned book, and might defend what they were pleased to call the outworks of the faith. Men of the Patristic school, who knew how little it accorded with the divinity they most admired, yet argued, œconomically, that it might serve the purposes of such an age as ours is, and might confute objectors who did not deserve to be acquainted with any higher truth. I acknowledge the dishonesty and faithlessness of both decisions; I feel most deeply the mischiefs which have followed from both; but I see how much there was to make them plausible. I believe it is only a peculiar discipline, and some very painful experience, which has led me to abandon them, and to say boldly, 'I must give up Archbishop Magee, for I am determined 'to keep that which makes the Atonement precious to 'my heart and conscience; to keep the theology of the 'Creeds and of the Bible.'

But though I should be dishonest if I pretended that I was approximating a step nearer to *Unitarianism*, because these seemingly impassable barriers are removed, I do think that they have separated us from the hearts and reasons of *Unitarians* most unnecessarily and mischievously. When the Atonement is defended as an opinion of ours which they are setting at nought, as a conception respecting the method of God's government, and the reasons of His conduct, which they are disputing, the indignation against them becomes greater, because the question at issue becomes more involved with our personal credit, ingenuity, security. We are on one side, they are on the other; the assurance that the divine Atonement is infinitely wonderful, mixes with a consciousness that we are making it petty by our mode of fighting for it. We revenge ourselves for the painful contradiction by increased violence, hoping so to convince ourselves that we are in earnest. When the Atonement is contemplated as the ground of a Gospel to men,—when I dare to say, God so loved the world as to give His only-begotten Son for it,—how closely does that belief bind me to Unitarians, of every class and hue! They may build their theology upon certain deductions of the intellect, or upon certain individual consciousnesses; mine rests on the Eternal Love, which overlooks all distinctions, which embraces the universe. They may glorify this or that material—this or that spiritual—notion and conception. I am bound to acknowledge a Son of God, who is the Lord of their spirits and souls and bodies as He is of mine, who took their nature as He did mine, who died upon the cross for them as He did for me. They may argue about the degree of sin in one or another of us; I am bound to think that I am as much a sinner as any of them can be, and that Christ is the Lamb of God who took away the sin of the world. They may think there is some other way to the Father than through the cross of the

Son; I must confess that there, He is as willing to meet and bless every one of them, as He can be to meet and bless me. I can only hope to know Him while I seek Him in One who perfectly humbled himself; what a lie and a blasphemy to exalt myself on the plea of possessing that knowledge!

ESSAY VIII.

THE RESURRECTION OF THE SON OF GOD FROM DEATH, THE GRAVE, AND HELL.

In the last Essay I spoke of the Death of Christ as it is connected with the Christian idea of Sacrifice and Atonement. But all people who know the tendencies of this age, and who know themselves, are aware how much more easy it is to contemplate this or any event recorded in the Scripture, as an idea, than as a fact. There are many who acknowledge the Death and Resurrection of Christ, in what they call a spiritual sense, to whom the plain words of the Creed, '*He was dead and buried, He descended into Hell, the third day He rose again from the dead,*' are merely words which they repeat because they have repeated them from childhood. Numbers more hold those words to be the relics of an effete superstition, out of which the world has extracted whatever good there was in it, and which may now be left to crumble. I wish to inquire whether the spiritual men, or these words of the Creed, meet the demands of the human heart best; whether these words, or those who cast them aside, are most favourers of superstition.

1. St. Paul says: 'The last enemy which shall be destroyed is *Death.*' Strauss, being at issue with him on most other points, appears to have reached the climax of opposition upon this. He says: 'The last enemy 'which shall be destroyed is the belief of man in his own 'immortality.' Some may suppose that he has merely uttered an audacious paradox, for the sake of startling us, and showing us how far his vehemence against our ordinary faith will go. I do not think so. If we question our own minds honestly, we may find that there have been many hours, days, weeks, perhaps years, in which we have practically yielded assent to his proposition. 'If I could get rid of this sense of immortality, if I 'could convince myself that my years would be rounded 'with a sleep, if I could be sure that there would be no 'dreams in that sleep,—what freedom I should possess! 'how I should be able to enjoy the threescore years, 'or the thirty or twenty years, which are allotted me 'here!' Surely the modern teacher has a large body of unconfessing, unconscious disciples; he must have known that he was the spokesman for thousands, whom some fear withheld from expressing their own feelings. And have I not been obliged to confess in former Essays, that there is a justification for these feelings? Cannot numbers tell of sad effects which the dread of the world to come has produced upon their conduct to other men,

upon their judgment of the beautiful world in which God has placed them, upon their thoughts of God Himself? Have they not been cold, hard, selfish, whenever their minds have been occupied with the one problem, how they may avert the doom which they fear is awaiting them hereafter? Have they not almost cursed the trees and flowers, the new birth of spring, the songs of birds, the faces of children, as if they were mockeries,—witnesses of some present life with which they cannot safely sympathise? Has not the vision of God been one of darkness and horror? When they have said, 'Our Father,' have they not intended one who might destroy them, and from whom they have wished to be delivered? Such experiences in themselves, interpret what they read in history. They see what frightful crimes have been committed by men for the sake of pleasing or appeasing those who may dispose of their future destiny; how these crimes have become a part of their moral system, sanctioned and promoted by those who had apparently more insight into the mind of their God or gods than they have; what poverty and filth, what neglect of relations, what slavery and cowardice have been engendered by the notion that the business of existence here, is to provide for the possibilities of another existence elsewhere.

> Tantum Relligio potuit suadere malorum

has been no unreasonable summary of this evidence. Is not this summary expressed in another form by the words: 'The enemy to be got rid of, is the sense of 'immortality?'

But practical men are driven to ask themselves another question. *How* is this sense to be got rid of? *How* is this enemy to be destroyed? No experiments for the purpose have succeeded yet; no theories of the universe, no new arrangements of it. When you have seemingly extinguished this consciousness, it starts up again; the arguments and schemes which were to exclude it, themselves suggest it and awaken it. And yet there have been such approximations to the extinction of this feeling, as show clearly the only way in which it ever can be reached. Each one may understand for himself that the more he cultivates a merely animal existence, the more he forgets that he was created for anything but to eat and drink and sleep, the less clear and strong is this sense of immortality. And if he could stifle all thoughts that carry him back into past generations, and onward into those which will be when he has left the earth; if he could disconnect himself altogether with family, race, country, social sympathies; if he could cease to think of himself as a person, and become merely a thing,—he might quit himself of this coil; not, I suspect, till then. As long as everything about him preaches of permanence and restoration, as well as of fragility and decay; as long as he is obliged to speak of succession and continuance and order in the universe, and in the societies of men; as long as he feels that he can investigate the one, and that he is a living portion of the other: so long the sense of immortality will be with him; he cannot cast it off. The philosopher to whom I have alluded, probably supposes that he can substitute a political immortality for a personal one; that he can teach men to be indifferent about their own continuance after death, by making them think of the life and endurance of their race. He will find that the more strongly one sentiment is developed, the more certain the other is to come forth; that if one perishes, the other must perish. For he who heartily believes himself to be the member of a family or society, for which it is worth while to fight, and to perish, has the strongest conviction of his own personality; he cannot separate his life from its life; if *it* has any being, *he* must have a being.

But on the other hand, it is most true that a man may become awfully conscious of his own personality, while he is standing apart from all human beings. This is what I spoke of, in a former Essay, as emphatically the sense of *Sin*, the experience of a dark, hopeless isolation, caused by one's own self, certain to continue while that continues. And this it is which unites *Sin* to *Death*, which makes it so hard for us to divorce them in our thoughts. Death, in the obvious aspect of it, is isolation; the separation of each creature from its fellow. The internal dread of it, strictly corresponds to this its outward manifestation. '*I said, in the cutting off of my days, I shall go to the gates of the grave; I am deprived of the residue of my days. I shall not see the Lord, even the Lord, in the land of the living. I shall behold man no more with the inhabitants of the world.*' This was Hezekiah's language; the most natural language that a man could utter; the revelation of the thoughts of innumerable hearts. He has in himself the sense of immortality. It has been nourished by all his faithful acts as a King, by all his sympathies with his nation, by all his efforts to preserve it alive, by all his confidence that God would uphold it from generation to generation. Now he is losing sight of all those with whom he has shared his hopes, his fears, his sorrows. He is losing sight of the temple of God, of all that has reminded him of His presence. Where shall he be? shall he not be alone? A living creature, but an exile from living creatures. No longer in an order; perhaps in a chaos. Oh! infinite horror; the horror of absolute solitude! what can be compared with it?

The German philosopher, then, has much to say for himself; but I think St. Paul has more. The sense of immortality *is* very dreadful, but the terror is not one which the thought of death relieves us of; the thought of death awakens it in us,—the nearer we come to death, the more it faces us. Death, then, is *the* enemy; we must grapple with that if we would overcome the other. And men do grapple with it. There is a deep conviction in their minds, that death is utterly monstrous anomalous; something to which they cannot, and should not, submit. Generations of moralists have done nothing whatever to enforce the experience of six thousand years. They go on denouncing the folly of men for thinking that death is not a necessity, for not yielding to the necessity; the heart of man does not heed their discourses; their own hearts do not heed them. There is that in them which rebels against death, which rebels against it all the more because it is a necessity. Till you explain what that is, till you justify it, you will not cure it. You may wonder why men are so unreasonable, why they dread death, hate it, defy it, and then again seem to long for it, to suppose that it is the only end of their struggle of pain and doubt and despair; but you will fall into the same unreasonableness yourself, you will repeat all these inconsistencies as soon as you pass from the professor's chair to the couch of actual suffering.

I cannot see that the belief in Christ's death would be any deliverance from these awful perplexities, if that death were an artificial arrangement for saving us from a future penalty, while the actual penalty which makes us tremble is incurred as much as ever. But it is not in this light that the Cross ever presented itself to a weary, heavy-laden man. He hears that there is One who has shared his death and the death of the whole world; One in whom God delights; One in whom each man may delight. If this news is believed, the separation of death, that which is indeed its sting, is taken away. It is now, for the first time, common to the individual man with his race. He shall not die alone. He shall not cease to see the Lord, even the Lord in the land of the living; no, nor man with the inhabitants of the world. A new and mysterious attraction holds him to both. Death becomes a bond to them. And it is no longer a mere necessity. Christ *chose* it because it is ours. We can choose it as His more than ours. What I am saying, has no direct reference to our belief in the issue of the death. That may be always implicitly contained in our belief of the death itself. We should not be satisfied with it if we did not see in it the pledge of triumph. But Jesus Christ, as the Crucified, has been an object of rest and comfort to multitudes who have not consciously dwelt on His resurrection. The fact is undoubted, and we do not rightly understand ourselves or our fellow-creatures if we overlook it.

2. Nor are we accurate observers of facts, if we roughly confound the feelings of men respecting death, with those which are awakened by the grave. Philosophers or divines may classify them together,—for actual men they are different. 'He is gone,' are the words by which those who are standing by a bed-side, declare that the person whom they knew, is not in the form which they look upon. But that form is sacred, and awful. It is the witness and pledge that he has been. They cannot look at it in its stillness and repose,

and satisfy themselves with any thoughts of a disembodied spirit. In some way or other, they must connect it with the friend who spoke with them, and cared for them. And yet the instinct, 'Bury the dead out of our sight,' is also deep and healthy; there is something essentially brutal in those people who, like the Tartars, can bear to leave corpses exposed. We call that which the earth encloses, that which it devours and assimilates to itself, 'remains;' or, 'what is mortal;' we have a horror of identifying it with the actual body which was so precious to us. We shrink from the mummy as from a weak, irreverent, materialistic experiment to preserve that which was meant to perish. The earth or ashes seem to us far better; we would rather cast the dearest form into the sea, than give it that horrible, unnatural kind of endurance. These are true feelings, which are found strongest in the truest minds; yet they are very inexplicable. The body associates itself with any thoughts we have of personality and immortality; that which lies in the earth, or is consumed with the fire, we naturally and inevitably associate with decay, putrefaction, destruction. It is easy for superstition to confound the feelings, and to invest relics with the sacredness which we must attach to body; none of its appeals to the heart have been so successful. But the conscience bears witness against the confusion, and longs for a deliverance from it. 'HE *was buried.*' He, the King of men, the true Man, the Son of the Highest, has been in the grave. He knows its secrets, not as a stranger, but as an inhabitant. I believe myriads of sorrowers have found comfort in that conviction, which all their speculations could not give them, but rather took away. His burial, they feel, ought to explain that which all others cannot explain. And they do get the explanation into their hearts, though their understandings may still be much bewildered.

3. But besides and beyond this narrow house, there are fields of speculation, in which men have lost themselves almost from the beginning of the earth until now. Lord Byron has brought Cain into the Abyss of Space, Lucifer being his guide thither. No conception can be truer. The first murderer must have traversed those regions; innumerable footsteps have followed his, all perhaps under the same conduct. A dark, formless world, in which there is nothing for the eye to dwell upon, for the heart to embrace, where all is vague and monstrous,—this may become, this has become, the habitation of human intellects, formed in God's image. We can come into such utter dreariness, because we are spirits, because we have a home and a Father, because we can have no rest till we find that home and that Father. If we were merely children of earth, we might be satisfied with its pictures and images; these would be all in all to us. Being better than this, we must make a hell for ourselves, if we cannot find a heaven. Yes, a hell! the simple language

is the best. I will not quarrel about the etymology of Hades. It may mean the unseen, or the formless. But the unseen becomes to the bewildered conscience the formless; the negation of a world, the darkest conception a man can have of that which is without himself. He brings into it a more terrible darkness, that which is *within* himself; the worm of conscience which he cannot kill, the fire he can never quench. To be delivered from *that*, is to be delivered from sin. But how may he be delivered from the imagination to which sin has imparted its own horror and confusion? What glimpse of daylight can he discern in the trackless abyss? 'HE *descended into Hell.*' Mighty words! which I do not pretend that I can penetrate, or reduce under any forms of the intellect. If I could, I think they would be of little worth to me. But I accept them as news that there is no corner of God's universe over which His love has not brooded, none over which the Son of God and the Son of Man has not asserted His dominion. I claim a right to tell this news to every peasant and beggar of the land. I may bid him rejoice, and give thanks, and sing merry songs to the God who made him, because there is nothing created which his Lord and Master has not redeemed, of which He is not the King; I may bid him fear nothing around him or beneath him while he trusts in Him. I may beseech him to watch continually, lest he should lose his confidence in the divine and human Saviour and Conqueror, or forget that He has saved and conquered for his brethren as well as himself. I may tell him that if he does, he will become again the self-seeking, self-worshipping, cowardly creature the Devil is always seeking to make him, and that then he will assuredly fall into a condition of utter falsehood, in which all real things will seem to him unreal, and all unreal real; in which the worm and the fire of conscience will become ever more and more intolerable.

4. The Gospel narratives of the Resurrection are only a little longer and more minute than those which record the fact of Christ's burial. The women go to the sepulchre, they find the stone rolled away, angels ask them why they seek the living among the dead. He is not there, He is risen. They tell Simon Peter. He and John go to the sepulchre. One stays without, one looks at the linen cloth and the napkin. They tell it to the rest. There is wonder and doubt.—This is the story. What! only this? no greater array of proofs to secure our assent for that which stands solitary in the history of the world? No more overpowering testimonies than that of these women and these fishermen, in support of an event which is to be the basis of a world-belief? No!—meditate the fact well—this is all. Diligent men, in later times, may have shown, with great skill, why these fishermen and women were entitled to credit; why their simplicity and their own doubts confirm their trustworthiness; what they endured for their

perseverance in their story, &c. Those to whom the word of the Resurrection first came, received it simply as a message which, through whatever feeble voices it might reach them, must have been sent them from a Father in Heaven, because no one else knew how much they wanted it. If they had a Father, if He wished them to know that they had, this, they felt, must be His way of telling them. Between them and God there had been a dark impassable gulf; if that were not in some way filled up, they might talk of Him, use His name in their petitions, dream that He meant them well, but nothing had actually been done for them; no one hope of their hearts had been satisfied, no dread had been taken away. If there was no person who was actually one with God and one with man, the gulf must remain for ever unfilled; if there was, it was not incredible that He had entered into man's death, grave, Hell; it was absolutely incredible that He should be holden of them. Everything such a Being did, must be actual, not fictitious; seeming could have no relation to His nature; what men knew of suffering and fear He must have known. But to suppose that His Father forgot Him, did not own Him, did not claim Him, because He was exhibiting the fulness of His love, and carrying out His purposes, would have been a shock to the heart and reason such as they had never been called to undergo yet. Here was the evidence for the Resurrection; with this did the preachers of it subdue the world.

And this, I believe, must and will be the evidence of it in all generations to come, as much as it was in the first. The testimony will be mighty, because the thing testified of is that which all men, everywhere, are wanting,—which some who do not crave for what is peculiar and distinguishing, who must have that which is human, are taught by many hard processes that they want. But though I hold this evidence to be the highest, and to be that which all other kinds of it only serve to corroborate, I am convinced that the experience of eighteen centuries,—our experience especially of the confusions and contradictions into which churchmen and church doctors have fallen respecting the state of men here and hereafter, the experience that is appealed to as conclusive against our Creed,—illustrates the words I have been speaking of in this Essay, as they could not have been illustrated in the first ages.

1. We speak continually of death as the separation of the soul from the body. If we try to give ourselves an account of what we mean by Soul and Body, we should say, I suppose, roughly, that the soul is that with which we think; the body that which moves from place to place, and to which certain organs of sense belong. If this be so, how little does our language correspond to the fact which it tries to describe! Death, so far as we can judge from any of the phenomena it presents to us, affects the powers of thinking, of motion, of sensation, equally; our *natural* impression would be,

that whatever influence it produces on one, it produces also on the other. But that strange 'sense of immortality' which the benevolent German is so eager to extinguish, would not allow people to follow this conclusion of nature; *something*, they said, must survive. The soul would go to Hades; the hero himself would be a prey to the birds and dogs. We have adopted the language very nearly; often we adopt it altogether, even though we have a confused impression that the soul has more to do with the hero himself, and the body with that which the dogs or birds devour. But when *that* conviction has thoroughly taken possession of a man, when his 'sense of immortality' has begun to express itself in the only language which can express it, and he says, '*I* shall survive, *I* cannot perish!' then, first, all that horror which Strauss would deliver us from is awakened; then, secondly, it becomes impossible for the man to divide his soul from that which has been, during all his experience of it, its yoke-fellow. If he has cultivated his powers of reflection, and has studied the forms of language, he may learn gradually to find that the names which have stood so distinct in men's discourses, have distinct realities answering to them. But he will not allow his imperfect psychology to interfere with the witness of his conscience—that he, who uses equally the powers of thought and the powers of motion and sensation which have been entrusted to him, is responsible for both;—that, however they may be divided or united, they are both intimately attached to his personality.

If, then, there comes upon him a much stronger sense of his connexion with deeds done in the body than he had while he was drawing those artificial lines, and also a much stronger conviction of the dignity and sacredness of the body than those can entertain who would separate it from the soul,—the marvel of death, which seems to extinguish soul as well as body, and yet which he can neither hope nor fear will extinguish *him*, presents itself under a new aspect. He *must* have a solution of it. The solution must be one which does not hide any part of the fact, which does not impose a notion upon him as a substitute for the fact. The Scripture says plainly, that Christ poured out His soul, as well as His body, to death. The description of His agony and crucifixion has been received by those who have believed it, practically, if not in name, as the history of the death of a soul as well as of a body. Those who have wished to represent His death as different from all others, for the sake of enhancing its worth, have dwelt upon this as its most wonderful characteristic. To me it seems the most wonderful, because from it I am able to learn what other deaths are,—what the death of man is. Christ gave up all that was His own,—He gave *Himself* to His Father. He disclaimed any life which did not belong to Him in virtue of His union with the Eternal God. It is our privilege to disclaim any life which does not belong to us in virtue of our union with Him. This would be an obvious truth, if we were indeed created and constituted in Him,—if He was the root of our humanity. We should not then have any occasion to ask how much perishes or survives in the hour of death. We should assume that all must perish, to the end that all may survive.

2. Such a conclusion would go far, I think, to help us through that terrible perplexity, into which I said we all fell, respecting the body and that which we commit to the ground. As long as we suppose the mystery of death to be the division of soul and body, so long we must cling, with a deep love, to those remains which yet we are forced to regard with a kind of loathing. We shall be ready to believe stories of miracles wrought by them, we shall be half inclined to worship them. Or if we reject this temptation,—because Romanists have fallen into it, and we think it must therefore be shunned,—we shall take our own Protestant way of asserting the sanctity of relics, by maintaining that at a certain day they will all be gathered together, and that the very body to which they once belonged will be re-constructed out of them. That immense demand is made upon our faith,—a demand in comparison of which all notions of cures wrought at tombs fade into nothing,—by divines who would yet shrink instinctively from saying that what they call a living body here, *is* a mere congeries of particles,—who would denounce any man as a mate-

rialist if he said that. This demand is made upon us by divines, who use as a text-book of Christian evidences 'Butler's Analogy,' the ground chapter of which, 'On the Future State,' is based on the argument that there is no proof that death destroys any of our living powers, —those of the body more than those of the soul;—and which distinctly calls our attention to the fact, that ordinary attrition may destroy the particles of which the matter of our bodies consists, more than once in the course of a life; so that nothing can be inferred from our depositing the whole of that matter at the moment of dissolution. This demand is made upon our faith by divines, who read to every mourner as he goes with them to the grave of a friend, that corruption cannot inherit incorruption; that flesh and blood cannot inherit the kingdom of God.

But though I speak of this opinion as 'a demand upon our faith,' I hold it to be the fruit of our unbelief. If we did attach any meaning to that expression upon which St. Peter at Jerusalem, St. Paul at Antioch, dwelt so earnestly, that Christ's body saw no corruption; if we did believe that He who was without sin showed forth to us in Himself what is the true normal condition of humanity, and showed forth in that body of His what the human body is,—we should not dare, I think, any longer to make the corrupt, degrading, shameful accidents which necessarily belong to that body in each one of us, because we have sinned, the rule by which we judge of it here: how much less should we suppose these to be the elements out of which its high, and restored, and spiritual estate can ever be fashioned?

It is impossible not to perceive, under this notion of a resurrection of relics,—of that corruption which our Lord did not see,—a very deep conviction that the body of our humiliation must be identical with the body redeemed and renewed. This conviction is so rooted in the heart, that it will absolutely force nature, fact, Scripture, everything, into accordance with it. I must be, in all respects, the same person that I was before I put off my tabernacle; *therefore* these elements, which were once attached to my body, must come from all the ends of the earth to constitute it. What a witness for the reality of a belief, that it can sustain such a contradiction as this rather than cease to exist! All through my life on earth, soul and body are groaning together under a weight of decay and mortality,—are crying for deliverance from it. An hour comes which seems to say that their emancipation has taken place; that these Adam conditions belong no more to the man; that as to them he is utterly dead. The preacher of God's Gospel runs about saying, 'Oh, no! it is a mistake! These 'witnesses of the fall,—these pledges of pain and shame, 'from which fever, consumption, cholera, after days or 'years of suffering, have at last set your friend free,— 'belong to him inseparably, necessarily, eternally. They '*are* that body, the most curious, wonderful, glorious, 'of God's works; they are not, as your consciences tell 'you, as the Scripture tells you, the proofs that this 'wonderful fabric has suffered a monstrous and cruel 'outrage; that it needs a deliverer to raise it and renew 'it.' A strange Gospel, one would think! And yet one which men receive, which they will continue to receive and hold, rather than think that they are to perish, or that they are to have merely a visionary soul-life.

'*As in Adam all die, so in Christ shall all be made alive.*' This is St. Paul's broad statement in that passage of his writings which deals specially and formally with this subject. It is in strict accordance with all his other doctrine. Christ is the Lord of Man, the Life-giver of Man, the True Man; Adam is the root of his individuality, of his disease, of his death. All is strictly in order. Death has its accomplishment: the Adam dies, and is buried, and sees corruption; Christ gives Himself to death, and sees no corruption. If a man has an Adam nature and is also related by a higher and closer affinity to Christ,—is the effect of that union that he shall be redeemed, body and soul, out of the corruption which is deposited in the grave, or that it shall be his future, as it has been his past, inheritance?

But has not St. Paul spoken of a change to take place in the twinkling of an eye? and has he not connected this with the last trump? I hope, at some other time, to examine the whole of this great chapter, and to see what it actually reveals to us. But I cannot refuse even here to meet this special objection, it is for many reasons so practically important.

If, then, there was no allusion to that last trump of the Archangel in this sentence, I do not think we should any of us have hesitated to believe that St. Paul, in strict conformity with all his teaching respecting our death in Adam, and our life in Christ, was unfolding the mystery, —so deep, so necessary to all, so contrary to all the notions of the Corinthians,—that men, instead of sleeping in their graves, would be changed in a moment, in the twinkling of an eye. And I believe no one could have hesitated in any particular case to have applied the words. Nay, I do not find that men hesitate, even with their customary notions and opinions, to apply them now. As they watch the last breath departing from a dear friend, they seize the language, they feel they have a right to it. They say, 'A moment ago he 'was mortal, and now he is free! It has been but the 'twinkling of an eye, and what a change has come!' Such are the unconscious utterances of men's faith and hope, grounded, as they surely think, and, as I am convinced they have a right to think, on St. Paul's words.

Nor does the thought then disturb them, that there is a want of identity between him that has been and him that is. Though the decaying, agonized frame is lying calm and at rest, they do not then doubt that he who spoke to them a few moments before, did not derive his powers of speech, any more than the celestial smile which still remains on the clay, from that clay. Faith and reason, however crushed and confounded, are too strong, in that hour of reality, for a notion so cold and so inhuman.

'But the trump of the Archangel! that seems to put all 'belief of a resurrection of the body to an inconceivable 'distance, and to make the hypothesis, which identifies it 'with a resurrection of remains, after all, the only scrip-'tural one.' And this opinion becomes so intertwined with the expectation of a great future judgment of the just and the unjust, and therefore with all the most sacred moral principles, that we may well tremble when we encounter it. If I did not feel that morality, and godliness, and the practical belief of a judgment, were put into the greatest risk by the confusions which we are tolerating respecting these words, I would gladly pass them by. But I dare not be silent, because I see what a mass of unbelief and indifference is congealing in men's minds under a thin coating of apparent orthodoxy.

I scarcely need ask any Protestant whether the words 'trump of the Archangel' convey to him precisely the impression which he would derive from the picture of Michael Angelo. He is likely to answer with, what I should think, rather excessive and unnecessary indignation, that none of his impressions are derived from pictures; that he has the greatest horror of their sensualizing effect; that of course he does not dream of a material trumpet. I do not use this language myself. I *have* learnt from pictures, and am willing to learn from them. I believe I might learn much from this one of Michael Angelo's, which would do me great good, which would give strength, distinctness, even depth, to my own convictions, and to the words of inspiration. But I accept the statement, from which I am sure no pious and intelligent Romanist would for an instant dissent, that the mere trumpet, whether read of in a book, or seen in a picture, though it may be helpful to the mind in delivering it from vagueness, is symbolical; that to give it an actual material counterpart, would be gross and superstitious in the last and lowest degree.

I should scarcely think it necessary to make this remark, if I did not perceive painful proofs that our zeal, —to a great extent, I think, an honest zeal,—against symbolism, sometimes involves us in a confusion, to which those who are educated in it, (being thereby, I allow, exposed to other temptations,) are not equally subject. We adopt what we suppose is a spiritual substitute for some literal or material representation. We find we have got only a shadow or phantom. We must fill up the hollow in our hearts by some means; and we unconsciously add on the very driest and most material conception, to the (so called) spiritual one, as a necessary support to its feebleness. I could give instances upon instances of this strange intellectual hocus-pocus; the neglect of them by divines is, I believe, contributing most effectually to the return of Romanist notions and habits. I do not therefore think it unnecessary to bring each person who speaks of the Archangel's trumpet distinctly to book, and to make him confess,—though he may be disposed to shrink from the acknowledgment as too obvious and humiliating,—that he does not mean such a trumpet as men play upon; that he would count it shockingly irreverent to let the thoughts of such an instrument dwell in his mind in connexion with such a subject.

But are we then to dismiss the phrase as if it imported nothing to us, because we cannot reduce it to this signification, which would be actually nothing? I apprehend that it has the most serious import, and that the Scriptures tell us what it is. The Prophets of the Old Testament, in whose ears the trumpet that sounded loud and long on Sinai was ever repeating its notes, did not allow their countrymen to rest in the old image. Every rending of the mountains, every earthquake, everything which idolaters looked upon as the sign of the wrath of the tyrant before whom they trembled, everything that the mere philosopher calls an ordinary convulsion of nature, was with them an Archangel's trumpet, declaring that the righteous and everlasting King was coming forth to punish the earth for its iniquities, and to set truth and judgment in the midst of it. This was the teaching,—the uniform teaching,—of the old seers, in whose school St. Paul's mind was formed.

Are we to suppose that he had a *less* comprehensive, less spiritual idea of the divine method than they had,—that he deserted them for some more heathenish conception? Are we not rather to conclude that he was carrying out their truth to its highest power; that whatever they meant he meant still more perfectly?

If you ask whether he meant that there would sound in his own day an Archangel's trumpet, which would call the nations,—his own first,—into God's judgment, and that a mighty change in the condition of them all, the beginning of what may be rightly called a new world, would follow upon that judgment, I should answer, Undoubtedly I think so; I can put no other construction upon his language; and I can put no other construction upon the facts of history, except that they fulfilled his language. But if you ask further how he connected this with the condition of each individual man, who might or might not be alive at that crisis in the world's history, I should say, Since he held that in Adam all die, and that in Christ all are made alive, he of necessity believed also that a day was at hand for every man, a day of revelation and discovery, a day which should show him what life was, and what death was; what his own true condition, what his false condition was. And everything which warned a man that such a day was at hand, which roused him to seek for light, and to fly from darkness, was a note of the Archangel's trumpet; a voice bidding him awake, that Christ the Lord of his spirit might give him light. And in a moment, in the twinkling of an eye, by a fit of apoplexy, by the dagger of an assassin, the vesture of mortality which hides that light from it might drop off from him, and he might be changed. What had merely sounded to him here as some common earthly note of preparation for death, would then be recognised as the Archangel's trumpet calling him to account, asking him whether the light that had been vouchsafed to him, whilst shadows were still about him, had been faithfully used, or whether he had loved darkness rather than light, because his deeds were evil?

In both these anticipations,—if they are, or can be separated,—I accept St. Paul and the other Scriptures as a guide respecting the condition of us who are living in this later period of the world. I look for a judgment of Nations and Churches to wind up our age, as he looked for one to wind up his age. I believe the trumpet of the Archangel has been sounding in every century of the modern world, that it is sounding now, and will sound more clearly before the end comes. But I do not, for this, allow myself to doubt that it is sounding in the ears of each individual man; that a time will come, when the light will burst in upon him, and show him things as they are; when he will know that there is all life for him in Christ, and that there is all death in himself. I cannot persuade myself that the eloquent words I have heard from preachers, in which this truth was pressed home upon the consciences of men, in which they were told how all personal and family visitations were messages from heaven, trumpets of the Archangel calling them to repentance, were merely fine metaphors which, if possible, were to produce a startling effect, but which meant nothing. It is indeed 'fiddling while Rome is burning,' for God's ambassadors to be indulging in fine talk about His judgment, which their congregation are not to take as real. I must suppose that they think such language not metaphorical, but the translation of metaphors into reality. And if so, there is nothing in this part of the teaching of St. Paul, to hinder us from accepting the other part as a confirmation, not a contradiction, of the inference which we should draw from the New Testament generally,—that Christ was buried in order that the body might be claimed as an heir of life; as redeemed from corruption.

3. Supposing this to be the doctrine which is involved in the belief of Christ's descent into the grave, another enormous weight would be taken from the human spirit, —a weight which the heart and the understanding have been equally unable to bear. We are told to believe in a *place* of *disembodied* spirits. According to all the maxims which we ordinarily recognise, place appertains to body; it is only of body that you can predicate it. And this logical principle, so far from being at variance with our higher instincts, entirely accords with them.

People *talk* of their friends as disembodied. When they *think* of them, they are obliged to suppose them clothed with bodies. They admit the necessity; it is part, they say, of their weakness. They *ought* to feel otherwise. They ought to compel themselves to imagine that which they cannot imagine; that which they do only imagine at the peril of a direct contradiction! 'But Scripture demands it.' How, and where? It speaks of the bodies of saints coming forth, and showing themselves after the Resurrection. It speaks of Moses and Elias appearing to the disciples. It records acts of our Lord on earth, by which bodies are recalled from the unseen region into ours. 'Oh! but these are exceptions.' Exactly; and Scripture presents nothing but exceptions to your theory. If, however, I accept the Scriptures as teaching me laws by instances, and so correcting my theories, and dispossessing me of them, I think I am at least as much bowing my neck to its authority as you are, even though the result may be that I am not obliged to force my conscience or my intellect into an impossible position.

'But are we not, then, to believe in a Hades?' It was not a duty, but a terrible necessity, which led men of the old world to speak of Hades. They did not *believe* in it; there was nothing to believe. The void beyond the grave had never been entered; they could do nothing but mark it down in their charts by some name which left an impression of its vague, inaccessible character. But the heart was so impatient of the void, that all earthly forms and pictures must be thrown into it, if, perhaps, it might be filled. It cannot be all Stygian darkness; there may be verdant meadows here and there, scattered in the midst of the desolation; the forms of human justice must be there; Æacus and Rhadamanthus will decide which of the shadows that pass by them shall be consigned to the better, which to the more hateful, region. The Jew, taught in the law of his fathers, dared not let his fancy indulge in such creations. There was no Elysium in his Hades. He fled from the frightful vision of mere death and darkness, to trust in the living God. The dead he was sure could not praise Him: if God had been his hope and deliverer all through his pilgrimage, He would not desert him at last. He would not leave his soul in Hades, nor suffer that which had been holy in His eyes to see corruption. Yet the fact of corruption was before his eyes; the grave did receive its victim; the worms did gnaw upon him. Was this confusion to last for ever? I believe that the words, '*His soul was not left in Hades; His body did not see corruption*,' are a removal of it, once and for ever. I have no right to speak again of an unvisited, trackless region beyond the grave; I have no right to people that region with forms of my fancy. Elysium and Stygian pools have vanished; I have no right to call them into existence again. I have no right to accept the darkness which haunted the minds of patriarchs and prophets, and in which they believed it was a sin to dwell, as if it were intended for us.

'But we mean by Hades, a place of Spirits; do not 'you believe in that?' Certainly, I believe in a place where Spirits dwell. This earth is such a place; we, who dwell in it are spirits. There may be a multitude more dwelling in it, who have cast off their conditions of mortality, or who have never been subject to such conditions; I do not know; there is nothing to oppose such a belief,—much, perhaps, to encourage it. As the butterfly in its free flight may drop upon the leaf or flower, and taste its sweets, on which it fed as a caterpillar, or in which it lay wrapped as a chrysalis, so those who could just see the glories of the earth through its decay, and were sometimes so entranced by them as to forget their own greatness and their Father's house, may now enter fully and safely into the beauty which overpowered them, and make it the occasion for thanksgiving, or may be instruments in leading us to an apprehension of it. There may be many more places for Spirits in those innumerable worlds which the Astronomer is discovering to us, and which we shall delight in and wonder at the more, as we become more convinced that they are God's worlds, and that not one of them can have been made without Him who is the Light of men. The question is, whether, above and beyond all these, I must invent a place which my senses do not tell me of, which Science does not open to me,—not for spirits, but for shadows; and must use the language of Scripture which, apparently, is meant to deliver me from such a dreary necessity, as the excuse for it.

'But Christ went and preached to the spirits in 'prison.' I rejoice to believe it. I do not, indeed, know, more than St. Augustine did, to what age or place that preaching is to be referred; I may think with him, that the words of St. Peter, literally taken, point more to the time of Noah than to a later time. But be that as it may, I thank God that Christendom, even in some of those traditions wherein there has been most of vagueness and fancy, has borne witness to the fact that Christ is the Lord of all spirits, who have lived in all times, and that He is the great deliverer of spirits. I thank God that men have been sure that there was a justification for that faith in Scripture, whether it is to be found in the particular texts to which they appealed, or not. But how that preaching to spirits in prison warrants me in building a prison for them, which, according to no laws that the Scripture teaches us about spirits, could hold them,—a place for the disembodied,—I have yet to be informed.

'But, your language, pushed to its consequences, might 'prove that there is no Heaven and no Hell.' Forgive me; that is the very consequence which I dread from the perplexity into which you have led us. I believe that Christ came into the world expressly to reveal the kingdom of Heaven, and to bring us into it. He and His Apostles speak of it as the kingdom of righteousness, peace, joy in the Holy Ghost. They present Righteousness, Love, Truth, to us as substantial realities, as the Nature of the Living and Eternal God; manifested in the Only-begotten Son; inherited by all who claim to be made in His image. And since they reveal Heaven to us, they of necessity make known Hell also. The want of Righteousness, Truth, Love, the state which is contrary to these, is and must be Hell.

'Mystical! mystical! States, not places! So we 'expected.' A danger to be feared; and one to be carefully avoided. I have tried to avoid it, by saying that I know of no place for disembodied spirits. I cannot understand how men realise a state except in some place. I do not try to understand it. I find some spirits in different places of this earth very miserable, and others in a certain degree of blessedness. I do not find that the place in which they are, makes the difference. The most fertile and beautiful may be the most accursed; the naturally sterile may be more desirable. I should conclude from these observations, if I had nothing else to guide me, that the moral and spiritual condition of the inhabitants is the means of making a heaven or a hell of this earth. Scripture sustains this conclusion. All it tells me of the kingdom of Heaven, shows me that man must anywhere be blessed, if he has the knowledge of God and is living as His willing subject; everywhere accursed, if he is ignorant of God and at war with Him. This, I have a right to say, *I know.* And if I believe God's revelation of His Son, I may know a little more. I may be sure that death,—as Butler maintains from analogy,—does not change the substance of the human creature, or any of its powers or moral conditions, but only removes that which had crushed its substance, checked the exercise of its powers, kept its moral conditions out of sight. I may conclude, even if Christ did not tell me so expressly in all His parables, that the laws of God's kingdom in its different regions are not different; that one must explain the other; that everywhere to know God, and work for God and with God, to help His creatures, to cry and labour for the extirpation of evil, must be the good of spirits formed in God's image; that everywhere sympathy, fellowship, affection, must be the condition of right human existence; selfishness, its plague and contradiction. I cannot believe the good anywhere, in any creatures, to have reached its climax, because the Scriptures and reason teach me that there must be a perpetual growth in the knowledge of God, and in the power of serving Him. And as long as there is any evil in the universe, I must suppose, seeing that God and His Son desire its overthrow, that good spirits also desire its overthrow. Further than this I dare not go. And this, it seems to me, should be enough to make our zeal in proclaiming the Gospel of men's deliverance from evil, and death, and hell, very strong and vehement, and in exhorting our brethren not to reject so great a salvation; seeing that left to ourselves, without a Redeemer and a Father, there must be a continual descent into a lower depth. It cannot signify much to me, or any man, whether I call that depth Hades or Gehenna. To me the Hades becomes a Gehenna, because my own self becomes one, if I cannot be raised out of myself, and brought into sympathy with God's order, and God's love.

4. When Jesus said to Martha, '*Thy brother shall rise again*,' she, taught in the popular school of the time, answered, '*I know that he shall rise in the resurrection at the last day*.' '*Jesus answered*,' says St. John, '*I am the Resurrection and the Life; he that believeth in me, though he were dead, yet shall he live. And whosoever liveth and believeth in me shall never die*.' It seems to me sometimes, in low and desponding moods, that in the nineteenth century of the Christian Church, we have got back to Martha's point of view,—that we believe just what the Pharisees had instructed her to believe;—that the glorious mystery implied in the words by which our Lord raised her out of that condition of mind, and in the act which confirmed them, has perished out of the circle of our convictions. But I am sure this is not so, and that it only seems to be so, because we judge of the inward belief of human beings,—of that deep and secret wisdom which they receive from above,—by the hard and formal propositions which they have caught

from us, and have probably misunderstood. This distinction,—which I find it more and more necessary to keep in mind respecting ourselves, that I may feel our sins, and God's mercy,—is also a great comfort in thinking of Unitarians. To me, nothing sounds harder and colder than their mode of talking about Christ's Resurrection. In old times they clung to the belief with great tenacity; it was the main article of their faith. The Resurrection, they said, proved the truth of immortality, which philosophers had always disputed. It proved also the truth of the Christian religion. Apparently the translation of the first statement is, that a stupendous violation of all the laws and principles of the universe was divinely ordained, to convince men of a truth which they had never been able to forget; which had haunted them, and given birth to the most frightful superstitions; from which the most modern wisdom hopes that we may at last be rescued. As to the second reason, a man is compelled to ask, 'And what is the religion 'which this stupendous anomaly is to establish?' for it cannot itself *be* the religion; it is described as a means to an end; a mere mode of demonstration. Is it to show that certain great moral maxims are sound and true, which would commend themselves to the conscience without any such evidence, and which cannot be obeyed at all the more, if it were multiplied a thousandfold? Both these difficulties would seem to have been increased greatly, by the perseverance with which Priestley and the earlier Unitarians maintained the simplest materialism, denying the existence of a soul, and holding that the body slept till some distant Resurrection-day. And yet I am sure that the faith of these Unitarians in the Resurrection was often most strong, most energetic. It bore them through many outward difficulties, made them ready to encounter popular indignation and contumely, saved them from the temptation,—which must have been often great, as the correspondence between Gibbon and Priestley shows,—to cast in their lot with the accomplished infidels, who respected them for their knowledge of physics, and despised them for their want of boldness in not wholly repudiating the supernatural. A belief which could bear these fruits, I at least feel that I have no right to speak slightingly of; nor do I discover that I have what German doctors call 'a theological interest' in undervaluing it. I rather think, that if I were thoroughly rooted in the principles which I have endeavoured to assert in this and the foregoing Essays, I should give thanks for these signs and witnesses that Christ is with those who seem to speak most slightingly of Him, testifying to them that He is risen indeed, and that they have a life in Him which no speculations or denials of theirs have been able to rob them of, even as we have a life in Him, which our sins often hinder us from acknowledging, but cannot quench. Since, however, it is evident that the younger Unitarians cannot retain the ground which their fathers held; since they must either give up all belief in the fact of the Resurrection, or find some divine basis for it, which was not perceived by *them*,—I do very earnestly ask them to reflect upon the deeds and words on which I have been trying to comment, and not to let the theories of my brethren, or mine, hinder them from uniting with us in a confession which existed before all these theories, and will live when they have perished.

ESSAY IX.

ON JUSTIFICATION BY FAITH.

WHENEVER such broad statements are put forward as those which I have endeavoured to defend in my last four Essays,—that Christ is the Lord of man; that He took the nature of man; that He reconciled man and God by the sacrifice of Himself; that He rose again, as the Redeemer of man, from death, the grave, and hell,—there arises in our minds a fear which is both natural and righteous. Does not such language overlook the notorious fact, that good and evil men are mixed together in this world,—that the evil far outnumber the good? Does it not break down moral distinctions, which it is our first duty to preserve? Does it not practically deny that God approves the just and condemns the wicked?

No one should be weary of answering these objections, or should complain because they rise up again and again after he fancies that he has disposed of them. Though the whole purpose of his argument may have been to show how essentially and eternally opposed Good and Evil are, how impossible it is that they ever can blend together; what, according to God's revelation of Himself, He has done and is doing to separate them,—he must not be the least grieved if he should be met at last with the observation, 'What you talk about the redemption of 'mankind, means nothing after all. It is a mere dogma 'or technicality, with which those who are not in contact 'with the actual world may amuse themselves. We who 'are, know that, instead of identifying ourselves with 'the mass of the creatures around us, we must learn how 'we may become most entirely unlike them, or we never 'shall be like Him who you say is perfectly Good and 'True.' Such words, even though they may be uttered in a very contemptuous tone, would not excite any displeasure in us, if our own minds were in a right and healthy state. We should welcome them as signs that the speaker had an honest and deep conviction which he will not part with, and which must be thoroughly satisfied before he takes in any other. And it is the less excusable to manifest any irritation when we are the subjects of this kind of animadversion, because we know, or ought to know, that this difficulty, in one shape or other, has given occupation to every age of the Christian Church; that it has been no sooner overcome by a mighty effort in one direction, than it has reappeared in another; that it has, therefore, all the tokens of being a practical human difficulty, and one of so grave a kind, that people have been compelled to seek an explanation of it; and that when they have sought, they have found. The past experiences of the world, in this and in all cases, are not warrants for discouragement; if we use them faithfully, they are full of hope.

1. The Church, after the days of the Apostles, was no longer contending chiefly with Jewish sects, which claimed to be portions of the one divine nation. It was in the midst of a huge empire which hated it, and with the principles of which it was at war. Its members must carefully distinguish themselves from those among whom they dwelt, with whom they trafficked, who were under the same protection or tyranny. Baptism was the sign of their fellowship. Baptism must separate the churchman from the common earthly man. It could not merely denote an outward contrast. The new dispensation had penetrated below the surface to the roots of things. Baptism must import the most inward purification, the removal of that common evil which all men had inherited from Adam. 'Then,' it was argued, 'he 'who wants this, is necessarily lying under that common 'evil; he can be looked upon only as a natural creature.' There were innumerable checks and counteractions to this opinion. It was incompatible with the interest which the more spiritual of the Fathers felt in the inquiries of Gentile philosophers, as bearing upon all the deepest mysteries of the Gospel; it was still more obviously incompatible with the view which they took of their own internal conflicts, before they entered into the fold of Christ. But it became the formal recognised

school maxim, and it could not be that, without having the most direct influence upon practice. The influence was felt more bitterly and painfully within the Church than without it. Many Christians were found to be leading as sinful lives as heathens. It could not be doubted that their responsibilities were greater, and that, therefore, their sin must be greater. An inference was speedily deduced from that fact. The blessings of Baptism were said to be infinite for those who first received it. Their sins were blotted out; they were new creatures. But the blessings were exhausted in the act. Every subsequent step, in the immense majority of cases, perhaps in every case, was a step out of purity into evil. The white robes were soiled; the divine offering for sin had been spurned; pardon could only be hoped for by continual acts of repentance and mortification.

In this instance, as in the other, the counteracting influences were most numerous. The Psalms were still the great book of Church devotion. They spoke of flying to God as a refuge from all enemies; of sins being forgiven and iniquities covered; of God not desiring sacrifice and offerings. The Creed proclaimed belief in forgiveness of sin, as part of the ordinary and necessary faith of a Christian man; the Lord's Prayer taught him to say, 'Our Father;' the Eucharist was a continual thanksgiving for a sacrifice offered and accepted. Still the doctrine of post-baptismal sin had been proclaimed; the understanding could not refute it;

the sin-stricken conscience confirmed it; the natural inference that it was much safer to defer baptism to the latest moment was drawn, and, as in the case of the first Christian emperor, reduced into practice. Constantine had settled the debates of the Donatists and presided at a Council concerning the deepest mysteries of the faith, before he received the rite of initiation. He availed himself of the delay to murder his son, and to leave orders for the slaughter of the most conspicuous members of his family.

If this memorable example of the moral consequences of the doctrine had been wanting, there was more than enough in the despair with which it inspired numbers of those who had received the Sacrament, in the experiments to which that despair drove them, in the utter confusion of their thoughts respecting the character of God and the services which He required of them, to startle its most resolute champion. But it continued to dwell in the minds of good men, because for them it was, to a great extent, inoperative; their love for God and His family, and for the whole world, made any opinion they held a reason for severity to themselves, and for tenderness to their brethren. They could not see any logical escape from this one; they conspired with bad men to suggest practices, for curing outward sins or removing the sores they left in the heart, which strengthened and deepened it. And thus it seemed as if the great line which separated the Church from the world was one which could not be wisely passed; for, by the Church's confession, the majority of those who were within it were not better than the rest of men, and were exposed to a more dreadful doom.

But if this line was not deep enough, others might be drawn. One class of baptized men might be allowed to rest contented with an ordinary secular life,—to marry, rule the household, and do those works which were considered godly by the patriarchs and prophets, and which St. Paul commanded the ministers, as well as the members, of the churches he founded, to perform; others might become religious,—might eschew, as far as possible, human ties and obligations, and give themselves to the service of God. Here was another experiment for the purpose of separating the righteous from the unrighteous. A church was to be set up within the Church. The whole fellowship was not one of saints, but it was one which might nurture saints. There were two great counteractions to the habit of mind which this division indicated. The first lay in the feeling of churchmen that they were meant to rule the world, and therefore must take part in all the most secular affairs of it, whatever danger there was of defilement from them. The second arose from the strange discovery, that those who were felt and confessed to be the truest saints in virtue of the influence which they exerted, were precisely those who broke down the barriers which had been raised between them and ordinary people. They ate and drank with publicans and sinners. They were especially witnesses to the people of a common Friend and Redeemer, who cared for all. But these existing agencies enable us to understand better the effect of the belief itself on the morality of the Church. Its dealings with the ordinary business of the world took a particularly cunning, sordid, debasing form, because that ordinary business was supposed to be destined only for a lower Christian caste; the very sympathies which were most truly human and divine looked artificial, because, according to the theory, they were portions of the saintly ideal, and the means by which it was exhibited to men. And the lowering effect of the scheme upon those who gathered from it that their calling was to shuffle through existence as they could, and only to expect that divine helpers would be found waiting for them at the close of it, no words can describe.

2. At last there came a clear and effectual testimony against these notions, and the practices to which they had given birth. And it took this form:—It said, 'You 'are seeking to make yourselves just or righteous before 'God. You cannot do it. There is but one Righteous'ness, that which is in Christ, for the worst and the best 'of us. You are seeking to deliver yourselves by this 'and that experiment from the sense of the evils you 'have committed. You cannot do it. Faith in the Son 'of God is the only deliverance for the conscience of 'any man. You are not free till you trust Him; till

'you are free, you cannot do the works of a freeman, 'but only those of a slave.' The Reformers who bore this protest were obliged to carry it still further back. They were forced to say, as St. Paul had said before them, 'God Himself is the justifier. He has given 'Christ for our sins, and has raised Him again for our 'justification. He calls you, each of you, to know that 'Just One, in whom you are accepted.'

It is impossible not to see that this was levelling language; it was breaking down, to all appearance, the barriers between the righteous and the wicked, barriers which centuries had been at work to build up. Nay, it seemed as if this language carried one beyond the limits of the Church: as if any man might claim the righteousness of Christ,—might have his conscience set free from sin,—might believe that God had justified him. The Romanists charged both these consequences of their doctrine upon their opponents. 'By preaching faith without 'the deeds of the law,' they said, 'you efface moral dis'tinctions; by speaking so generally as you do of Christ's 'death and resurrection, you seem to take away the pri'vileges of the baptized man.' The Reformers retaliated. 'You,' they said, 'are guilty of the sin you impute to 'us. You have overthrown all difference between the 'pure and the impure; you have done so inevitably, 'because you have destroyed all difference between those 'who believe and those who do not believe.' That being the danger which they dreaded most, they set themselves to consider how they might most successfully avoid it. The result was a new set of experiments to separate the Church from the world, and then to create a Church within the Church. Faith justifies, but it must be ascertained who have faith. Christ's is the only righteousness; but to whom is that righteousness imputed? God calls men to the knowledge of His Son; but if He calls, does He not also reject? It seemed to Protestant divines and laymen just as necessary to invent plans for dividing the faithful from the unbelieving,—those who belonged to Christ from those who had no relation to Him,—the elect from the reprobate,—as it had ever seemed necessary to the Romanist to divide heathens from baptized men, ecclesiastics from the laity, the saint from the ordinary Christian. And I think it must be owned, that the effects in each case have been similar. The great moral distinctions, which God's law proclaims, and which the conscience of man affirms, have not been deepened but obliterated; fictitious maxims and standards have been introduced, which are as unfavourable to the common honesty of daily life, as they are to any higher righteousness which we should seek as citizens of God's kingdom, as creatures formed in His image. It seems as if faith signified a persuasion that God will not punish us hereafter for the sins we have committed here, because we have that persuasion; as if some men were accounted righteous, for Christ's sake, by a mere deception, it not being the fact that they are righteous; as if God pleased of mere arbitrariness that certain men should escape His wrath, and that certain men should endure the full measure of it. I find it hard even to state these propositions, without being guilty of a kind of profaneness, and a kind of uncharitableness, so shocking do they sound when they are put into plain words, and so wrong is it to suppose that any man holds them in the sense which those words seem to convey. But it is not wrong,—it is a great duty,—to set them out broadly and nakedly, that those who have dallied with thoughts which are capable of such a construction may shudder, and may ask themselves whether this, or anything like this, is their meaning; or, if not, what they do mean. Provided always, that we admit, in this instance, as in that of the Romanists, what enormous influences there are at work to neutralize these notions and statements; even to change them into their direct opposites; how strong and earnest *their* desire is for freedom from sin, and *their* willingness to bear any punishment rather than be slaves of sin, who seem as if they thought their faith was merely to procure them an exemption from penalties which others must suffer; how serious *their* zeal for God's truth, who seem, by their words, as if they could bear to suspect Him of a fiction; how thoroughly in their hearts *they* acknowledge God to be without partiality, and to be altogether just, whose phrases ascribe to Him a principle of conduct upon which they would themselves be ashamed to act. I repeat what I said before; the more frankly and thankfully we make these admissions, the more we are bound to labour, that the faith which is in the hearts of men may not be extinguished in them and utterly misrepresented to their children, by the perilous unbelief which they allow to mingle with it. For the sake of the precious good, we must wrestle with its counterfeit. And this, I believe, we can only do by resolving once for all, that since every attempt which has been hitherto made to draw lines and limitations about the Gospel of God, for the purpose of dividing the righteous from the wicked, has tended to confound them,—to put evil for good, and good for evil,—we will abstain in future from all such attempts, and will ask seriously whether God has not Himself established eternal distinctions, which become clear to us when, and only when, we are content to be the heralds of his free and universal love. I think it may be shown, not only that these distinctions are most recognised when we look upon all men as interested in Christ's Death and Resurrection, but that we cannot do justice to the zeal of Romanists for Baptism, of Protestants for Faith, that we cannot reconcile the one with the other, paying the highest honour to each, till we claim the wider ground from which they are both inclined to drive us. I think that we shall find that the Scriptures interpreted simply, interpreted especially in connexion with the fact of the Resurrection which has lately occupied us, explain and vindicate each of these apparently inconsistent tenets, but explain and vindicate them by taking from each its exclusive and inhuman, and with that, its fictitious and immoral, character.

3. If we start from the point at which we arrived in the last Essay, and believe that the Christ, the King of man's spirit, having taken the flesh of man, willingly endured the death of which that flesh is heir, and that His Father, by raising Him from the dead, declared that death and the grave and hell could not hold Him, because He was His righteous and well-beloved Son, we have that first and highest idea of Justification which St. Paul unfolds to us. God justifies the Man who perfectly trusted in Him; declares Him to have the only righteousness which He had ever claimed,—the only one which it would not have been a sin and a fall for Him to claim,—the righteousness of His Father,—the righteousness which was His so long as He would have none of his own, so long as He was content to give up Himself. '*He was put to death in the flesh, He was justified in the Spirit;*' this is the Apostle's language; this is his clear, noble, satisfactory distinction, which is reasserted in various forms throughout the New Testament. But St. Paul takes it for granted, that this justification of the Son of God and the Son of man was his own justification,—his own, not because he was Saul of Tarsus, not because he was a Hebrew of the Hebrews, but because he was a man. All his zeal as an Apostle

of the Gentiles, all his arguments against his own countrymen, have this ground and no other; the one would have worn out from contempt and persecution, the other would have fallen utterly to pieces, if he had not been assured that Christ's resurrection declared Him to be the Son of man, the Head of man, and therefore, that His justification was the justification of each man. He had not arrived at this discovery without tremendous personal struggles. He had felt far more deeply than Job did, how much he was at war with the law of his being, the law which he was created to obey; he had felt far more deeply than Job, that there was a righteousness near him, and in him, in which his inner mind delighted. He had been sure that there must be a Redeemer to give the righteousness the victory over the evil; to deliver him out of the power to which he was sold, to satisfy the spirit in him which longed for good. He had thanked God through Jesus Christ his Lord. And now he felt that he was a righteous man; that he had the only righteousness which a man could have,—the righteousness of God,—the righteousness which is upon faith,—the righteousness which is not for Jew more than for Gentile,—which is for all alike.

How impossible, then, was it for him to receive Baptism as if it were merely the outward badge of a profession, a sign which separated the sect of the Nazarenes from other Jews, or other men! If it marked him out as a Christian, that was because it denoted that he would no more be the member of any sect, of any partial society whatever,—that he was claiming his relation to the Son of God, the Head of the whole human race. It must import his belief that this Son of God, and not Adam, was the true root of Humanity; that from Him, and not from any ancestor, each man derived his life. It must import his acknowledgment, that in himself, in his flesh, dwelt no good thing; but that he was not obliged or intended to live as a creature of flesh, as a separate self-seeking being; that it was utterly contrary to God's order that he should. But if Baptism imported so much, it must import more. Paul had not devised it, or invented it. An act which expressed the giving up of himself, could not be one which only signified that he had made a choice between two religions, abandoning one, adopting another. He had done nothing of the kind. He had not abandoned his Jewish faith; he was holding it fast, maintaining that it had been proved to be true throughout. He was not adopting a Christian religion. He was simply submitting himself to a Son of David as being also the Son of God. Baptism, then, he accepted as the ordinance of God for men, as His declaration of that which is true concerning men, of the actual relation in which men stand to Him. If He had justified His Son, by raising Him from the dead,—if, in that act, He had justified the race for which Christ had died,—then it was lawful to tell men that they were justified before

God, that they were sons of God in the only-begotten Son; it was lawful to tell them that the act which, by Christ's command, accompanied the preaching of the Gospel to all nations, signified this, and nothing less than this. If Christ was not the actual Mediator between God and man,—if His resurrection did not declare that God confessed Him in that character, and thereby confessed men to be righteous in Him,—Baptism was a nullity, a mere delusion; it ought not to be associated with the proclamation of facts so stupendous; a message professing to come from God, who is a spirit, and concerning all the mysteries of man's spiritual life, should not be linked to a poor petty rite which denoted merely his external position.

By declaring in plain words, that they who were baptized into Christ were baptized into His death, that they put on Christ, that they were to count themselves dead indeed to sin, but alive unto God, risen with Christ, St. Paul pointed out the ever-effectual protection against the error into which the Church afterwards fell; the one great divine distinction for which it substituted its awkward and mischievous theories and practices. So long as Baptism was really felt to denote the true and eternal law of man's relation to God, so long it could give no excuse for those notions respecting post-baptismal sin, out of which such enormous and complicated evils were developed. How could those who believed that God had declared His Son to be the root of righteousness for every man,—that they were baptized into Him, adopted to be sons of God in Him,—teach any human creature that he had had a certain righteousness, justification, freedom from evil, for a moment, but that when he had yielded to the lusts of the flesh, or the power of the Evil Spirit, these blessings were his no longer? Of course it would be so, if his righteousness were his own property, if it could ever become his own property. But if what baptism proclaimed was precisely, that it never could, that the notion of a self-righteousness is false in principle, the greatest of all contradictions, then it must be the right and duty of men at all times to turn to Him in whom they are created, redeemed, justified; their trust was either lawful at no time, or it was lawful at every time; on no principle, save that of continual trust in the Lord of his spirit, could a man assert the privilege and glory of his baptism, and rise above his enemies. Whatever doctrine robbed him of that trust, or led him to build his life and conduct upon distrust, was earthly, sensual, devilish.

The Reformers, I conceive, were not denying the strongest assertions of St. Paul respecting baptism, when they used this language, and called on all men to believe in the Son of God for their justification. In fact, they appealed to these assertions continually; they were their most effectual weapons. Nor, I conceive, did they pervert or weaken these words, when they said that the Church was falling into the condition of a mere world, and that faithful men must be the instruments of raising it out of that condition. Faith, they said,—and the conscience of men confirmed their words,—is the ground of right hearty action; unbelief makes it impossible.

'Yes,' replies the Romanist, 'and your Protestant 'mode of reforming the universal Church was to split it 'into a thousand sects; your Protestant way of asserting 'the preciousness of faith was, to leave us nothing in 'which we should believe.' The mockery is severe, and it is deserved. Sectarianism has been the effect of the schemes which Protestants have adopted for the purpose of defining who have a right to be members of Christ's Church, and who have not; the loss of a distinct and common object of faith has been the effect of the schemes which Protestants have adopted to ascertain who have and who have not the gift of faith, or the right to believe. They have sought to be wiser than God, and God has confounded their vanity. He has laid one foundation for a Universal Church, and they thought they might make foundations for themselves. He has established the great distinctions, that there is in every man a spirit which seeks righteousness, and a flesh which stoops to evil; that there is with every man the Christ, who would quicken his spirit, and deliver his soul and body out of death; and with every man an evil power, who tempts him to become the slave of his flesh, and so to destroy his soul and body; that in Christ, the true Lord of their spirit, men are claimed as sons of God, and that they, by distrusting Him, and yielding to the devil, become utterly unlike Him, forming themselves in the image of the father whom they have chosen. And we, for these great practical divine contrasts, which will be brought out in the clear light of God's judgment-day, and which nothing in earth or hell or heaven can alter or modify, must have our own sets of spiritual and carnal men; of those who can make it clear to us that they believe, and of those who cannot: divisions which are so many premiums to hypocrisy, so many hindrances to honest men, so many temptations to him whose experiences have acquired for him the title, 'religious' to think that he has not a world and flesh and devil to struggle with, while he may be convincing a looker-on, by his ordinary behaviour, that he is an obedient slave of all three; which tempt those who are treated as carnal and worldly, to believe what they are told of themselves, to act as if they had not that longing for good, which they yet know that they have, and which God does not disown, for His Son has awakened it, though His servants may be stifling it.

Most assuredly the curse of God is upon these Protestant devices, and we shall feel it more and more. But is the refuge in going back to those who have been guilty of framing devices for the same ungodly end; devices, the condemnation of which is written in the history of the world? Is it not rather in the bolder, freer proclamation of God's universal Gospel, of a Church founded on Christ the Son of God and the Son of man, of His justification of each man as a spiritual creature, a child of God created to trust Him, to know Him, to exhibit His likeness?

I have alluded to the sympathy which existed between orthodox English Churchmen and Unitarians in the last century, on the subject of the conversions and spiritual struggles upon which the Evangelical teachers dwelt so much. There was an alliance also between these same parties against the leading Evangelical *doctrine.* Both alike foretold that the consequence of holding and preaching justification by faith, must be the weakening of moral obligations. 'A high-flown pedantical morality 'might be cultivated by those who adhered to this tenet; 'plain home-spun English honesty and good faith would 'be undermined by it.'

When the Evangelical teachers appealed to our Articles, in defence of their proposition, they used a good *argumentum ad hominem* for one division of their opponents; it had no weight at all for the other. The evidence *they* required was of a different kind, and it was not wanting. The Edinburgh Review, by adopting Sir James Stephen's delightful Essay 'On the Clapham School,' has practically declared, that the cause of which it was the ablest champion forty years ago, is not now defensible; that the men who, if the words of its accomplished clerical ally were true, must have been utterly fantastical, as well as fanatical,—governing themselves by some absurd imaginary principle, which has nothing to do with the business of the world,—were really simple, clear-hearted, clear-headed men, who were faithful in their callings, who infused a new and juster spirit into commercial life, who compelled politicians to acknowledge other maxims than those of party, another object than that of advancing themselves. There can be now no manner of doubt that the existence of such men had the most purifying, elevating influence upon English society; that they did very much to overthrow that morality of sentiment, which the Anti-Jacobin could only ridicule, and to counteract the stock-jobbing tendencies of the day, which some of those whom the Anti-Jacobin most lauded were nurturing. Their one great testimony, that a man can never be a chattel, was the most significant practical commentary on all they said of the worth of the individual soul; a proof how thoroughly their doctrine possessed their lives; an example to all after generations; seeing that the very time they chose for making this protest was the one in which the doctrine of the individual rights of men was frightening them and most of their political associates, seeing that they were accused of promoting Jacobinism as well as of putting the wealth and commerce of the great English cities in peril, and that they nevertheless persevered, in the faith that evil must be denounced at all hazards, and that that which is wrong in the tendencies of a time, can only be effectually resisted by the assertion of the right which is most akin to it. This was faith, and these men were in the true sense 'just by faith.' Their outward acts proceeded from a principle; that principle was, Trust in an unseen Person.

Why do those who talk most of justification by faith in our day exhibit no similar fruits? Why is English society not raised or purified by their presence in it? Why are the tradesmen among them as ready as any others to mix chicory with their coffee? the merchants and politicians to job? the divines to slander? Is it not because they believe justification by faith, instead of believing in Christ the Justifier? Is not the whole principle changed? Is not the formula which represents the principle doing duty for it?

I know well how many there are in the modern Evangelical school who imitate the faith as well as the works of their fathers. I know how deeply they are grieved by the crowd of heartless and noisy champions who defend their cause because it is the popular and patronised one now, as they would have cursed it and slandered its professors fifty years ago. I entreat the Unitarians to compare these two classes;—those whom they cannot for one moment suspect of hypocrisy, to whose honesty and simplicity of character they are willing to do homage; and those whom they have a right to condemn as loud, talking, unreal bigots, bitter against all who differ from them, in proportion as they feel their own ground insecure. I entreat them to ask themselves whether the most striking characteristic of the former, so far as they are able to judge, is not faith in, and devotion to, a living Person, whom they reverence as their Lord, and to whom they cleave as their Friend? whether the others are not as evidently fighting for a notion or a theory? Supposing this to be the case, then are not the former holding with a strong grasp that very belief, which the Unitarian idea of Christ would wrest from them? Would not the loss to the other, if that idea were forced upon them, be very inconsiderable indeed? If the anti-orthodox faith obtained the ascendency which it once held among the Vandals in Africa, and were as persecuting as it was among them, is there not the highest probability that this latter class would supply a band of ready, promising, very soon vehement, converts to the new system? is it not certain that the former would withstand it to the death?

There is one fact recorded by the faithful and affectionate biographer of the Clapham school, which I should be very dishonest and cowardly if I suppressed. It is, that one of the neighbours of Mr. Wilberforce and Mr. Thornton, who was united with them in many of their benevolent projects, and in close personal friendship, was professedly and notoriously a Unitarian. It must have puzzled him greatly at first, to explain how all the plain and practical virtues which he saw in them, not only accompanied,—that he might have accounted for on his general maxims of toleration,—but manifestly flowed out of, the faith which he had been taught was so likely to beget immorality. It may have puzzled them almost equally to understand how he, an opposer of that faith, not only performed right acts, but exhibited, as we are told he did, that habitual rectitude, which they would ordinarily and rightly attribute to some deep root. I suppose he came at last to some solution of his difficulty which satisfied him. I should think their faith in Christ the Justifier must have been the solution of theirs. As that grew stronger, they must have said more and more frequently, 'Thou, O Lord, art more than all our systems and calculations. Thou mayest perchance have rule in a thousand hearts, where they are not admitted, even as it is clear Thou dost not rule in many where they are received.' And that conclusion, instead of leading them to Latitudinarianism, will have saved them from it. How could they ever give up their faith in Christ as a living Person, when they traced, not only all that was not evil in themselves, but all that was good in any man, to Him? If they had not only seen that truth at certain times, but had been able to state it fully at all times, from how much of misery might they have saved some of their contemporaries, from how much vagueness and infidelity their descendants! Need Cowper have sunk into despair, if he had believed that Christ was in him at all times, and was not dependent upon his apprehension or faith? Would his evangelical biographers have been reduced to the miserable—not always the successful—apology, that his madness was not caused or aggravated by his Christianity? Might they not have had to give thanks that that was the cure of it? If Blanco White had ever learnt to extend that belief to all men, would he have approached the confines of speculative atheism?

I ask these questions with fear; but I think, for many reasons, that they should be asked. And since the last of them has a very close interest for the new school of Unitarians, I would venture to offer one or two more thoughts for their reflection. They have learnt from Mr. Carlyle and others, to speak of faith in a tone altogether different from that which was common in the last generation. I would respectfully inquire of them, whether they are not, ever and anon, falling into the error which I have attributed to our modern Evangelicals, and which infects many beside them,—that of making Faith itself an object of trust, almost of worship? I know how they will escape from the charge. 'Oh no!' 'they will say, 'we mean, not faith in Faith, but faith in 'an idea. Don't you know what Mr. Emerson says of 'the Mahometans, that they overthrew hosts, because 'they were horsed on an idea? What we object to is, 'your doctrine that faith in a *Christian* idea is the only 'faith.' I beg to disclaim any such representation of my doctrine. I acknowledge that Mahomet triumphed over hosts, I acknowledge that he triumphed by faith.

Yes! by faith in a real living God. His opponents were horsed upon ideas; (or rather conceptions of their own mind;) therefore the horses and the riders were cast into the sea. I think that his faith could overcome much, because it was faith in a substance, a reality, a Person. I do not think it could overcome the world, or the flesh, or the devil. I think all three have proved, in the issue, too strong for the Mahometan. I accept the Apostle John's explanation of the two conditions which are necessary to a complete victory. It has stood the test of much experience, and will, I think, stand the test of all. '*This is the victory that overcometh the world; even our Faith.*' '*Who is he that overcometh the world, but he that believeth that Jesus is the Son of God?*

ESSAY X.

ON REGENERATION.

Mr. Combe's Essay on the Physical Constitution of man has, I am told, had an enormous circulation, both here, and in Scotland. I cannot wonder at its success; nor do I regret it, though I might not easily find a book from the conclusions of which I more entirely dissent. It has, I think, brought the question of education, and many other questions, to the right issue. What is the constitution of man? We want to know that. Till we know it, we connot educate; we cannot do much to benefit the condition of men, individually or socially. When we know it, our main business will be to ask what there is which has hindered men from being in conformity with their constitution; how they may be brought into conformity with it. That I understand to be Mr. Combe's main principle, and I heartily assent to it. I do not think it is now for the first time announced. I believe men have been trying to act upon it. But I believe also that many causes have prevented us from stating it to ourselves consistently; that notions of education and reformation, inconsistent with this, have intruded themselves into our minds; that they are confusing us greatly; that any one who recals us to this sound and orthodox doctrine, is doing us a service. Mr. Combe, however, claims for himself an honour which did not belong to our ancestors. He says, that they knew little or nothing of man's physical state, of the laws of his body, of the condition under which he exists as a citizen of this earth. I am not inclined to dispute either the charge against them, or the pretensions which he puts forth for himself. I have no doubt this was their special ignorance, and that it was the mother of a multitude of false theories and mischievous practices. I think God has given us great means of removing the primary error, and its fruits; and that we are guilty in His sight, if we do not use them.

But, further, Mr. Combe assumes that this knowledge which we have attained, repecting men's physical condition, is the only secure knowledge, the only knowledge upon which we can act. All other, he thinks, all which our ancestors supposed they had, is a mere collection of guesses. They did not agree about it themselves; we agree about it still less. How can we teach men guesses? How can we apply them to practice? When they are put into one scale, and ascertained laws into another, must not they kick the beam? Practically, therefore, even if we have ever so much hankering after these guesses,—ever so much of what we call Faith in them, —we must leave them out of our calculation. And is it not probable that we shall find, at last, that we had the best possible right to leave them out; that, in fact, these physical laws explain them; that if we understand *them*, we understand the whole constitution of man?

To these questions I answer distinctly: Whenever guesses are balanced against laws, guesses *must* kick the beam; if divines and moralists have nothing but guesses to produce, and Mr. Combe has laws, it is not a matter of doubt but of certainty, that he will be the teacher of the world, and that they must make their way out of it as fast as they can. I admit, further, that there are a great many appearances in the history of the world and in our present position, which may, very naturally, lead Mr. Combe and thousands of others to the conclusion that divines and moralists *are* guessers and nothing else. Not a few of them have almost admitted that they have no certain ground to stand on. Many of those who do not, rest the proof that they can teach things which may and should be believed upon reasons which do not satisfy the understandings and consciences to which they are presented. The divisions of Christendom, which have increased, and are increasing, seem to make out the strongest *primâ facie* case in favour of Mr. Combe's practical decision. If every other method of education is laid aside and his adopted, as the only one which States can sanction or which is available for men universally, he and those who have joined with him in advocating it will be much less answerable for the result, than we who have opposed him.

After what I have said in previous Essays, it would be great affectation to pretend that I have any doubt as to the final issue of that experiment. As I have throughout been tracing feelings and consciousnesses in men which point to some spiritual object, and which are uneasy, feverish, tormenting, precisely because that which they seek they cannot find, and because some faint, obscure image is offered to them as the substitute for it; as I have maintained that these feelings and consciousnesses are not less active now than in former days, but, perhaps, more active,—active in quarters where the influence of Church doctrines is utterly repudiated; as I have differed from my brethren chiefly in confessing the wider extent of these consciousnesses, the evidence which proves them to exist where we should be inclined to ignore them; as I have been reasoning with those who would build a new scheme of divinity on these very consciousnesses,—one which is, they say, to be universal, and to displace our exclusive doctrines; it cannot be very necessary that I should enter at large into my reasons for not supposing that we can provide for all the necessities of human beings, or set them altogether right, by treating them as creatures possessing a stomach, a liver, and a brain. It is, of course, an obvious and familiar theory, that these consciousnesses are secreted in the stomach, the liver, and the brain; I am quite willing that any one should hold that theory, and should try to work it out. I believe that in the course of his workings he will do much good; that he will continually observe, and may enable us to observe, the close connexion of these bodily functions with the thoughts and moral state of human beings,—their action and re-action upon each other. I believe that the more the facts which establish that relation and inter-dependence are noted, the better; that the more they are meditated upon, the better. And this because the thorough patient observation and meditation of them will, I am sure, set right a great many crude notions of ours, and will also convince the inquirer that his scheme must fail; that when he has got all priests and traditions out of his way, he is only beginning the process of clearance which is needful for his success; that he must get the thoughts and convictions which have helped most to raise and civilize human society out of his way also; that if he does not, they will perplex and torment him continually. And I do tell him plainly and confidently, that, tolerant man as he is,—honestly tolerant, I have no doubt, and eager to rid the earth of us, because we are intolerant,—he will not be able to expel an infinite number of religious experiences, fancies, notions, by medicines allopathic or homœopathic; he will be obliged to resort to older, more tried methods. He must—I would say it to him in the lowest whisper—but I must say it, and he and the world will find whether I am right,—he must *persecute.* The inconvenient consciousnesses, which do not let the physical constitution act freely and healthily, will have to be prohibited. And since it is not easy to reach *them* by decrees and swords, the expression of them must be checked; because it will be found that they are just as infectious as scarlet fever, or small-pox. I do not speak these words lightly or inconsiderately. The history of persecution by all sects, governments, churches, in all families and neighbourhoods, seems to me most clearly to show that it originates with a desire,—(often an honest desire,—it was so in Trajan and Marcus Aurelius, when they ordered the deaths of Ignatius and Polycarp),—to put down that which is found to interfere seriously, either with the quiet of society, or with the comfortable working of some system or theory, which we have convinced ourselves is salutary and needful for human beings. That I think is an account of it which includes all cases, the particular motives and influences being of course most various. And I cannot understand how those who think that there are certain common tendencies in all men, call them physical or what you please, should suppose themselves free from *this* tendency, which experience shows to be so general; or, at least, why the world should suppose them free from it. I rather think the danger of their yielding to it is greatly increased by their apparent conviction that it never can assail them.

I do not, however, dream that warnings of this kind will deter any one from reducing Mr. Combe's theory to practice; most certainly I do not wish that they should hinder any one from giving it the most serious consideration. There are some eminent moralists among ourselves, formed in the school of Butler, who will be inclined to dismiss it rather superciliously, on another ground. They will exclaim, 'Why, are Mr. 'Combe's disciples really ignorant that a much closer 'observer and deeper thinker than he is, has been in 'this field before him, and has shown us clearly and 'satisfactorily that there is a *moral* constitution in which 'all human beings are sharers? Have they never heard 'that Butler has proved social affections to be an integral 'part of our human nature, a far more essential part of 'it than the senses or the power of locomotion? Do 'they not know that he has proved self-love and re-'sentment to have a moral basis? Have they forgotten 'the evidence by which he has shown that the Conscience 'is not only one of the faculties of our nature, but the 'lordly, sovereign faculty, to which all owe obedience? 'Will any one say that the processes by which these 'positions have been demonstrated are less legitimate or 'less scientific than those to which Mr. Combe has had 'recourse?'

I, at least, feel no temptation to maintain that paradox. I should find it difficult to say how much I honour Butler, or how much I owe to his discourses on Human

Nature. But I cannot help perceiving that there are causes which give the exclusive believers in a physical constitution,—immeasurably inferior as they may be to him,—a very decided advantage over him. Though Physiology may be even yet in its infancy, the physiologist speaks confidently of some facts and laws which he has ascertained. As Butler is commonly interpreted, he assumes all moral principles to depend merely on probable evidence. Some of his disciples seem to look upon that as his most characteristic doctrine.

Again, there are certain diseases of the body which can without any hesitation be traced to certain conditions of the atmosphere, which are the effects of bad drainage, neglect of ventilation, want of cleanliness; others, which can be directly referred to drunkenness or profligacy. The former are positive evils directly curable by physical remedies, the latter, which we commonly call moral, might be avoided by a man who noticed how much of sickness, pain, poverty, they produced. But when our social affections and our self-love are diseased, it does not appear that Butler has pointed out any satisfactory method of setting them right, of restoring their healthy activity. He shows that they are meant for us, and that they are meant to be in harmony; but suppose they are dormant, how are they to be awakened? suppose they are in discord, what is to reconcile them? Is it not likely that a man will say, 'Mr. Combe helps me to a certain extent. He shows 'me some influences which may seriously derange the 'economy of my individual life, and of the world. He 'tells me how I may avoid those influences. Till you 'can give me some aid that is more efficient, I must avail 'myself of his.' The student of Butler's doctrine on the Conscience, is often forced even more painfully upon this conclusion. For he will say to himself, 'My conscience 'ought, you say, to be a king. But it is not a king. 'It is a captive. How shall it be raised to its throne? 'And when it has got a temporary ascendency, can I 'trust it? Does not Butler himself admit the possibility 'of superstition acting upon it, and deranging its de-'cisions? Is that a slight exception to a general maxim? 'Does not all history show that the decrees of this great 'ruler may be made contradictory, monstrous, destructive, 'by this disturbing force, which Butler notices, but 'hardly deigns to take account of?'

And thirdly, it must not be forgotten that so intelligent and ardent (I dare not say, so excessive) an admirer of Butler as Sir James Mackintosh, has complained, that while he is bold and clear in asserting the fact of a conscience, and its right to dominion, he is timid and hesitating in affirming what it is, and how its prerogatives are to be exercised. Is not this remark strictly true? Is not every practical student of Butler obliged to put the question to himself: 'This faculty belongs to my nature, 'then:—What, to *me?* Is the conscience *mine?* Do *I* 'govern it, or does it govern *me?*' The school-doctor may dismiss this difficulty with great indifference. For the living man everything is involved in the answer to it.

I have taken Butler as the highest specimen and best known representative of a noble class of thinkers and writers, to whom I believe we are under the greatest obligations; who have brought to light truths which we could never less afford than now to lose sight of, but who are in danger of being utterly supplanted by a race of mere physical philosophers, or of mere spiritualists, if we are not prepared to examine in what relation they stand to both. The great facts to which Butler bore so brave a witness, cannot, I think, be explained, while we regard them *merely* as facts in man's nature. The more we look into them, the more they imply an ascent out of that nature, a necessity in man to acknowledge that which is above it, that which is above himself. When we take in this necessity, as implied in our constitution, the difficulties which beset the most full and masterly explanation that can be given of these facts, gradually disappear. I will endeavour to explain what I mean, and to offer one more evidence that Theology is the protector and basis of Morality and Humanity.

The word REGENERATION occupies a prominent place in all summaries of Christian Theology. It seems to many who hear it, and to many who use it, as if it imported a principle most inconsistent with that which Butler has defended in his Sermons on Human Nature. 'If a man requires to be regenerated,' they ask, 'before 'he can be that which God requires him to be, that 'upon which He looks with approbation, how can human 'nature in itself be the good thing which Butler would 'have us believe that it is? Must he not be at variance 'with the Scriptures, at variance with the testimony of 'our hearts, which confess the Scriptures to be true, 'and ourselves to be evil?' I am always glad when I hear a person who has really a reverence both for our great moralist and for the Scriptures, asking this question; it is nearly certain to lead him into a clearer apprehension of both. I am always sorry when I hear a person asking it who wishes to prove Butler wrong; it is nearly certain that he will be confirmed in the notion that he himself is perfectly right, and that in his eagerness not to twist the Bible into conformity with Butler's notions he will twist it into conformity with his own.

Regeneration *may* mean the substitution, in certain persons, at some given moment, (say in the ordinance of Baptism, or at a crisis called conversion,) of a nature specially bestowed upon them, for the one which belongs to them as ordinary human beings. No doubt it has this meaning for a great many Protestants, as well as Romanists; no doubt this meaning mixes with another, in some of the purest and noblest hearts to be found in either communion. Such a doctrine of regeneration, I apprehend, is quite incompatible with the doctrine of a moralist, who supposes the human constitution,—

that which belongs to us not as special individuals different from the race, but as members of the race,—to be good, and any violations of it and transgressions of it to be evil. There is no possibility, so far as I see, of bringing these two schemes of thought into reconciliation; they are directly, essentially antipathic. For, to suppose that they can coexist in any human heart or intellect, merely because one has the label 'moral,' and the other, 'theological,' is to suppose that heart or intellect a mere shop or warehouse of opinions, in which no living processes are going on, but where goods are kept to meet the inconsistent demands of different markets.

Regeneration *may* mean the renovation or restitution of that which has fallen into decay, the repair of an edifice according to the ground-plan and design of the original architect. This meaning is in accordance with the common usage of language. It is more like the sense which either a popular writer or a philologer would put upon the word, supposing he did not know that it had acquired another. And it is a signification which cleaves to the word in the discourses of the most religious people; one which Romanists and Protestants adopt consciously in the way of argument, and fall into unconsciously in their prayers and exhortations. It is obvious that *such* a signification need not in the least contradict Butler's idea of a human constitution, but might remarkably illustrate it. There being a certain constitution intended for man by His Creator, and certain influences about him or within him which weakened or undermined it, the author of the work might look lovingly upon it, and devise certain measures for counteracting those influences, and bringing it forth in its fulness and order. Some such theological complement of his moral system we may suppose gave coherency and satisfaction to the mind of Butler himself.

But there is a great difficulty in our way, if we seek to put this idea of Regeneration in the place of the one which I set forth previously. Such a regeneration may be intended for us; there may be processes leading some men, even leading the world, towards it; but are there any signs that it has been accomplished? Is the order, in this sense, restored? Can even good men be said in this sense to have recovered what the race had lost? Theologians therefore dwell on a restitution or reformation, or complete renewal of the divine image in individuals, as an object of *hope*. Many of them connect with that, a restitution and reformation of the earth and of the order of human society. But they contend, as earnestly, that there is something already obtained by Christ, for those who will receive it. This something, they say, is very real; we are partakers of it now, not to be partakers of it in some future ideal state; it is the necessary beginning of, and preparation for any such state. And the words 'birth' and 'generation,' which they find recurring so continually in Scripture, do, they contend, suggest another thought than that which the restoration of an edifice suggests. They must indicate a life communicated from a Father. A life of this kind they affirm they have received; it is renewed every hour; they cannot possibly wait for it till the world recovers its primitive glory; they want it as the pledge that they shall not sink into utter debasement.

Those who use this language, refer to the 3d chapter of St. John's Gospel, as containing the full interpretation of the doctrine which is so unspeakably precious to them. All Christians admit that this is *the* passage by which their opinions respecting Regeneration must be tested. No humble reader, I suppose, thinks that he has fathomed the depth of the discourse with Nicodemus. Every humble reader probably feels that he has caught glimpses of light from it which he would not exchange for the most costly treasures of the world. He perceives from the very letter of the Evangelist, that the birth is from above; that a Divine Spirit is the author of it; that it is the birth of a spirit; that it is the condition of entering a kingdom; that it has something to do with Baptism. He suspects that the latter part of the conversation, concerning earthly things and heavenly things, the Son of Man who came down from Heaven and is in Heaven, the serpent that was lifted up in the wilderness, the love of God to the world in sending His only-begotten Son, that whosoever believeth in Him should not perish, but have everlasting life; the light which is come into the world, the condemnation which consists in loving the darkness, cannot be separated from the former part. But he is bewildered by the number of different opinions that present themselves to him respecting the relation which the portions of this truth, as our Lord sets it forth, bear to each other. 'How comes 'the external rite of baptism,' he inquires, 'to be so 'linked with an inward operation? What has a king-'dom to do with a new life? Is it a future state that is 'denoted by the term Heaven; or if not, what is it? 'How is the Son of Man said to be in this Heaven, even 'while He is upon earth? Why should the exaltation 'of the Son of Man upon the cross be referred to in *this* 'connexion, all-important as it may be in reference to 'the doctrine of redemption, or the expiation for sins? 'Why is God's love to the world brought into a passage 'which seems to speak expressly of the condition of those 'who are separated from the world? Is not the con-'demnation of men this, that they do not partake of this 'divine and spiritual birth? Why is it declared to be 'that they love darkness rather than light'?

All our disagreements, intellectually considered, arise from the answers which are given to these questions. Each of us is disposed to fix upon some one of our Lord's statements, as that to which he shall refer all the rest. If we desire to have our thoughts orderly, not loose and incoherent, not mere qualifications or contradictions one of another, there must be a centre round which they revolve. But it is unspeakably important that we should not choose this centre and so create a system for ourselves; but that we should find it. Then we may find also what are the orbits and inter-dependencies of the bodies which it illuminates. Will any one say that I am wrong if I affirm that God Himself is the centre here, that the love with which he loved the world, is that to which our Lord is leading us, that if we learn from Him what that love is, what it has designed, what it has accomplished, we shall be in a better condition to apprehend all that He is teaching us respecting the birth from above?

Starting from this point, then, it seems to me that this love is declared to have manifested itself in setting forth the only-begotten Son, not merely as the author of forgiveness, but as the very ground and source of man's eternal life. Looking up to the cross as the exhibition of God's love,—as the exhibition of the true and perfect Man,—the man does not perish by the bite of that serpent which is continually stinging him, that spirit of selfishness which is continually separating him from God and from his brethren. He sees that Eternal Life which was with the Father, and which in the Divine Word is manifested to us; he becomes an inheritor of it. But his perception does not make the fact which he perceives. The Son of Man, who is one with men and one with God, who is in Heaven, in the presence of God, whilst He is walking on earth, has come down to establish the kingdom of Heaven upon earth, to unite earth and heaven in Himself. He has come to claim men as spiritual beings capable of this spiritual life, inheritors of this spiritual kingdom. Baptism declares this to be their proper and divine constitution in Christ. All who receive it claim the kingdom which God has declared to be theirs. They take up their rights as spiritual beings. He bestows His Spirit upon them that they may enjoy these rights; that they may be as much born into the light of Heaven, into the light of God's countenance, as the child is born out of the womb into the light of the sun. That countenance is shining upon them, the Spirit is with them to open their eyes, that they may take in the light of it. And this is the condemnation, and this will be the only condemnation, that they do not come to it, that they shut the eyes of their spirit to it, that they love darkness rather than light, because their deeds are evil.

We have considered three views of Regeneration, each of which was plausible, each of which had arguments from Scripture and arguments from experience to allege on its behalf. The first of them was directly opposed to Butler's doctrine of a moral constitution for man. The second was compatible with it, but scarcely accorded with the exact language of Scripture. The third promised something like a kingdom or constitution to man hereafter, but seemed to make the existence of a spiritual society at present rather an anomaly and an exception among human societies. If we may take Christ's own exposition, if we may assume Him to be the Regenerator of humanity, a light seems to fall on all these different aspects of the theological doctrine; we need not despair of their being reconciled. And that same light enables us to remove the practical obstacles which hinder the application, even the acceptance, of Butler's ethical principle.

First, that great and serious objection of his affectionate critic, Sir James Mackintosh, is taken away. The name, Conscience, would seem to import, not a power which rules in us, but rather our perception and recognition of some power very near to us, which has a claim on our obedience. I think this interpretation of the word is fully borne out by the most familiar, and at the the same time by the most serious and thoughtful, usage of it. The most conscientious man does not speak of his conscience as *giving* him a law; he speaks of it as confessing a law which he dares not violate. No one, I believe, felt this more strongly than Butler. Again and again one perceives how much it penetrated his whole mind. If the *individual* conscience undertakes to lay down laws of its own, his idea of a *human* constitution, that is, of a law or order for all human beings, is absolutely set at nought. And yet he was *forced* to say, that in our nature, conscience is the lordly faculty, the one entitled to speak and to be obeyed. But if I am entitled to say, 'There is a Lord over my inner man to 'whom I am bound, apart from whom I cannot exercise 'the functions which belong to me as a man, according 'to the law of my being,' conscience can be restored to its simple and natural signification; it does not demand sovereignty, but pays homage. And since it is the witness of His authority who governs all the faculties and energies of man, since it claims their service for Him, since it testifies of every act of disobedience done by any of them to Him, it does occupy that position relatively to all of them which Butler has assigned it. They are all out of order when they do not listen to its voice; they are all in harmony when its suggestions are heeded. It may in the most true sense be said, that we are only in our *natural*, that is to say, in our orderly and reasonable state, when everything within us is preserving its subordination to its righteous ruler. It can be said with equal truth,—and one assertion illustrates instead of contradicting the other,—that *naturally*, that is to say, when we follow our own inclinations, when we set up to govern ourselves, and forget that there is a supernatural government established within us, we become disorganized and bestial.

The habits of Butler's time, perhaps, did not allow him to use this language. Hence that hesitation and timidity which Mackintosh so livingly and admirably describes. We may see in it the shrinking of a reverent thinker when he approaches an awful truth, interwoven with his own being, which he is not able distinctly to express. But what was reverence in him, would be, it seems to me, cowardice in us. We have been driven forward into a new position, in which we must either grasp a higher truth, or let the one go which he vindicated. I feel that I am not confessing Christ before men, that I am ashamed of Him and of His words, if I do not say that it is of Him my conscience speaks, that I am under His government, in His kingdom. Nor dare I hide from any man the good news that *he*, too, is a subject of this kingdom, that the Regenerator of humanity is his Lord and Master, or the warning that if he chooses another condition than this, he is declaring war with his Creator, with his fellows, and with himself.

Next, if this truth be accepted, Butler's honest admission respecting the possible effects of superstition in perverting the decrees of the conscience will no longer be fatal to his principle. Till the true Lord of the conscience has made Himself known to it, of necessity it must go about seeking rest and finding none. Every false king will assume dominion over it; as it bows to the impostor it will become beclouded in its judgments; the more it tries to regulate its vassals, the more mischief it will do them, the more cruel they will feel its tyranny. It may prescribe those very outrages on physical rules, which I said would oblige the disciples of Mr. Combe to coerce it. It may prescribe outrages on the social affections, and so may drive the disciple of Butler, with all his reverence for its authority, to coerce it. Butler confesses the necessity; the appeals which he makes to our fears when he most desires to convince us that we have, in ourselves, a love of right for its own sake, are an acknowledgment of it. But if we believe that Christ is the ruler of this conscience, how beautifully that distinction of St. Paul between the flesh and the spirit, to which I alluded in my last Essay, would interpret the mystery of His divine government; what a solid basis would it lay for ethics and practical education! All the actual punishments which overtake wrong doing, all the fears of punishment which visit the wrong doer, are needful for that evil nature in us, which is always seeking to break loose from law, and which would reduce us into mere animals. But the Christ, the true bridegroom of man's spirit, is ever drawing it towards Himself,—is holding out to it freedom from evil, and the knowledge of Himself as its high reward. Owning Him, the man rises out of dark superstitions, out of immoral practices; he recognises the fitness of all God's arrangements in the physical and moral world; he claims for the body as well as the soul a redemption from all which corrupts and degrades it.

The full bearing of the principle that Christ is the regenerator of humanity, upon Butler's view of the human constitution, is not however understood till we have sought to apply his doctrine that we are essentially social beings just as much as we are individuals. I say, to *apply* it; for nothing is easier than to state the maxim;

it may sound to us like the veriest common-place. But when we have tried, in any particular case, to 'bid self-love and social be the same,' we have, probably, found that we could utter that command, just as we could call spirits from the vasty deep; but that self-love and social did not do as they were bid, any more than the spirits came when they were called. The theoretical common-place then becomes the hardest of all practical paradoxes: and yet in its very difficulty there lay the strongest witness of its truth. I am certain that I have no self that I can love,—nay, that self must be an object of intense torment and hatred to me, unless I am the member of a body. I am certain that I cannot be the member of a body consisting of persons, unless I am myself a person; that I cannot love another person unless I do also love myself. Bring in the belief of the one Head and Brother of each man, the one Centre of society, and that great moral contradiction is felt to be a great moral necessity; one which we can welcome and rejoice in, and act upon.

'But after all,' the disciples of Mr. Combe will say, 'you have not proved these positions. They have not 'the certainty which belongs to our statements respect- 'ing the physical constitution of man. Butler, in his 'Analogy, fairly admits that he is dealing only with 'probabilities and chances. That is affirmed by his 'disciples, his religious disciples especially, to be his 'great merit. You may pretend that you have given 'certainty to what was doubtful in his speculations by 'adding to them the words of Scripture. But you have 'only given us your interpretation of those words, which 'is surely not entitled to any great weight. It is but a 'guess sustaining a guess.'

Now I am bound to own that Butler did use words addressed to the loose thinkers of his day, the men of wit and fashion about town, which seemed to confound probabilities with chances, to suggest the thought that we ought to calculate the odds for and against the truth of a religious principle, and that, if there is a slight balance in favour of it,—nay, none at all,—we are to throw in the danger of rejecting it, and so force ourselves into the adoption of it. I mourn over these words as I read them, feeling how much a great and good man sacrificed of what was dearest to his heart for the sake of an *argumentum ad hominem*, which after all was not an argument that ever reached the conscience of any man, or that could do so if the conscience is what Butler affirms it to be. But I have mourned more deeply when I have seen these passages culled out by persons of great acuteness,—acuteness cultivated in an Aristotelian, not a Baconian, school,—and used first as a representation of the whole plan and purpose of Butler, secondly as the basis of a theory which was to save English divines from the necessity of demanding either the dogmatical certainty which Rome promises to her children, or the scientific certainty which Protestants seem to be craving for.

Thanks be to God, that house of cards has fallen down. The ingenious architect has, himself, undertaken to expose its instability.* How much better for him that he should be seeking even such a temporary standing-ground, —sandy and shifting as I believe it to be,—as Rome can afford him, till he finds an eternal rock, neither of authority nor of probabilities, on which he and the Church may rest;—nay, how much better that one in whose heart there is, I am convinced, a real, even a passionate, love of Truth, should pass through all imaginable subtleties, distortions, impostures of the intellect, in his way to it, than that he should be content with a scheme which shuts out Truth from men as an unattainable, scarcely desirable, treasure! How much better for us that we should incur the bitterest hatred and scorn, expressed with the most admirable cleverness and wit, of one who I yet doubt not is capable of all generous affections, than that we should be saddled with a theory which was leading numbers of young men to think that the main, perhaps the only, reason for believing in a God is, thet if there should happen to be one, He might send them to hell for denying His existence! I am sure that the thought of tempting any to such an opinion would have been horrible to this writer at all times; I have dared to put it into words, that it may awaken

* Compare Father Newman's book on "Romanism and Popular Protestantism," with the masterly demolition of his theory of probabilities in his "Essay on Development."

horror in the minds of those who are left among us, and may lead them to reflect on the infinite peril of resorting to plausible arguments for Faith, which may prove to be hiding-places for Atheism.

But to return to Butler. I entirely deny that either these conclusions of his disciples, or his own inconvenient statements in some passages of the Analogy, represent his design or his method as it comes out in the first part of that great work, or in the Sermons at the Rolls Court. On the contrary, he is pursuing precisely the same end as the physical inquirer, by an inductive process as nearly as possible the counterpart of his. He is as unwilling to accept hasty generalizations as every disciple of Bacon must be; he is as ready to look at facts and test them; he seeks to be delivered from vague hypotheses that he may feel the ground upon which he is actually standing. What more can Mr. Combe do? He knows perfectly well that he cannot lay down conclusions which shut out further inquiry; that he would be a very mischievous man if he could; that he cannot have certainty in this sense; that he disclaims it. He must collect facts respecting the condition of men in different circumstances; respecting their states of health and of disease; respecting the treatment, mischievous or beneficial, which has been applied to them. Such facts must not be merely observed, loosely and carelessly: they must be submitted to a series of searching experiments. There must be experiments on the bodily frame which illustrate those on the influences to which it is exposed; the anatomist, physiologist, chemist, geologist, must each contribute his quota of observation and thought, to the confirmation or correction of the other. Then, after many theories have been accepted, and thrown aside, some simple law is brought to light, the great test of which is its power of explaining facts, new and old; so far as it can do that, it sustains its character; when it fails, it is not discarded, but it is supposed that some deeper, more comprehensive law is yet to reward the toil and humility of the inquirer. What can be better or truer than investigations of this kind? What duty can be greater, than to avail ourselves of the results to which they lead? But the more we study them and admire them, the less shall we adopt those loose expressions which represent this evidence as something altogether different in kind from that which is open to moralists and divines, if they like to make use of it.

They may scorn facts; they may cling to anticipations and definitions which they bring with them; just as all the old physical students did; but if they take that course they depart from all the precedents of the wisest of their predecessors; they depart still more from the precedents of Scripture. For the Bible is a book in which God is teaching His creatures induction by setting them an example of it. Nothing is there taught as it is in the Koran, by mere decree; everything by life and experiment. It offers us the severest tests of its own credibility. It meets the facts of human life and the difficulties of human speculation; it undertakes to interpret the one, to show us the source of the other. If we accept Revelation for this purpose we do not put our own sense upon it; we go to it in our great necessity, to see whether it can give us the help we need; we expect that if it is God's, He will do for us what we cannot do for ourselves. If that which was a presumption before,—a presumption which I could not disown without disowning all my own processes of thought and judgment, but yet which I did not dare to pronounce certain, because I was afraid lest some idiosyncrasy of my mind should, in spite of my watchfulness, have mixed itself with these processes, and falsified the result,—becomes clothed with a new force, illuminated with a new brightness; if it comes back to me, stripped of all that was merely my own, and yet I recognise it as more mine than ever,—I do not know what the reason can ask for besides, to quiet it, and satisfy it. That, and more than that, I think the belief of Christ as the Regenerator of humanity does for all the questionings and demands of human suffering beings; that and more than that, for the speculations of the faithful moral student who has been painfully tracing the vestiges of an order and constitution in the thoughts and doings of himself and his fellow-creatures.

What I say is to be tested by life, and cannot be proved by words. But since Mr. Combe and his followers are rightly and naturally disturbed by the discords and contradictions of Christian divines,—by their practical contradictions even more than their speculative,—by the evil acts and courses which have seemed to follow from their dogmas, and by their eagerness to enforce them,—I shall draw the evidence I produce from this source; I shall maintain that these can be distinctly traced to the *unbelief* of Christians in the fact that Christ is the Regenerator of man; that this faith, had they maintained it, must have made their conduct and their influence on society very different from what they have actually been.

1. It may sound like the strangest of all charges against Romanists to say that they have undervalued the Church; that they have thought meanly of it in relation to God and to man, of its work and of its powers. But I do believe that that is the very charge which we have most right to bring against both Latins and Greeks; it is for this sin, I hold, that they have been called, and will be called, to give account before the tribunal of Him who has committed to them their stewardship, and before those for whose use they have received it. Do you say, 'They have done their 'very utmost to exalt the Church; they have boasted of 'it as divine; they have said that there was nothing in 'earth or heaven that it could not bind and loose; they 'have, till men became too enlightened to believe them, 'reduced their doctrine to practice, and made the priest

'the ruler over the spirits, souls, bodies of men?' Even so; your words are true; they establish my position. The Apostles, instead of *doing their utmost* to exalt the Church, did nothing. They spoke of the Church as being *in* God the Father and in Jesus Christ; they told those who belonged to it that they were created and redeemed in Christ Jesus and called; they bade them remember that they had no worth or greatness of their own; they said that they were to be witnesses to all men of the redemption which had been wrought out for them by the love of God, through the sacrifice of Christ; they said that in proportion as they renounced idols, and devil worship, and parties, and claimed the dignity of spiritual creatures, and acted as if they were sons of God and members one of another, they would be such witnesses. How could men who *had* this position make one for themselves? What had men who could *exercise* such a mighty power over the world to do with asserting or vaunting of it? No Jew or heathen believed that they had it; but *they* believed it, and acted as if they did. When the Church's faith in its divine birth, in its regenerate position, in God's calling, was growing weak, then it must begin to say how very divine it is. When it no longer understands itself to be in Christ, to be by its very nature and constitution spiritual, it must begin to assert that a certain mysterious spirituality had been conferred upon it, apart from Christ; it must suppose that He had *delegated* His functions to those who should have been the witnesses that He was continually and in person exercising them; at last the notion must be adopted, and be regarded as necessary to the unity of the Church, that one person was representing Him in His absence, was His commissioned vicar.

Every pretension of the Church, which has been felt as tyrannical and intolerable by the inward conscience and reason of mankind, has arisen from this low and imperfect view of its own position. It must force men's assent to opinions, because it did not believe that it had power to elevate them into a knowledge of the Truth; it must hold down human thoughts and energies, because it did not believe that it had a commission to awaken and emancipate them; it must be the worst of all civil rulers, the most miserable of policemen, the most despicable of intriguers, because it did not feel that the God of Truth was with it; that it might make men citizens of His kingdom; might raise them out of the inner corruptions, the evil results of which troubled the civil ruler—demanded the aid of the policeman; that it might deliver people and their rulers from the habit of lying one to another.*

But the Church has done—all honest modern historians, infidel as well as Protestant, confess it—other

* See the Essay on "the Unity of the Church," where I have endeavoured more fully to work out these statements, in connexion with the doctrine of an Indwelling Spirit, which I have not touched upon here.

works than these. However strange it may be to say that, having committed all these abominations, she has yet been a civilizer and educator of human beings; has given a new principle to society; has helped, at least, to break the chains of the serf; has made the new world quite unlike the old; this has been said, and must be said. Those who cannot bear the inconsistency, cannot bear history. If they want it to utter either fact without the other, they must write it afresh; it is not what God has written. Both facts must be explained in some way. If I find that men who have acted in the faith of God having regenerated the world in Christ, and who have thought themselves called as churchmen to proclaim that fact and bear testimony to it by their lives, have been the great instruments of good to the world, and if I find that men—possibly these very men at some other period of their lives, or at the very same period—who have acted on the opposite hypothesis, who have behaved as if it was their business to make human beings something else than God has made them, have produced all manner of mischief and confusion; I have a right to say, that my explanation is not altogether unreasonable.

2. But Protestants have said,—Englishmen especially have said with great energy:—The habit of magnifying the Church, which Romanists, and Greeks also, though not perhaps in an equal degree, have indulged in, has been utterly injurious to ordinary morality and human

life, because the state and civil order, and ultimately, domestic order, have been disparaged, for the sake of glorifying it; for the sake of maintaining a certain spiritual or ideal life, which is supposed to be the most truly Christian. Undoubtedly all this has happened; the complaint has the best possible foundation. And why has this been so? Because Romanists and Greeks, whatever they have professed, have not believed that Christ came into the world to regenerate all human society, all the forms of life,—all civil order, all domestic relationships;—because they have not really confessed that, when He took human flesh, and ate common food, and sat at the marriage feast, He declared these to be connected with Him, to have a divine, eternal, spiritual, basis, and not to lose that character because they are connected with the earth and the body. A secret Manicheism has been infecting the practice of the Church, while she has denounced the heresy in terms; and that Manicheism has gained strength, and must gain strength every hour, till the idea of a regenerated humanity supersedes and extinguishes it. You may try other expedients, and you will try them in vain. The office of the magistrate will be scorned as secular, marriage will not be held to be honourable nor the bed undefiled, till neither king, father, mother, wife nor child, are loved more than Christ, till all are honoured and loved, because He is acknowledged as the bond of their union. What, then, are Protestants doing to maintain that which it is the peculiar glory of Protestantism to maintain, when they deny the renewal and regeneration of society in Christ; when they insist that we may not claim for our children the glory and privilege of the new birth, of being members of Christ; that this is the special distinction of a few persons who have been brought to know that they possess it? How can they defend the honour of kinghood or fatherhood, or of conjugal life, against Romanists, while they surrender their true position for so feeble a one?

3. And thus I am brought back to Mr. Combe and the Physical Constitution of Man. 'That has been very 'often disparaged by churchmen; the body has been 'spoken of contemptuously by them; health and clean'liness have been treated as vulgar things.' Assuredly; to our shame be it spoken; it has been even so. And why? Because we have forgotten that Christ took a human body, and spent the greater part of His time on earth in healing the sicknesses of it: because we have not confessed that the body and the earth are as much redeemed and regenerated by Him as our spirits, or intellectual powers; because we have not confessed the meaning and power of the Resurrection. A man who fully believes in Christ's Regeneration, must regard every physical study as a sacred study, physiology as the most sacred of all; must desire that they should be pursued manfully and fearlessly, with no other check than that which every true student voluntarily submits

to,—the check upon his own pride and impatience,—that restraint, which tends to the highest freedom, which every scientific man covets, that he may be a true discoverer of God's laws, and a benefactor to his brethren. We ought to feel that all God's judgments by fever and cholera, are judgments for neglect of His physical laws, but that *they* will not be obeyed till men obey His moral laws, by ceasing to live to themselves, by feeling that it is their business to care for their fellows and for the earth.

4. An able and benevolent man* has complained that we have been talking and arguing about Baptismal Regeneration, while our brethren of the working classes are discussing the question, whether there is a God. He means to intimate that we know next to nothing of what is going on in their minds, that we are quarrelling about our technicalities, while they are occupied with first principles. I feel the truth of much of the charge, and desire to take it home to myself. There is a sad chasm between us and them; the cause is all too well indicated by this remonstrance. But I cannot admit that we are discussing theological technicalities, when

* Since these words were written, he to whom they referred has left a blank in many hearts, and has been taken from the evil to come. The sentence I alluded to occurs in a beautiful lecture by the Rev. F. Robertson, of Brighton. If I objected to the mere form of his complaint, it was with the full consciousness that he knew infinitely more about the working classes than I did, sympathised with them far more deeply, was teaching them much better the mystery of spiritual and social Regeneration.

we are talking about Regeneration; I believe we are discussing the most radical principle of human life. I cannot admit that the working classes are strangers to the word Regeneration, or to controversies about it; it is one of their favourite words; they are continually thinking about plans of social regeneration. I cannot believe, finally, that they will ever come to the settlement of that primary question, whether they have a God to believe in and worship, till they are taught whether He has done anything, or is doing anything, for their regeneration.

Our fault, I conceive, is, not that we have spoken too much on this great subject, not that we have been too earnest in asserting that God has regenerated us, and has given us a simple sign and pledge that He has done so, but, that we have not made the people understand, because we have not understood ourselves, that we were needing such a Regeneration as they want and feel that they want,—a social as well as an individual Regeneration. If we did see our way to tell them this; to explain that we regard Christ as the Restorer of Humanity to its true and proper condition; as the King of kings, and Lord of lords; as the Head and bond of a universal brotherhood; as the righteous Judge and Punisher of all that violate their relations to each other, and set up self in opposition to society; I think we might, in time, bring some of them to feel that the Church was their friend and deliverer, not as they now, with great excuse, consider it, the bitterest of their foes.

Let any one, however, who shall determine to speak and act on this principle fully count the cost, and determine with himself whether he is ready to incur it. Let him be sure that he must offend all parties, without a single exception. He is a silly dreamer, if he fancies that he shall conciliate High Churchmen because he defends Baptismal Regeneration, or Low Churchmen because he says that faith in Christ as the Redeemer and Regenerator is the ground of all right Christian action. He must offend priests, monarchs, nobles, for he must tell them they have sinned against Christ, who has appointed them to take care of His sheep. He must offend those who denounce priests, monarchs, and nobles, because he recognises their appointment, and does not conceive that the Church, being a brotherhood, is therefore a democracy. He will displease those who say that you must reform the individual before you reform society, for he declares that Christ is the Reformer of both, and that the individual who claims any relation to Him, must own himself the member of a society. He must displease those who talk of reforming Society, as the only way of reforming the individual, because they understand by the reformation of society, the alteration of its circumstances, not the assertion of a spiritual root and ground of it. He must count upon the hostility of those who wish to keep things as they are, and who dread change lest the whole social fabric should fall to pieces, because he is certain that it will fall to pieces, unless Christ, who sacrificed Himself, is acknowledged as its foundation, and unless all maxims and practices, religious, political, commercial, which assume another and contrary foundation to this, are abjured and cast aside as anti-social, immoral, destructive. He must count upon the active opposition, or profound contempt, of the whole new school of philosophers and reformers, because their greeting to each other is, 'Christ is *not* risen;' their message to the tyrants and wrong-doers of the earth is, 'You need not fear the wrath of Him that sitteth upon 'the throne, or of the Lamb;' their gospel to the prisoners in Neapolitan or Roman dungeons, 'The deliverer 'of captives has not come; it is a figment of the priests 'that there is such a one.' Whereas, his only hope of that which shall be, lies in his acknowledgment of that which has been and is. His assurance that the bands of death and hell have been loosed, is his only ground for confidence that they will be loosed; his certainty that Christ is the Judge of the earth is his only reason for believing that it will be one day purged of all its oppressors; his trust that the King has actually been one of the sufferers, and the chief of them, is his warrant for declaring that the earth shall not cover the blood of any of her slain,—that what has been done of good or evil to the least of Christ's brethren, has been done to *Him*.

I cannot tell what amount of sympathy has been expressed by Unitarians generally with Mr. Combe's doctrines, but I should imagine that one class of Unitarians, being sincerely philanthropical, and more or less strongly inclined to materialism, must be very favourable to them. I have no arguments to urge upon them in reference to these doctrines, besides those which I have addressed to my countrymen generally. Some of them, I know, are admirers of Butler, and regard his doctrine of human nature as a valuable counteraction to our favourite theological dogmas,—to that especially which they understand us to associate with the word Regeneration. If I have succeeded in showing that this dogma, interpreted not according to some peculiar theory of mine, but in the way most consistent with the profession of Churchmen, explains Butler's moral constitution, and proves that we need not reject it because we do all honour to Physics, I shall at least prepare their minds (and this is all I desire) for a calmer and less prejudiced consideration of the whole subject.

As men earnestly interested in politics, I also claim their attention. They will see, I trust, that a clergyman may concern himself with politics, not merely as they bear upon the interests of his order, not merely as they contribute to make the office of the priest more honoured either on civil or ecclesiastical grounds. And this not because he thinks meanly of his order, or entertains any theories about a universal priesthood which interfere with the acknowledgment of individual priests; but because he counts it a most degrading thing for a priest to assert his powers instead of using them, and because he believes those powers must be used sinfully and shamefully, if they interfere with those which are committed to any other functionary, and if they do not promote the moral and civil freedom of the community in which they are exerted. The elder Unitarians are, I believe, commonly Whigs. And so far as Whiggism implies the recognition of a constitution for each particular nation, the principles and forms of which are adapted to the character and circumstances of its inhabitants, and are brought to light through its history, I heartily sympathise with them, and would only suggest that in our day we can scarcely understand or defend such particular constitutions, unless we are willing to inquire whether there is a constitution for mankind,—one which does not destroy, as so many universal constitutions that men dream of do, but upholds, the order of each country and each family. But if by Whiggism they mean merely a compromise between the past and the present, between order and freedom, I who hold that a faithful care of the treasures of the past ensures the brightest hopes for the ages to come,—that there cannot be an excess of order or of freedom,—must part company with them as wholly unsatisfactory teachers, from whom no practical good can be obtained, and betake myself to some of the younger men of the sect who, I suppose, would prefer the name of Radicals.

That name, too, I hold in sincere reverence, and wish that I were worthy to claim it. I fear we have none of us been radical enough, that we have all been too content with superficial changes, not demanding a full and thorough reformation. After thinking, with some earnestness, how that may be attained for us in England and for men everywhere, I have come to the conclusion which this Essay expresses. I hinted at it when I begged the new school of Unitarians to tell me plainly what kind of a Church it is which they look for in the future;—whether it has anything to do with that which has existed in the world for eighteen centuries; whether He who is declared in our Creeds to be the Corner-stone of that, is also to be the Corner-stone of this. I press the inquiry again, now that I have told them my mind frankly upon it. I will add this only: that if I accepted the doctrine of some of those with whom they are associated, and whom they sometimes proclaim to be the heralds of a new dispensation; if I thought that the world which is to arise out of the wreck of that in which we are living, were one of which some other than Jesus Christ, the Son of God, was to be the king; I should have no more fervent wish, supposing I could then form a wish,—I could conceive no better prayer, supposing there was any one to whom I could offer a prayer,—than that I and my fellow-men, and the whole universe, might perish at once, and for ever.

ESSAY XI.

ON THE ASCENSION OF CHRIST.

It is a favourite practice among some writers and thinkers of our day, to contrast the vulgar, low-minded, animal Jew, with the refined, imaginative, spiritual Greek. The comparison is dwelt on especially by those who wish to deliver us from what we have been used to call the facts, from what they call the legends, of the New Testament. All these, they say, had an ideal truth for the old Greeks, and furnished them with the hints of a thousand beautiful stories. The hard, definite forms in which they have obtained currency throughout Christendom, they owe, we are told, to the intellects of a few Galilæans, below even the average of their countrymen in cultivation, beyond them in coarseness and superstition.

This charge applies more or less directly to all the records of our Lord's life in the Evangelists; to all the articles of the Creed which I have been considering in my recent Essays. But it bears most strongly upon the words, "He ascended into heaven, and sitteth on the right hand of God the Father Almighty." 'Here,' it is said, 'we have a great idea sensualised and mate- 'rialised. Humanity is continually longing and striving 'to ascend above itself. There is always a mysterious 'heaven, which it desires to reach. Ever and anon 'it feels that it has actually gained a vision of the 'Infinite, towards which it aspires. The Greeks, pos- 'sessing the creative faculty, had various modes of 'expressing this truth. The people rejoiced in the 'symbols; the wise men, indifferent to them, perceived 'that which was latent in them. The poor Jew could 'think only of an actual body ascending into some 'actual Heaven. The Christian Church, unable to divest 'itself of the same dry habit of mind, has accepted the 'Jewish dogma. But she has felt the restraint which 'it imposes. The notion of a present Christ alternates 'in her teachings with that of One who has gone 'away. The doctrine of Transubstantiation has repre- 'sented and perpetuated the contradiction. Protestants 'have tried to rid themselves of it. They will not do 'so,' these teachers continue, 'till they are content to 'receive the kernel without the shell, to take the idea of 'the Ascension, and to cast away the story of it.'

I have ventured already to encounter the idealists in some of their favourite positions; I can have no wish to shrink from a fair examination of these. I should be taking a very strange course if I denied that the Galilæans were the most ignorant part of a race which was specially inclined to animal worship, which had exhibited that tendency throughout all its history. The Scriptures tell us so; as I accept their testimony, I must believe that it was so. Nor can I make any exception in favour of the fishermen, from whom our Lord chose His Apostles. If I did, I should contradict their own repeated statements. No doubt they were immeasurably less imaginative than the Greeks, very little able to conceive of a world beyond the range of their senses, or to people it with bright forms. Not only had they little natural capacity for this kind of creation; it was restrained in them by laws, institutions, traditions. They were told that the Lord God, the Creator of heaven and earth, had chosen their fathers to know Him, and to spread abroad the knowledge of Him. They were told that they must not think of Him as being like anything in heaven, or earth, or under the earth. They had a great hankering to do so. It was very hard to help such thoughts. What could He be like if He were not like some of these things? From time to time they were ready to fancy Him like the meanest of them; foreigners might suggest that He was like the worthiest, like a man: they were not insensible to the suggestion; still they clung to the law of their fathers.

Were they never to have any knowledge of this Being except what they got from their books and their traditions? How strange and sad it was to read the books, to hear the traditions, if that was the case! For all whose stories were related to them had spoken of actually knowing His name for themselves, of taking refuge in Him, of delighting in Him, of finding Him a high tower from the face of their enemies. Was all this changed? Was He removed to an infinite distance from them,—He who had seemed to promise that the ages to come should know Him better than those to whom He spoke; who had encouraged the fathers to hope that they should leave a richer legacy to their children than any that had come to them, and that it would go on increasing for their heirs?

At times they felt that this could not be; at times they *knew* that it could not be. What times were these? Were they hours of some special freedom from their ordinary cares and dulness, when the peasant was for an instant transfigured by the sight of some glorious sunset, when the fisherman looked into another world below the lake, and heard voices tempting him to come down and behold its wonders? No! it was not then; it was in hours of special toil, sickness, oppression; it was when the child or the friend was taken away; it was when sorrow for the past, doubt in the present, terror of the future, were griping them fast; it was then that the conviction dawned upon them, 'He still is;' 'He may be known by us.' 'We may find in Him a 'refuge, even as David or Isaiah did.' And then they perceived how it was that He must be known, if the knowledge was to do them any good, to bring them any comfort; that their hearts, not their eyes, were crying out for the living God; that with their hearts they must perceive Him, if they were ever to throw off their burden and enter into rest.

It was but for a little while they retained that confidence, and that clear understanding; they tried, perhaps, to keep both alive, by asking aid and instruction from some scribe or doctor of the law. He might give them words which would sink into their memories and their hearts, to come up again at some other day; he might give them rules which would bind them with heavy chains, from which afterwards they would struggle in vain to break loose, because they were rules for fitting them to seek that intercourse into which they must enter before they could be fit for it; or rules which bound them to those earthly things and those shameful recollections, from which they wanted to be set free.

But at last there came a Teacher, not removed from them like the Rabbis, a peasant, even as they were,—One who had grown up in their villages, and walked about in their cities,—One who went into all companies, but who seemed to care for no society so much as theirs. And He spoke to them as one having authority. He did not tell them of a God, who had been in other days, with whom it was possible for Moses and the prophets to hold converse. He spoke to them of a

Father who knew them, the fishermen of Galilee, and whom they might know. He spoke of having come forth from Him. He spoke of His kingdom as the Kingdom of Heaven, and yet as one in which they, the meanest sons of earth, could dwell, the secrets of which they might understand, the powers of which they might exert, which they were to assure their own countrymen was at hand, the gates of which they would ultimately open to the world. As He interpreted to them the nature of this kingdom, they more and more felt that He was drawing them from a world which they looked upon with their eyes, into an unseen world which another eye that He was opening must take in; yet a world which was intimately united to the one they were walking in, which gave the forms of that world a distinctness they had never had before. When He wielded the powers of His kingdom, they felt more and more that He governed the secret heart of nature and of man; that spirits were subject to Him; that through them He was acting upon bodies; that all His influences proceeded from within, though at last they left the clearest marks upon that which was visible and outward. It was strange how they were continually striving against this education, trying to invert it, translating His words and acts of power into some low, material, ineffectual sense. But it was stranger still how His teaching met all their thoughts and anticipations, in spite of this opposition; how natural it seemed to be, how exactly framed and devised for them; how it harmonized with all they had heard in their Scriptures of a righteous and invisible God, who cared for His creatures, and desired that they should seek Him and find Him; how it raised them above those animal inclinations of theirs; what a new feeling of humanity it kindled in them! But the Teacher Himself; what was He? Might not He who was leading them out of all visible idolatry Himself become the object of it? Could they help regarding Him with such a reverence as interfered with the reverence for Jehovah? Did not the Pharisees continually reproach them with this sin, and Him with encouraging it? There *was* this danger. What was He doing to deliver them from it? When Simon Peter said, '*Thou art the Christ, the Son of the living God*,' He said, '*Blessed art thou, Simon Bar-jona, for flesh and blood hath not revealed it to thee, but my Father in heaven.*' When Simon Peter said, '*That be far from Thee, Lord*,' that Thou shouldst be rejected of the chief priests and scribes, and be put to death, He said, '*Get thee behind me, Satan; thou savourest not the things that be of God, but the things that be of men.*' For a moment He was transfigured before them, and His face became bright and glistening; then a cloud covered Him, and a voice came out of the cloud, '*This is my beloved Son; hear Him;*' and He began to speak of His passion, and, He came down into the crowd about the boy who had fits. Thus a sense of inward glory belonging to Him, which spirit might apprehend, but the eye could not, was awakened in them; while they saw Him crushing and humbling all that they looked upon, all that they could make an excuse for idolatry. And at last the humiliation became complete. They saw Him in agony. The Jewish law sentenced Him as a blasphemer. The Gentile ruler gave Him up as an impostor, who pretended to the crown and the purple. He was not stoned, but crucified. Whatever could put contempt upon a Son of God, or a King, was poured upon Him. The night before His passion He spoke words, so St. John tells us, which the Apostles could not at all interpret. '*For a little while*,' He said, '*they should see Him, and then a little while, and they should not see Him, because He went to His Father*.' '*What is this*,' they said to themselves, '*which He saith, a little while? We cannot tell what He saith*.' And then '*when He saw they were desirous to ask Him*,' He spoke of a day of bliss to them, which should succeed a night of sorrow; a day when they should feel like the woman who remembers no more the anguish of travail, '*for joy that a man is born into the world*.' That same night, we are told, '*He took bread and blessed it, and gave it to His disciples, and said, Take, eat, this is my body, which is given for you;*' and poured out wine, and said, '*Drink ye all of this; for this is my blood, the blood of the New Testament, which is shed for you and for many, for the remission of sins*.' What such words signified, they knew not, and could not know. His body was there; within a few hours it was taken down from the cross and laid in a sepulchre. That He would ever rise out of it, they say, they had only the faintest dream, in spite of words which encouraged the belief. But then, they add, that when He did rise, this seemed to them the explanation of all that He had done, and said, and been. They report words which they say they heard of Him: '*Ought not Christ to have suffered these things, and to enter into His glory?*' If there was such a Son of God and Son of man, as He had led them to believe there was, then it seemed to them strange and monstrous that He should die, but natural and reasonable that He should rise. And soon they seemed to have felt it scarcely less natural and necessary that He should ascend to Him from whom they believed that He had come. They relate, in a few simple words, how they arrived at that conviction, how He educated them into it. He appeared to them while they were met together, the doors being shut for fear of the Jews. He showed them His hands and His side; He ate with them; He vanished out of their sight; He breathed on them; He commanded them to go and baptize all nations; He said, '*All power is given unto Me in heaven and earth;*' He said, '*Lo! I am with you alway, even unto the end of the world.*'

I repeat their story. If it sounds unnatural, inconsistent, grotesque to any, I certainly shall not make it less so by translating it out of their words into mine. But at all events this was clearly the effect of what they heard and saw, or fancied or pretended they heard and saw. They felt, 'This Lord of ours is actually related to 'us now as He was before He was crucified. He is 'related to His Father now as He was then. His body 'is the very body which He had then. But we are not 'henceforth to see Him often in that body. Our 'intercourse with Him will not be helped or hindered by 'the eye. It will be, as it has always been, intercourse 'with a divine Teacher, with a Guide and Enlightener 'of our spirits. It may be—must be—immeasurably 'more perfect than it has been, because He has been 'Himself cultivating and preparing us for it so long. 'But it must be, as He has always taught us to expect, 'intercourse with Him as the Head of a great kingdom, 'as the Lord of men, as One who has a work for us to 'do on behalf of men. It will be real and blessed if we 'enter into that work; if we do it as those whom He 'has called to do it; if we do not seek to appropriate 'Him to ourselves, to confine Him within our bounda- 'ries; if we remember that He is to fill all things, to 'bind earth and heaven in Himself. It must be— 'as He told us it would be—henceforth awful intercourse 'with the Father through Him, so that as in Him God 'has stooped to us, in Him we may ascend to God.'

'We may ascend to God! Why that is the ideal 'language. You are now translating Hebrew into

'Greek.' If I am, I am doing what the Apostles did. Their minds—the minds of these dull Galileans—*were* idealised, spiritualised. It is what I wish you to observe; and I wish you to observe also the process by which this strange transformation was wrought. A person whom they had known, with whom they felt that they were inseparably, eternally united, had gone out of this world; to what place they knew not, nor cared to know; but certainly to His Father, certainly to Him with whom He had always been one, with whom He had come to make them one, whom He had declared and proved to be their Father, as well as His Father. It was the great witness and demonstration to them that they were spirits having bodies, that they were not bodies into which a certain ethereal particle, called spirit, was infused. That which conversed with God was not something accidental to them, but their substance. And this too was that by which they held converse with each other. Without this there was no possibility of their feeling together, suffering together, hoping together. With this, it was possible to feel, suffer, hope with all men, with the whole universe. But was it necessary to forget that Christ had a body in order that they might enter into this fellowship with His Father and with His brethren? If they did forget that, the fellowship would cease, and their spirits would fall again into their old slavery. For this is the pledge of their union to Him; His victory in the body, over the body, for the body, is theirs also. They could claim the dignity of spirits, because they were one with Him who had redeemed the body and made it spiritual. They could have fellowship with all sufferers in the body, because He had suffered and died, and was the common Lord of all. They could rise to communion with the Father of Spirits, because there was One in a body who was His well-beloved Son, and who had offered Himself for them.

The disciples of Christ, having gained this learning, could enter into the force of those words spoken at the Paschal supper, which had been at first merely bewildering. They could remember how at Capernaum He had spoken of his flesh being meat indeed, of His blood being drink indeed; how He had said that His flesh would be given for the life of the world; how, when some were offended, He said, '*The spirit quickeneth, the flesh profiteth nothing;*' and how He had connected these apparent contradictions with the question, '*What and if ye shall see the Son of man ascend up where He was before?*' And now, as they ate the bread and drank the wine, according to His commandment, they could receive these tokens as the surest pledges that they were risen with Him; that they were in His presence as much as ever; that they had no life in themselves; that the life of the world was in Him; that His flesh and blood were indeed the bond between the creatures and the Creator, between the creatures and each other.

You see, then, how careful the Apostles are to impress us with that fact, which wise men, who do not in general consider them trustworthy authorities, are also so anxious to impress us with, that they were very stupid people,—on a level with the most stupid. Thus they show that the great experiment of what man is and what he is meant for, was made *in corpore vili ;* so that none could say, 'This lesson is not for me ; I cannot claim to be a 'spiritual being, and to be risen and ascended with 'Christ.'

These Galileans, not being men of any gifts of soul, not men whose race or general culture led them to magnify the soul above the body, yet came to such an apprehension of the spiritual condition and glory of man,—to such a practical apprehension of it,—as no sages in any country had ever reached; I say of *Man ;* for this was necessarily involved in the discovery that they were not better than the worst of their countrymen, and that Christ had cared for the worst and taken their nature. Though, as their mission was to the lost sheep of the House of Israel, all they needed, generally, to proclaim was, that the silliest of *those* sheep,—the one who had wandered furthest,—had an interest in the sufferings and triumphs of the good Shepherd.

But there came a time when a Jew of Tarsus felt that he was called to go forth and tell Greeks that they were possessors of the blessings of the children of Abraham. The blessings of the children of Abraham!

What a message to bring to the most graceful and refined people on the earth, that they might share the privileges of those whom they accounted the most coarse and inhuman! To assure those who believed that they must be meant, in one way or other, to bear rule over mankind, because they had souls and the majority of men only an animal nature, that they might become what some of the least intellectual of that miserable majority already were! And yet this was the proclamation of the Jewish tent-maker. And instead of its seeming to him or to his countrymen a message which flattered their national pride, Saul declared that, until that pride was crushed in him by a revelation of Jesus the Son of God,—until he knew Him to be indeed the King of his own spirit, and the risen and ascended King of the whole earth, he could not endure the thought that the Greek was cared for by the God whom he worshipped, and was a member of the same body with himself. When he did with his whole heart acknowledge that truth, and was convinced that he had a commission to declare it, Greeks, who had been given up to dæmon-worship, and whose thoughts of that which was divine had found the most exquisite visible forms to clothe themselves in, turned with wonder and awe to the invisible Lord whom the poor Syrian tribe had for centuries been confessing; claimed Him as the common Father of them and the barbarians; owned that one perfect human image of Him had been manifested, and that all the images which they had formed must be cast away; believed that a way was opened into His presence for them and for all, through the Mediator, who was in their nature at His right hand. On this ground a church of men, taken out of all nations and kindreds, stood; this was the bond of their fellowship; this destroyed the divisions which locality, race, individual temperament, old traditions, private judgments, had established among them. And when they met, as St. Paul told them they were to meet, and kept that feast which Christ had instituted the same night that He was betrayed; they met to have fellowship with a Lord who had ascended in that body which He had offered up, and which death could not hold; they met in the assurance that they were risen with Him and brought into His presence; they met to realize their union with the whole family in heaven and earth, which was named in Him the elder Brother of it; they met to give thanks in Him, to the Father who had made them meet to be partakers of an inheritance with the saints in light.

But St. Paul discovered in each one of these churches, tendencies which were threatening the existence of this communion, and were bringing back all Judaism, all idolatries, all local divisions, the materialism of old traditions, the spiritual conceits of those who had not been taught to suspect themselves and to know that they knew nothing. He encountered each of these tendencies as he saw it rising; traced it to its source; pointed out the habits that were akin to it, and that were fostering it. Among the Corinthians he discovered the love of faction and party leaders, which was so specially Greek; among the Galatians, the influence of teachers who persuaded them that the Jew had still a position higher and diviner than that of all other men, and that they must become Jews if they were to have God's favour; in the Colossians, speculations about angels, dæmons, emanations; all that constituted the philosophised mythology of Orientals or Greeks. There is something peculiarly adapted to this last habit of mind in the words which we find in the third chapter of the Epistle to the Colossians: '*If ye then be risen with Christ, seek those things that are above, where Christ sitteth on the right hand of God.*' He wished to remind the philosophers who were trying to scale heaven by their theories, that they would be baffled, as all the giants of former days had been. He wished to show them that what they called spirituality was not that at all; that it was merely the exaltation of the soul at the expense of the body, of the sage at the expense of the common man, and that it led by a very direct road to the degradation of Humanity. He wished them to see how —not the soul or the sage—but the man, had been exalted in the exaltation of Christ; how the whole Body, and not some of its choice members, might claim to be risen with Him; how impossible it was for any one to rise who tried to rise by himself, or to set himself in anywise apart from his brethren. But though there is this special appropriateness in the words, they are generally applicable to all conditions of the Church, which St. Paul discovered then, or which he expected might exist hereafter. They point out, I think, what would be the source of various diseases, and what would be the one remedy for them.

When we hear the words, '*If ye be risen with Christ*,' our first inclination is probably to say, 'It is not an '*actual* rising, of course, which he means; the lan- 'guage is metaphorical. We are to rise, as one of the 'collects expresses it, in heart and mind.' Now Paley, who had a broad, simple, English nature, who was a utilitarian by profession, and who had as little tendency to mysticism as any one who ever lived, was struck especially by the business-like quality of St. Paul's mind. You may say, Paley was an advocate, he held a brief for St. Paul. No doubt; but he need not have chosen that peculiar merit for his panegyric; there were a thousand stereotyped common places about devotion, intrepidity, self-sacrifice, which would have done as well. He would certainly have resorted to them, and not to this phrase, if he had thought Paul was in the habit of using metaphors when he was writing on grave practical topics. No man of business would do that, and therefore Paley, whatever construction he might have put on, or have abstained from putting on, such passages as these, which are so familiar to every reader of St. Paul, so characteristic of his style and of the man, certainly must have concluded that they were not pieces of fine writing, not flourishes of rhetoric; that they were unlike those expressions of poets or philosophers, which are far from being unmeaning or nonsensical, but which he would have deemed so, about the wings of Psyche, or the ascent of the divine in man into its native element. Our Archdeacon must have perceived, with his shrewd northern common sense, that St. Paul, though very unlike him in most respects, was just as substantial as he was, just as little of a dreamer or a sentimentalist; that there was a connexion between what he said of spirit and 'business.'

It is precisely this connexion which I have been endeavouring to trace, and which marks out St. Paul as 'a Hebrew of the Hebrews.' The Teacher whom the other Apostles had known after the flesh, trained him, by discipline not less regular, mysterious, and severe than theirs, to know that the spirit is the substantial part of man; that he *is*, because he is made in the image of God, who is a Spirit; that he is in a fallen, anomalous condition, when the senses which connect him with the earth are his rulers, and he judges what he is from them; that he is in a restored, risen, regenerate condition, when he is able to assert his glory as a spiritual being by asserting his relation to God. Believing, therefore, that God had regenerated and restored Humanity in Christ, that He had called men to claim their relation to the Father through the Son, he could say boldly, 'You are risen with Christ.' 'It is not a 'metaphor or fancy that you are; you will be always in a 'region of metaphors and fancies, always shaping some 'dream of a nobler life out of the coarse material of 'your earthly existence, until you take up this position. 'Then all becomes simple and real. There is no more 'a straining after some high ideal; the most quiet, 'reasonable life you can lead is that of creatures who 'are raised into union and fellowship with a higher 'nature; who are continually looking up to Him, in 'weakness and dependence leaning upon Him, confident 'that He can lift you, and is lifting you, above all the 'things which He has put in subjection to you, and is 'giving you the power to use them as your ministers, 'and to consecrate them to Him. And because you 'know how these things have corrupted you, and en-'slaved you, and become your idols, therefore as risen 'creatures, as regenerate sons of God, seek the things 'that are above, where Christ sitteth at the right hand 'of God. Claim your portion in the eternal Truth, and 'Love, and Righteousness, which He has manifested to 'you, and of which He has made you heirs; have done 'with all earth-born phantoms, superstitions, conceits, 'fears. They will cling about you, as all grovelling 'lusts and filthy imaginations will likewise. But give 'entertainment neither to one nor to the other. You 'can disengage yourselves from them. For you are 'members of Christ's body, and Christ is at the right 'hand of God. And if you say, "But the earthly 'attraction is too mighty, and the sense of past evil and 'slavery recurs continually, and the moment we seem 'to rise we are fallen again, and when we seek to be 'united to our brethren, then come in all low, petty 'thoughts about ourselves; and when we want to rule 'the world for God, the world gets the mastery, and 'rules us for the Devil;" then, I say, remember the 'words, "*My flesh is meat indeed, my blood is drink* '*indeed.*" Be assured that He who is at the right hand 'of God is not merely a spiritual being separated from 'you; He is in your nature, He has taken your flesh. 'He has redeemed it, glorified it! Come, then, brother 'man, not as a fine, dainty, selfish epicure, to seek some 'special and solitary blessings for yourself; but come 'as one of a family, to seize a common food which is 'given to all, a sacrifice which has been offered for all. 'Come, and eat it in haste, with your shoes on your feet 'and your staff in your hand, as a man who has a 'journey before him and work in hand, as a pilgrim, not 'as a philosopher. But again: eat it, all of you, as 'risen men, as spiritual creatures; not as those who are 'peeping into the ground and muttering, to ask the aid 'of some familiar spirit; not as those who come with 'cowardly prostration before a dæmon whose favour they 'are bribing; but as those who have their habitation and their polity with Christ, their Representative and 'Intercessor.'

If the Greeks, with their high spirituality, had anything to produce which was more spiritual than this,—if, with their Humanity, they had anything which was more human,—it is a pity they did not bring it forth in those three centuries when they were struggling, with every possible advantage, against the Christian Church. But I think the more we look into the history of that Church in those centuries, and in all that have succeeded them, the more we shall perceive that it has become earthly, debased, superstitious, inhuman, just in proportion as it has lost hold of this truth of Christ's actual ascension, just in proportion as it has substituted a mere symbolical or ideal ascension for that, just in proportion as the Greek notion of men rising and ascending by dint of high gifts of soul into gods, has superseded the notion of the fishermen and the tent-maker, that they and the humblest men are risen with Christ, and may therefore seek those things that are above.

My readers will perceive at once that this is a natural and direct inference from the doctrine I maintained in my last Essay. I showed then how many of the mischiefs and abominations which had tormented the Church, and made her the oppressor of mankind, arose from her disbelief in Christ as the Regenerator of man. There are some special applications of this statement which belong to the subject I am now considering.

The resurrection and ascension of Christ having been taken by a great portion of the Church as merely extraordinary, anomalous events,—not as events which could not have been otherwise, which exhibit eternal laws, which vindicate the true order and constitution of human existence,—while at the same time there has been an assurance that they were necessary to men, and that they must in some way be *pattern* events, examples of that which men were to be and to do,—a series of acts, attesting the power of spirit over body, the capacity of men to overcome the powers of nature, the possibility of rising into communion with the infinite, has been imagined. These have been considered strange exceptions in the order of the world; and being such, the whole inventive power of the human spirit has been employed in decking them out and connecting them with the life of some favourite saint or hero. By degrees it has been discovered that a number of these triumphs may be referred to ordinary principles and laws, which govern the human frame and the course of nature; that other portions of the stories are traceable to mistake, confused reporting, or direct fraud. Still not merely the affections of men, but their consciences, have clung to these instances of an actual connexion between the spiritual and the external world, and of the dominion of the first over the second. In vain you produce the clearest evidences of imposture; in vain you talk of natural causes. The heart of man says, 'Here are signs 'of a *faith* which was not false, but true; here are tokens 'of that which is not natural, but supernatural.' And now a new change is evidently taking place. Science itself is becoming dynamical rather than mechanical; powers and agencies are discovered in nature itself, not less mysterious than those which miracle-workers spoke of. Man is able, through science, to exercise such powers as seem to attest the dominion of spirit over nature more completely than any signs they wrought. The victories of the old artist over the marble, the mysterious energy by which he compelled it to express the thoughts and emotions of living beings, are leading many whom these facts do not impress, in the same direction; the legends of Greece are received as striking commentaries on the powers of her sculptors and poets. The Romish priests, as teachers of youth, see that a movement is going on very like that which the popes rashly encouraged at the revival of letters. Some of them cry out that it must be checked. 'Let us have as little science as we can. The old notions 'about the sun are safer than the new. They must be 'restored if possible. Let us banish the classics from our 'schools. The Greek legends are corrupting our youth. 'They and profane art must be proscribed.' It is impossible not to see that many in Protestant England, who hate these priests on other grounds, would be ready to join them in their prohibitions. There are those among us who think that the facts of science, unless they are well sifted and sorted by religious men, and mixed with religious maxims, are likely to disturb the faith of the people, and that the beautiful forms of Greek sculpture, especially if they are not clothed, and made unnatural, must corrupt their morals. I shudder at these notions, but I do not wonder at them. It seems to me that the Romish protesters are wise in their generation. If their disciples are to learn fictions, it is better they should not be able to compare them with facts; it is not well that they should know how many of their stories are borrowed from Pagan sources, and how much less pure the copies are than the originals. On higher grounds they may be right in thinking that those who are not allowed to read the Scriptures in their simplicity and breadth, have no standard for judging of what is good and evil in other literature, and had better be kept from it altogether. The existence of such feelings amongst *us* is far less excusable. Our education in the Bible ought to have taught us to believe in a God of Truth; to reverence facts, because they must be His facts; to long that laws should be discovered because they are His; to fear nothing but what is false, that being certainly of the Devil. Our Bible culture ought to have made us understand that nothing is impure save the corrupt and darkened conscience and will, and that that may convert all things, even the holy words of inspiration, into its own nature. The breadth, simplicity, nakedness of the Scripture language should have taught us to dread what is disguised and dressed up for the purpose of concealment as immoral and dangerous; to regard the study of forms as they came from the divine hand, with the beauty which He has impressed upon them, as safe and elevating. Such has been the effect of the Bible upon the daughters of England; if her sons manifest it less, the Greek legends are not to blame. Those, like Milton, who have been most deeply penetrated by the meaning of these, if their minds have had a sound Hebrew root, have been the purest and the bravest. I do not believe any single man of us can look back and say, 'It was this 'culture, or my diligence in seeking it, which has done 'me injury.' It was a want of zeal and sincerity somewhere else. It was that the words the boy heard in church or was compelled to learn about the religion of his countrymen, did not present themselves to him as connected with those which he was reading in his Greek or Latin form. One did not illustrate the other; they seemed to be mere contradictions, intended for different creatures. If the heart acknowledged a fellowship and sympathy with the one, it seemed as if the other was frowning disapprobation. The Hebrew Scriptures, and the Creed, and Catechism, were taken to be setting forth a theory about God. The Greek world was human. And what had the human and divine to do with each other? Yes!—let the words be rung in the ears of our divines till they have taken in the full force of them—our youths ask, What have the Divine and human to do with each other? in a country which receives as the cardinal tenet of its theology, that Jesus Christ is very God and very Man.

'We accept that tenet certainly in a sense.' Yes, and, in the name of my countrymen, of our faith, and of God, I demand in *what* sense? Is it a real sense, is it a fundamental sense? Is it one which explains the facts of Humanity, or leaves them unexplained? Because if it is, be assured people will get their explanation elsewhere. The Greek legends, all feeble as they are because they interpret God by human measures and do not bring men to a divine measure, will yet be preferred to a mere doctrine which puts God at an infinite distance from man, and makes Him an object of dread not of confidence to the creatures who are declared to be formed in His image and who are craving for the knowledge of Him.

These thoughts must press heavily on the heart of every one who studies the condition of England,—especially of her young men,—at this time. The struggle between the tendencies which incline them to regard Christianity as utterly hopeless,—as convicted of incapacity for giving any relief to the efforts of human beings after a higher state,—and to accept a Christianity which guarantees the salvation of their souls if they will abjure all such efforts, and surrender to a system that which their consciences tell them they can only surrender to God,—this struggle is more tremendous than any of us know. Their English hearts solemnly protest against either alternative; but it is impossible for men, whose minds are awake, to live in a perpetual see-saw; nothing, they feel, is less English, less manly, than such a position. What evil may not be awaiting us, if all the sounds which reach such perturbed spirits are loud ravings against Rationalism and Romanism, while nothing is offered them but what looks less sincere and hopeful than either! But oh! what good, beyond anything I can think of or dream, may God be preparing for us through this conflict! What a day of joy may succeed a night of travail, if the message is indeed brought to us, 'The Man is born into the world!' And is not this the message which is contained in the old story of Christ's ascension to the right hand of God, if we take that story not as a legend, but as the fulfilment of all legends; not as an idea, but as the substantiation of an idea in a fact? With what delight might we then trace the unfolding mysteries of science, believing that each new fact is revealing some step in an ascending scale of creatures, the lowest of which is an object of creating and redeeming love, the highest of which is in communion with the Son of God! How the triumphs of art would then be felt as witnesses for the subjection of all things to man, a subjection accomplished in Him who has gone through death and has ascended to His Father! What joyful testimony would every mythological story then bring in, not to the wishes and aspirations of men only, but to God's satisfaction of them! Why may not the countrymen of Bacon, and Shakspeare, and Milton, aspire thus to declare to all mankind, the significancy of science and art, the essential and practical connexion of earth with heaven, of the human and the divine?

But they have still a higher work to accomplish, which perhaps must precede the other. I have alluded more than once in this Essay to that feast which the Galilean fishermen were told to keep when they sat at the Paschal supper; which St. Paul said that he was commanded to perpetuate in the churches which were gathered by the preaching of his gospel from the different tribes of men. For eighteen centuries Christendom has kept this feast; there has been no other like it in the world. It has spoken of the union of rich and poor, of men of all races, kindreds, educations, opinions, with each other, and with a divine Lord who had died for them. All the sections of Christendom have kept up some form of it, save the Quakers, and *they* affirm that they keep it in a higher sense. All the sections of Christendom have made it the symbol of their separation from the rest. That which was to unite all men, of every kind and degree of intellect, has been made the subject of the most subtle, intellectual distinctions. That which was to deliver men from the bondage of sense, has been made the minister of the senses. The doctrine of Transubstantiation has gathered up all idealism and all materialism into itself, is a compendious expression of all the contradictions in the hearts and understandings of human beings. Yet what hold it seems to have upon those hearts! How it defies the skill of Protestant divines, the wit of Protestant scoffers! How it mixes itself, unconsciously, with their theories! How mightily it has stood its ground against all notions that the bread and wine were but the memorials of an absent Lord, or that the believer created a Presence which, but for His faith, would not be! How it is strengthened by all Quaker experiments to make spiritual feelings and notions, which appertain to the few,—the expression of which is intelligible to still fewer,—the media of intercourse, instead of those symbols which speak of food and life for mankind! My dear countrymen are puzzled by all these observations which their experience forces on them. They are impatient of theories, unskilful in forming them. Yet it seems to them as if they must have a theory, either compounded of all theories that have ever existed, or the negation of all:—some grains of Paschasius, a few globules of Luther, an infusion of Zwingle, shaken together, and plentifully diluted with the *aqua pura* of George Fox. Then tired of a mixture, which must be either tasteless or nauseous, this man plunges into Romanism; that exchanges sacraments for some transcendental exposition of them; another who discovers the flimsiness of the exposition, flies to the open worship of Mammon, to *his* sacraments, in which the outward sign and the thing signified are so perfectly consubstantiated. Oh, brethren! must we, being such blockheads, as our German and Gallic brethren consider us, and as we know ourselves to be, in all metaphysical conceptions, always try to rival them? Is it not possible God may have some other work for us, not so satisfactory to our pride, but, on the whole, if we perform it faithfully, not less serviceable to mankind, or less to His glory? Has it struck you that we are not *merely* countrymen of Bacon, Shakspeare, or Milton, but also of some millions of men, living on our own soil and in our own day, speaking our tongue, who work with their hands, and who have, besides those hands, senses which converse with this earth, sympathies that should unite them to each other, spirits that might hold converse with God? I do not know that they want theories about transubstantiation or consubstantiation, Romanist dogmas or transcendental dogmas, Le Maistre or Schelling. But I do know that they want occupation for these senses, these hearts, these spirits. And I do know that you can, if you will, say to them, one and all, 'Brothers, here are the pledges that we have a great 'Elder Brother, who was a suffering peasant here on 'earth, who died and rose again, and who is at the 'right hand of God. These tell us that we are one 'with Him where He is. We need not ascend into 'Heaven to bring Him down; we need not go down into 'the deep to bring Him up again. You may hold con-'verse with Him where He is. He has proved you to be 'spirits. He has given you this bread and this wine, 'these common things which belong to us all alike, that 'we may claim a participation in that body and that 'blood which were as real as yours, which were given 'for you, raised from death for you, glorified at God's 'right hand for you. Take, eat; receive this New 'Testament in His blood. Confess your selfishness, 'your divisions, your heart-burnings. Claim the unity 'which belongs to you. Go your ways; work like men; 'till the earth, and subdue it for God; make it bring 'forth corn for the sower, bread for the eater. In due 'time it will be all God wants it to be. Meantime you 'have a city that hath foundations; a house not made 'with hands, eternal in the heavens.'

And there is something besides which perhaps we have forgotten. Though it has not pleased God to make us clever in building systems, He has seen fit to bestow on us an empire on which the sun does not set. He has committed to our care some hundreds of millions of human beings, who have certainly the same flesh and blood with us, and who show by the strange speculations which their sages (often rich in the gifts we are so deficient in) express in words, and which are for the people embodied in acts, that they are spiritual beings, and that they know they are. Most of our civil and military servants, though they have done some parts of their business admirably, and have taught these people to believe that there is truth and justice among men,— alas! they have often doubted and denied their own position,—have felt that with this part of their mind, though the most radical, though affecting their whole existence, they could not meddle. Missionaries have gone forth with the noblest aims; not seldom they have effected blessed results. Yet the officials say, nay, many of them say themselves, that the majority of the natives have only derived from their presence a vague impression, that all they had held themselves is false; and, that we could offer them in exchange the choice of some twenty different religions, manufactured in Europe, and belonging to white men. Suppose we could go to them and say, 'There is an Advocate and Intercessor, 'not for Europeans, but for men, at the right hand of 'God. And here are the witnesses that you as men, 'having flesh and blood, and being, as you know, 'spiritual creatures, are one with Him, sharers of His 'nature, and, therefore, children of God, fellow-heirs, 'with all men everywhere, of His kingdom,'—does it not seem possible that the animal and the human sacrifice, the fearful invocation to Kali, the prayer-machine of the Buddhist, might disappear more quickly, than while we merely argue with them for opinions respecting which we are divided as well as they?

These are thoughts which I have addressed specially to English Churchmen, who, if they heeded them, might, perhaps, in due time, first bring the sects in their own land to meet them in a common sacrifice and a common Lord; secondly, might reconcile Protestants and Romanists abroad, instead of hovering uneasily between them, or showing a contempt, which is amply returned, towards both.

I now lay these same thoughts before my Unitarian brethren, of both sections. What I have said of Paley, may show those whom the younger school stigmatise as materialist or utilitarian, that I do not feel separated from them; that I do not think it is needful for them to go through an initiation in any German or American school, before they can understand St. Paul or St. John. Good manly sense seems to me so precious and noble a gift, that I am afraid I often speak intolerantly of those who put spiritualism and philosophy in place of it. But I have no right to do so, for I have felt that temptation strongly; and if I have felt also the punishment for having indulged it, and the reaction against it, I should be the last to cast stones at any offender. Most earnestly, therefore, do I call upon all of the spiritual school to join with those from whom they are in part alienated, and with me, in believing that there is One ascended on high, and on the right hand of God, who is our Mediator and theirs; who claims us as spirits now, and can change the body of our humiliation to the body of His glory, by that power whereby He is able to subdue even all things to Himself.

ESSAY XII.

THE JUDGMENT DAY.

There is no question which exercises the minds of moralists and politicians so much as the question of responsibility. How are you to make ministers of state, legislators, judges, responsible? To whom are the highest officers in every state responsible? Are they to be practically ruled by those whom they profess to rule? Is the sovereign a sovereign only in name? Is the ultimate authority vested in those who, by a fiction, are called his subjects? Or is he governed only by some code written in letters which he has himself the power of interpreting, with which he may even at times dispense? Or is he an autocrat, whose own will is the last court of appeal, that to which all must not only in name, but in deed, do homage? We all know in what an infinite variety of forms these questions present themselves, how they force themselves upon us in the business of every day life.

The notion which prevails mostly among ourselves

is, I think, something of this kind. In a civilized country,—above all, in one which possesses a free press, —there is a certain power, mysterious and indefinite in its operations, but producing the most obvious and mighty effects, which we call public opinion. If this can be brought to bear upon the acts and proceedings of any functionary, we suppose that there is as much security for his good behaviour as can be possibly obtained. He lives under the conviction that his acts, as a public servant, are open to a vigilant and suspicious scrutiny; experience assures him that no nice or accurate line will be drawn between this part of his life and that which he might wish to claim as private—his domestic relations, his opinions on the different topics which interest his fellow-men. Thus his whole existence is in a great measure exposed; his sphere of independent action or judgment is very limited. Though the right of thinking for himself may be one which he is anxious to assert, nay, which the habits and rules of the times require him to assert, the actual power of thinking for himself can only be exercised under strict conditions; practically, the circle in which he moves, or the world at large, or those, be they who they may, who direct the world, think for him.

When public opinion has been for some time deified in this manner, there comes a strong recoil. 'Is it 'possible,' men ask, 'to live honestly upon such terms 'as these? Has the progress of civilization, as it is called, 'not brought us into greater freedom, but only into more 'hopeless slavery? If we are to have masters, should 'we not know who they are? Should we not, at least, 'know what is their right over us? Should they not have 'some claim to our reverence, if they have no hold upon 'our affections? What can be so ignominious as this 'subjection to judges whom we do not in our hearts 'believe to be wise, to whom in secret we attribute little 'sincerity or truth, who are the sport of a thousand 'accidents and influences, as vulgar as any of those 'which could pervert our own judgments if we were left 'to ourselves? Is it not the business of a man to shake 'off such a yoke as this, to say that he will *not* have his 'deeds or thoughts moulded by this opinion, that he will 'not bow down and worship an image, which has been 'set up he cannot tell when or by whom, but which exacts 'devotion to itself under the heaviest penalties? Should 'not a minister of state, a legislator, a judge, hold him-'self responsible to some other tribunal than this? Must 'he not do so, if the words which go forth from his lips, 'if the deeds which he performs, are ever to be of any 'worth to ages to come, even to his own?'

These complaints are uttered. In youth, many strong resolutions are often founded upon them,—many bold and eccentric courses taken in pursuance of them. But again and again the man is driven into the old rut. He finds that the world was right in saying that self-will is a perilous and fatal guide. He thinks in vain where a substitute for this strange force of opinion is to be found; how wicked men are ever to be curbed, if it is not held up to them as an object of fear; how well-disposed men are ever to be kept in an even course, if they have not some hope of its protection. 'It is vague, 'indefinite, intangible enough, no doubt; but is not that 'the case also with all the powers which affect us most 'in the physical world? The further men advance in 'the study of nature, the more of these uncontrollable, 'invisible forces seem to make themselves known. If 'we think with awe of mysterious affinities, of some 'mighty principle which binds the elements of the 'universe together, why should not we wonder also at 'these moral affinities, this more subtle magnetism, 'which bears witness that every man is connected by 'the most intimate bonds with his neighbour, and that 'no one can live independently of another?'

It may easily be admitted that a reflection of this kind is suggested when we meditate upon public opinion,—the insignificance of the agents by which it works, and the greatness of its results for good or for evil. But I apprehend no one is able to derive this lesson from it, or at least to turn it to any practical use, till he has risen in some measure above the terror of it; any more than he can estimate the sublimity of a storm, while he is trembling lest it should in a moment destroy him and all that are dear to him, or than he can think of all the hallowed associations which a churchyard at night-time might call up, while he is dreading lest he should be pursued by some pale spectre. If we could learn the secret of overcoming this power, of acting as if we were indeed responsible to some other and more righteous one; if that conviction could be as present to us as the thought of the judgment which our fellow-creatures pass upon us; if our whole lives were moulded by the one belief as much as they are wont to be moulded by the other,—we should be able to understand what the world's judgment can do for us as well as what it cannot do; the very same principle which keeps us from obeying it would keep us from despising it; we should be saved from setting up our own tastes, caprices, nay, our own most deliberate judgments, against the tastes, caprices, judgments of our own or other ages; just because we should have courage to say to them, one and all, '*Whether it be right in the sight of God to hearken unto you more than unto God, judge ye.*'

Divines have thought that the words, '*We must all appear before the judgment-seat of Christ,*' might be so taken into the hearts of men, and become such a strong abiding conviction there, that all the opinions of contemporaries, all fear of popular assemblies—even of the most august earthly tribunals—should shrink and dwindle before them. They have, therefore, presented to their disciples the picture of a great assize, to which all ages and nations shall be summoned. What has been the effect of such descriptions? We feel ourselves at leisure to analyse our own emotions in listening to them, to compare the methods in which the subject is treated by different artists, to criticise their skill. We observe how much more powerful and judicious Jeremy Taylor is than others, because he has gathered together distinct groups, such as 'those whom Cæsar Augustus did tax,' instead of trusting to vague, cloudy abstractions. Surely this is proof sufficient that the preacher has failed of his purpose. He has not given us some mighty conviction before which we must bow,—which will go with us where we go, and stay with us where we stay. The fabric of this vision, raised by however noble an architect, fades more surely, more rapidly, than that of any of the earthly temples which he tells us are perishing. As it departs, it leaves the impression on our mind that the vulgarest, pettiest motives, which act upon us in the bustle of the common world, are more efficient than the most magnificent anticipations of that which is to be, in some far-off period. We may mourn that it should be so; we may utter some common-places about the weakness or depravity of human nature; but in some way or other we reconcile ourselves to the discovery.

Have earnest, devout men, then, deceived themselves in this matter? Were they wrong in supposing that the belief in Christ's judgment ought to be a mighty belief for mankind? Was it not a mighty one for their own hearts? I am sure they were not deceived. The thought of Christ's judgment was their strength in prosperity and in calamity. It saved them from floating with the current of their times when it was gentle,—from being swept away by it when it was strong. But I do not conceive they would have derived the least support from the anticipation of standing before Christ in some distant day, if they had not believed they were standing before Him in their own day. They were sure that for them the judgment was already set, the books were already opened; that they were every hour of their lives in the presence of One who knew the intents of their hearts, and who was calling them to account for these and for the acts to which they gave birth. It is for the efforts which they have made to ground us in the same habitual persuasion that we are chiefly beholden to them. Whatever light they have thrown on the Scripture doctrine of a judgment to come has proceeded from the light in which they were continually walking. If they have ever darkened that doctrine, or coloured and distorted it by their fancy, we may trace the error to their forgetfulness of that truth which the writers of the New Testament never suffer us to forget,—that Jesus Christ is the same yesterday, to-day, and for ever.

Perhaps you will say, 'After all, these descriptions 'which you represent as so ineffectual, even when the 'ability displayed in them is greatest, are only the 'expansion and realization of the words in the Creed: '*From thence He shall come to judge the quick and the* '*dead.* If one is weak, the other must be weaker; if the 'picture which tries to embody the fact is of such small 'worth, what can be the use of merely repeating a bare 'announcement of it?'

The objection would be most reasonable if the words, 'HE shall come to judge the quick and dead,' could be separated from all that has gone before,—if no pains had been taken to tell us who *He* is. But if the Creed has been declaring Him to be the Son of God our Lord; if it has been exhibiting Him, first, in the closest relationship with God, secondly, in the closest relationship with man,—this relationship not being created by any acts which are recorded afterwards, but being the ground and explanation of those acts, not being the consequence of His Incarnation, or Death, or Resurrection, or Ascension, but the cause of them;—then I apprehend the practical difference between the dry statement and the brilliant translation of it is immeasurable. According to the one, it is impossible, without violating the law of my being, the eternal order and constitution of things, that I should separate myself from Christ. He is the Lord of my own self, of my spirit; whether I confess Him or not I must continually hear His voice, be open to His reproofs. Wherever I am, whatever I am doing, He must be there; He must be the standard of my acts; the right in them must be that which has originated in

Him,—the wrong must be the revolt from Him. No present or possible conditions of our being can change this order. Death, it has been proved, does not dissolve our relation to Him; He has entered into it for us. The Resurrection from the dead is a resurrection for us as well as for Him; it has vindicated man's true condition, not subverted it. The Ascension, if we admit it to be a fact, not a mere idea, proves, as I urged in the last Essay, not that we are divided from Him, but that place cannot divide us; that we are spirits; that when we act as if we belonged to the bodies which we are meant to rule, we stoop knowingly, and are condemned by our consciences. Such a doctrine, I said, so far from being at variance with the facts of history and the laws of the physical universe, is confirmed by both. History shows how confident men have been in all times that they were meant to ascend above their earthly conditions, and to have fellowship with an unseen world; their noblest dreams have had this origin,—their wildest and most degrading superstitions have arisen from their incapacity to claim what they felt was their right. Physical science shows how many violations of true and divine laws men commit when they become slaves of their bodies, and into what ignorance they fall when they accept the testimony of their senses as determining those laws; in either case they are evidently not obeying reason, but setting it at naught. What follows? This exclusion of Christ from the eyes of sense is not, as men fancy, an interruption of that judgment which He, as Lord of their spirits, is continually pronouncing; they are not less in His presence, open to His clear, all-penetrating vision, now, than if He were walking in their streets. The disciples who accompanied Him when He journeyed from Galilee to Jerusalem, and sometimes were amazed at the mystery of His being and at His knowledge of their thoughts, understood first when He was parted from them how entirely independent that being and that knowledge were of the accidents which then surrounded Him,—how much these accidents had interfered with their recognition of Him. As long as they had any notion that they stood to Him only in the peculiar relation of disciples to a Master, as long as *that* relation seemed to them an external fleshly relation, they wanted the real awe and check, as well as the real help and support, of His presence. It was when they understood that this relation was common to them with a multitude of persons no-wise bound to them by kindred, occupation, race; it was when they learnt that the real bond between a disciple and a Lord is not a visible, but an invisible one, that they exercised themselves to have consciences void of offence, being certain that all things were naked and open to the eyes of Him with whom they had to do, and that to be reproved by Him was a far more serious thing than to be reproved by Sanhedrims or Proconsuls. The Creed, then, affirms, for you, and me, and mankind, first of all this discovery of theirs,—that Christ, ascended on high at the right hand of God, is our judge, the judge of the living and the dead. I do not say that this is all which the words signify; I do not think so; but I say that whatever else they signify, they signify this, and that we never can enter into the other part of their signification if we do not acknowledge this as the groundwork of it. And though this meaning may be latent in our popular discourses on a great judgment day,—and I have no doubt it is,—I cannot think that the hearers or readers of those discourses commonly detect it; they suppose that they are, at some distant, unknown period, to be brought into the presence of One who is far from them now, and who is not now fulfilling the office of a Judge, whatever other may be committed to Him.

There is another difference, not less radical and essential, which, I think, we must all at times have perceived, if not when we were repeating this article of the Creed, at least when we were reading those parts of the Scriptures which most illustrate it. What is this office of a Judge? If we follow the popular representations of the great Assize, we should conclude that it was fulfilled when certain persons were subjected to an infinite penalty for their transgressions, and certain others were absolved from that penalty,—perhaps acquired, by some means, an infinite reward. It is obvious that those who make these statements, *intend* to accommodate themselves to the ordinary maxims of men; to those which are recognised in earthly jurisprudence. They rightly assume that there must be an analogy between the divine procedure and that which we own to be righteous here. 'The difference of degree,' they would say, 'does not 'prevent the inspired writers, and ought not, therefore, to 'prevent us, from resorting to the same language to re'present both.' I fully accept this statement, and, therefore, I would put it to any English jurist, whether such an account of the function of a judge as this, satisfies any conception that he has formed of it? Would not he say at once, 'It is a very secondary part of this 'function to assign penalties or rewards: that, in a 'majority of cases, is done already by the law which 'the judge announces. But to discern who is right and 'who is wrong; amidst a multitude of shifting, dis'tracting appearances, to find out the fact; to detect 'the lie which is hidden under the plausible coherent 'story; to justify the true and honest purpose which may 'have got itself bewildered in a variety of complications 'and contradictions,—*hic labor, hoc opus;* here is, indeed, 'a sphere for the exercise of that judicial faculty, which 'we all esteem so highly,—scarcely any of us enough.' And I am certain we shall find that, when the Scriptures speak of a divine Judge, it is *this* correspondence, *this* analogy that they mainly suggest to us. You hear of the Word of God, who is quick, and powerful, and sharper than any two-edged sword; who divides asunder soul and spirit, joints and marrow, who is a discerner of the thoughts and intents of the heart. You hear St. Paul declaring that though he is not conscious of anything against himself, he does not judge himself, but He that judgeth him is the Lord. You find him using, in the same passage, the remarkable expression which occurs again and again in his writings, and to which I shall have to refer presently for another purpose, that it is a very little thing for him to be judged by a *human day.** Such an expression, so strikingly denoting the kind of light which men were able to throw upon the secrets of the heart, is a key to thousands of others in the New Testament—nay, I will be bold to say—a key to the language of the Bible, wherever there is an allusion to the judgments of God, or to Christ as judge. Everywhere the idea is kept before us of judgment, in its fullest, largest, most natural sense, as importing discrimination or discovery. Everywhere that discrimination or discovery is supposed to be exercised over the man himself, over his internal character, over his meaning and will. Everywhere the substitution of any mere external trial or examination for this, is rejected as inconsistent with the spirit and grandeur of Christ's revelation.

Nowhere is this difference more remarkably brought out than in the words which we have translated, '*For we shall all appear before the judgment-seat of Christ.*'

* 1 Cor. iv. 3, ἀνθρωπίνης ἡμέρας.

When we hear these words without examining them, or their context, we are likely enough to say, 'Here is the 'old story of Minos and Rhadamanthus again; St. Paul 'knew that it was familiar to the ears of the Corinthians. 'He altered it, and adapted it to his Christian notions.' I am far indeed from denying that St. Paul was anxious to preserve the eternal truth which lay hid in those legends. He would have been most grieved if he had, in any one point, made the Greeks, to whom he proclaimed a faith, unbelievers. It was his duty to avail himself, as far as it was possible, even of the forms of language,—especially if they were not merely Greek, but human forms, appealing to the feelings and consciences of men in all countries,—which had been associated with old convictions. To this extent I am ready to admit that the word 'judgment-seat,' or 'tribunal,' was intended to remind the Corinthians both of the courts with which they were familiar in their own city, of the more solemn Areopagus, and of those which their imaginations had fashioned on the model of these for the pale spectres in the world below. But if this were his object, mark what the process of transformation is. In the first ten verses of this chapter, and several of the preceding, he has been working out the doctrine that man stands in a twofold relation; to an earthly visible tabernacle which is dissolving; to an invisible Lord. The dissolution of that perishable tabernacle will not, he says, involve homelessness, nakedness. There is a new clothing provided for him; a house not made with hands, eternal in the heavens. Here there is much groaning; the body bears the signs of suffering and death. He longs to put on one which shall be free, living, immortal, '*that mortality may be swallowed up of life.*' He believes that God is working in him to produce such a renovation, and has given His Spirit as an earnest of it. He is confident, therefore, and had rather be absent from the body which is making such demands upon him, that he might be present with the Lord of his spirit. '*For we walk,*' he says, '*by faith, not by sight.*' We do not see Him to whom we are united; we only believe Him and trust Him. And whether that vision at any time is strong or weak, whether we are crushed by the external tabernacle, or are rising above it, we are still ambitious to be well-pleasing to Him, '*For we must all*'—not appear—but 'BE MADE MANIFEST *before the tribunal of Christ.*' A time must come when it will be clearly discovered to all men what their state was while they were pilgrims in this world; that they were in a spiritual relation just as much as they were in relation to those visible things of which their senses took cognizance. That which has been hidden will be made known; the darkness will no longer be able to quench the light which has been shining in the midst of it, and seeking to penetrate it; each man will be revealed as that which he actually is, that every one may receive the things done in the body according to that he hath done, whether it be good or bad.*

This language is, I think, strictly and beautifully consistent with all that the Apostle has taught us of Christ as the Redeemer and Justifier—with the whole purpose and method of His Gospel. But it certainly suggests to us the thought, that the tribunal of Christ is one which is not to be set up for the first time in some distant day, amidst earthly pomp and ceremonial, but that it is one before which we, in our own inmost being, are standing now, and that the time will come when we shall know that it is so, and when all which has concealed the Judge from us will be taken away.

'But if that is the sense of St. Paul's words, why do 'we speak in the Apostle's Creed of His coming *thence* 'to judge the quick and dead? why do we say in the 'Nicene Creed that He shall come *again* in glory?' These questions are so important, and they connect themselves with so many thoughts which are occupying and agitating men's minds in the present day, that I am most anxious fairly to consider them.

If I read the words, *From thence He shall come*, following immediately upon the account of an ascension into heaven, which is described as a great triumph for Him and for mankind, I do not think my first notion would

* *Ἵνα κομίσηται ἕκαστος τὰ διὰ τοῦ σώματος, πρὸς ἃ ἔπραξεν, εἴτε ἀγαθὸν εἴτε κακόν.* I do not think any one can be exactly satisfied with our rendering of this sentence, though I am not prepared to suggest another.

be that they implied that He would descend from that state—that He would assume again the conditions and limitations of the one which He had left. The favourite scriptural analogy of the sun coming forth out of his bridal chamber, after the dark night, would present itself as, at all events, much more obvious. No doubt a great many considerations might induce me to reject this sense and accept the other. I might find that express words in the New Testament or a general current of meaning obliged me to take up with the more difficult hypothesis. But, in fact, express words and the current of sense force me out of the difficult hypothesis into the natural one. When St. Paul wishes to teach us about the coming or the judgment of Christ, the word he most commonly uses is *ἀποκάλυψις*, or 'unveiling.' He looks forward to the unveiling of Christ. He bids His disciples in all the Churches live in the expectation of it. Or else he speaks of *φανέρωσις*—'a manifestation'—as in the passage I referred to just now, and as in that celebrated passage in the eighth chapter of the Epistle to the Romans, where he describes the whole Creation as looking forward to deliverance from its travail at the manifestation of the sons of God. Each of these words, especially the first, receives the greatest illustration from the Apostle's own history. Whenever he gives the story of his conversion, he describes it as an unveiling of Christ to his bodily eye; when he lays open the principle and meaning of his conversion, he represents it as the revealing or unveiling of Christ *in* him. This idea, in these two different aspects of it, therefore, possessed his whole mind, and penetrated his teaching. His Gospel to men was a manifestation or revelation of Christ to them, as one who had proved himself to be their Lord, by entering into their death, and by redeeming them from their tyrants. His assurance to each man was, that if he yielded to his Deliverer, and struggled against all that were trying to enslave him, Christ's power and presence would be revealed to him more every day. His hope for the world was, that Christ would in due time reveal himself completely as its Conqueror and King, and would bring all men to see that His universe was built on truth and righteousness. In strict accordance with this teaching, he uses 'day' to express the coming or revelation of Christ; 'day' being taken, as the reader will perceive if he turns to the thirteenth chapter of the Epistle to the Romans, or to the fifth chapter of the First Epistle to the Thessalonians, in opposition to *night.* Hereby he explains that use of the words 'human day,' to which I referred before, as expressing the judgment passed by men upon himself; hereby he brings forth the full force and intention of that phrase which recurs so continually in the prophets of the Old Testament—'*The day of the Lord.*' *

* I have dwelt so much upon the use of this language, in my Sermons on the Kings and Prophets of the Old Testament, as well as

And there is this further—I think, quite unspeakable —benefit arising from his use of this form of expression. Instead of allowing us to dream of a final judgment, which shall be unlike any other that has ever been in the world, he compels us to look upon every one of what we rightly call 'God's judgments' as essentially resembling it in kind and principle. Our eagerness to deny this doctrine,—to make out an altogether peculiar and unprecedented judgment at the end of the world,—has obliged us, first, to practise the most violent outrages upon the language of Scripture, insisting that words cannot mean really what, according to all ordinary rules of construction, they must mean. Secondly, it has obliged us to treat with most especial contumely that solemn discourse of our Lord with his disciples when they showed Him the buildings of the Temple, and almost to deny His assertion that that generation should not pass till all the things he spoke of were fulfilled; though he adds to it a sentence which might have made us serious in our belief of Him, if anything could:—'*Heaven and earth shall pass away, but my word shall not pass away.*' Thirdly, as I hinted when I was alluding to this subject in connexion with the doctrine of the Resurrection, it has driven us into the perilous notion that we are only using metaphors when

in the previous volume on the Old Testament, that I did not wish to enlarge upon it here; especially as it will come out more properly when I speak of the Epistles to the Thessalonians, in the book I have mentioned in the preface to this Edition.

we speak of God as coming forth to judge the world in any crises of war or revolution. Certainly the Bible justifies that language, as not metaphorical, but most real. It speaks of all such crises as '*days of the Lord.*'

The 'coming' of the Apostles' Creed, and the 'coming again' of the Nicene Creed, must both indicate, if we derive our interpretation of them from the Scriptures, not that Christ will resume earthly conditions, or will take a throne in some part of this earth, but that He will be manifested as He is. The Nicene phrase, 'coming again in glory,' which is taken from our Lord's own words, '*The Son of man shall come in the glory of His Father, and of the holy angels*,' seems expressly intended to guard against the notion that He should be invested with some of those vulgar ensigns of royalty which the sense-bound Jew supposed were needful to make Him a King, while He proved Himself to be one by healing the sick, and casting out devils. In our day, many of those who are most busy in the study of prophecy, complain of the Creeds, because they do not set forth, distinctly, *their* notion of a second coming of Christ to reign on the earth, but only speak of a judgment of quick and dead. I can sympathise, to a considerable extent, with their feelings, though I am convinced that the Creeds are right, and that they are wrong.

If the belief of a judgment takes the form, which it certainly has taken in the minds of many of us; if we look upon it only as something exceedingly terrible, which we are to set before our readers when all ordinary resources of argument and rhetoric have failed,—when we can no longer move them by any testimonies we bear concerning the mercy of God or His redeeming Love; if the thought of Christ as a Judge is one which we are to shrink from, though we may find satisfaction in thinking of Him as a Saviour;—then it is, indeed, utterly unintelligible why the writers of the Old Testament should so continually call upon God to rise and judge the earth; why this should be the great burthen of their prayers, the ultimate point of their hopes; and why the writers of the New Testament should exhort their disciples to lift up their heads, and to desire, above all things, the Revelation of Jesus Christ. To escape from this amazing contradiction, it has been natural for men to invent a theory and say, 'He is coming, but not *only* 'for this end, not *first* for this end. He is coming to 'reign over His saints,—to give them rest from their 'enemies; then the judgment of the world will follow.' It is better, I think, that men should cherish this belief, than that they should contemplate Christ as one who has saved heretofore, but is coming hereafter only to punish and condemn. For though some connect no better thoughts with this faith than the expectation of their own supremacy,—and from the supremacy of those who can indulge so dark and selfish a dream, good Lord! deliver Thy bleeding earth—no tyranny that has ever existed upon it, would be so godless and so intolerable,—there are numbers of true-hearted Millenarians, who rejoice in it only because it is identified in their minds with the victory of Christ over what is evil, with the establishment of His gracious dominion over all people. Such men felt themselves tied and bound by the notion of the religious world, that Christ had taken the nature of man and died on the Cross, only to save a few elect souls. They were sure that He must intend to bless mankind, to redeem the earth. Most glorious conviction, which no Creeds that men have ever framed, must tempt us to part with, for the Bible witnesses of it in every page; the truth and love of God are involved in our holding it fast! But the Creeds differ in one respect from the supporters of this pre-millennial Advent. They teach us that 1800 years ago, He who was crucified under Pontius Pilate, asserted and proved that He was the Lord of man; that while the Jews were confounding a real king with an emperor clothed in purple, He demonstrated wherein kingship consists, and what are the highest powers which belong to it. A creed that speaks of a Son of God and a Son of Man, has no need to tell us,—could not tell us without contradicting all its other statements,—that at some distant day He will assume an authority which He has never exercised yet. But it may tell us, it should tell us, that He who sat as a King, and judged as a King, when the city and temple of Jerusalem fell, and the old world passed away with a great noise; He who sat as a King, and judged as a King, when the mightiest empire the world had ever seen was broken in pieces by a stone cut out of the mountain without hands; He who has been confessed as a King by all the most civilized nations of the Western world; in whose Name kings have reigned and decreed justice; He who has been proving that the powers which they used were His, by sweeping away dynasties, and putting down nations, the cup of whose iniquities was full; He from whom all that has been righteous, gracious, gentle, orderly, civilized, in the economy of nations, families, churches, has come; He against whom all that has been cowardly, cruel, slavish, superstitious, in that economy, has been rebelling,—will most assuredly be manifested, not in some little obscure corner of the earth, where pilgrims may go to look for Him, but as the lightning shineth from the one end of heaven to the other; will be manifested, not changed and shrivelled from the crucified, risen, ascended Lord, to the miserable Cæsar the Jews fancied Him to be; but 'coming as He went,' in the glory of His Father, so that every eye may see Him, so that every king, and judge, and priest, who has professed to rule or teach by His authority or for Him, shall be forced to own to himself and to the universe, whether he has been serving truth or a lie; whether he has been serving Christ, or Mammon, or himself; whether he has bowed down to the judgment and opinion of any public, religious or secular, or has walked as a child of the day in that light which lighteth every man who does not choose the darkness. Surely a sound creed should tell us this, and should therefore convey to us the needful assurance and comfort, that all events have been working under a divine guidance to a divine issue; that nothing which has been good can ever perish; that nothing which is evil can abide in that kingdom of righteousness, and truth, and peace, which is the kingdom of God and of His Son, and therefore can have no end.

In spite of my conflict with the Idealists in my last Essay, I am quite prepared to hear the charges that I have now been defending an ideal, and not an actual, judgment day, and that I confound the spiritual kingdom of Christ with His reign over the earth. I can only answer, as I have answered before, that I have found the current notions of a judgment, not exactly ideal, but exceedingly fantastic, figurative, inoperative, and that I have tried to ascertain whether Scripture does not give us the hint of something more practical and more substantial. If the popular notion on this subject is thought necessary to produce terror in the minds of thieves and vagabonds, I own that I am ideal enough to think the constabulary force a more useful, effectual, and also a more godly, instrument. That does assert the existence of an actual present justice; that does awaken in the consciences of evil men the sense of a law, which never loses sight of them, and may find out their darkest deeds; that holds out to their merely animal nature, which requires such discipline, the prospect of a sure and speedy punishment. If, again, the popular notion on this subject is wanted as an influence to act habitually on the lives of ordinary worldly men, and it is alleged that I have substituted for it the notion of a mysterious judgment, of which it is impossible that such men can make any account,—then I reply, that it is precisely this kind of mysterious judgment which these men do recognise, and to which they pay habitual homage under the name of Public Opinion. But if you require this popular notion for the sake of religious men, or of those who are looking forward to some great improvement in the constitution of the world, then I say it is quite clear that such men are not in the least satisfied with it, but are inclined rudely to discard it. Such men demand for *themselves* an habitual government, inspection, judgment, reaching to the roots of their heart and will; such men demand for the earth some complete deliverance from all that defiles it and sets it in rebellion against a true and righteous King. The religious men must have a kingdom over their own spirits; do not they see that only such a kingdom can be of any worth to any human being whatsoever? Has not Christ claimed to be King over both the spirits and bodies of *men?* over their bodies, because over their spirits; over all things whatsoever, because over the creature to which all things are put in subjection. Do we need a return to the lowest Judaism, the lowest Heathenism, in our notions of the relation between spirit and matter, the eternal and the temporal? Do we not require a redemption of all that is human from its changeable accidents; a judgment and separation which shall come from the revelation of Him who has redeemed and glorified our whole humanity, between that in us which is His, and that which we have contracted by turning away from Him? Do we not ask for a day in which all the scattered limbs of Christ's body in heaven and earth shall be gathered together in Him, for a day in which light and darkness, life and death, shall never be mingled or confounded again? Is there any one who seriously believes that it is a day of twenty-four hours in duration which we are thus expecting? Is it not one which has dawned on the world already, which our consciences tell us we may dwell in now, which therefore Scripture and reason both affirm must wax clearer and fuller till He who is the Sun of righteousness is felt to be shining everywhere, and till there is no corner of the universe into which His beams have not entered?

I do not intend these Essays as a commentary on either of our Creeds. We have, I suspect, more commentaries on them than we want. In most cases, I have preferred to take my titles from popular and recognised names of doctrines, not to express them in the words of our formularies. I have spoken of the Incarnation, of the Atonement, of Justification by Faith; not of Christ being conceived by the Holy Ghost, or born of the Virgin Mary, or suffering under Pontius Pilate. For my object has been to examine the language with which we are most familiar, and which has been open to most objections, especially from Unitarians. Respecting the Conception, I have been purposely silent; not because I have any doubt about that article or am indifferent to it, but because I believe the word '*miraculous*,' which we ordinarily connect with it, suggests an untrue meaning; because I think the truth is conveyed to us, most safely, in the simple language of the Evangelists; and because that language, taken in connexion with the rest of their story, offers itself, I suspect, to a majority of those who have taken in the idea of an Incarnation, as the only natural and rational account of the method by which the eternal Son of God could have taken human flesh.*

But I have deviated from this practice in three cases. I have used the express words of the Creed as the text of my remarks upon the Resurrection, the Ascension, and the Judgment. I have done so, perfectly well knowing that I am laying myself open to the displeasure, not

* I have expressed my thoughts on this subject in a Sermon "On Marriage," in "The Church a Family."

only of the Unitarians, but of the other Dissenters, who would have a much better opinion of me, if I had defended the same principles without appealing to what they consider dry and worn-out documents.

I do not know whether I can find a better opportunity than this for addressing myself directly to the feelings of Unitarians on this point. They have a great horror of a Creed. But *tenets* they must have. The other Dissenters have a great many. *Their* list, they boast, is reasonably small. The tenet of a Judgment to come, or Resurrection of the just and unjust, however, is included among them. I do not know whether they very distinctly define their opinions on this subject; but a respectable, well-conditioned Unitarian would be very sorry if his orthodox neighbour supposed they were widely at variance upon it. I conclude, therefore, that the same vague, superstitious apprehension, which I have said that *we* derive from Heathenism, he must have derived from it also. The sense of a judgment to come is so kindred to our nature, so rooted in our nature, that we must hold it under one form or another. The old Minos form, or one that is akin to it, will be the form which this tenet assumes so long as it is merely a tenet. What I contend is, that it assumes a higher, nobler, more practical form when, ceasing to be a tenet, it becomes part of a Creed. When it is viewed as one of the acts of a living Person, a Son of Man, and a Son of God, then its coating of superstition falls off from it: it becomes identified with the greatest triumphs that humanity has yet won; with its present struggles, with its most glorious hopes.

I submit this remark to the earnest consideration of all classes of Unitarians, but especially of those who are becoming discontented with the tenets of their forefathers. They very naturally argue in this way,—'We cannot bear the yoke which is upon our 'necks already. You would put a heavier one upon 'them. We have been beaten with rods; you would 'beat us with scorpions.' The other Dissenters press the same argument upon their disciples: 'You complain of 'us for compelling you to accept dogmas which you do 'not feel to be reasonable, nay, even for preventing you 'from appealing to Scripture against them, because, after 'a congregation or school has accepted a certain interpre-'tation of Scripture, it is bound by that. What would 'become of you, then, if you were connected with a 'Church which formally and avowedly holds its members 'to a certain Creed?' I am not careful to answer this argument. I am a very bad proselytizer. If I could persuade all Dissenters to become members of my Church to-morrow, I should be very sorry to do it; I believe the chances are, they might leave it the next day. I do not wish to make them think as I think. But I want that they and I should be what we pretend to be, and then I doubt not we should find that there is a common ground for us all far beneath our thinkings. For truth I hold not to be that which every man troweth, but to be that which lies at the bottom of all men's trowings, that in which those trowings have their only meeting point. But what I cannot and would not do, I believe, the experience of a great many Dissenters will do for them. They will be driven to Creeds by their weariness of tenets. They will find that they are at the mercy of every tyrannical congregation, of its wealthiest member, of every dogmatist who rules a school, of the public opinion of the sect which rules him. They will be compelled to ask, 'How does this happen? Is there 'no escape from these oppressive judgments of human 'beings,—no escape, but into absolute doubt and denial? 'not even an escape into *them*,—for what intolerant 'dogmatists there are among doubters and deniers!' If they want freedom for their reason and wills, the old Creeds speak of One who came to deliver them. If they feel that the language of Scripture cannot be tied down by the language of a formula, Creeds oblige us to look out of themselves to some book which shall unfold the person and the acts of Him of whom they are bearing witness. They never can put themselves in the place of our reason or of Scripture, till their words are perverted, and the sense of them contradicted. Why there should be such documents in the world, I can explain no more than I can explain why any part of the order of Nature should exist, or why it should be in harmony with any other part. I find it so. I give

God thanks that it is so. I hope, in the day when He is revealed, and we are all called to answer for the use or abuse we have made of His gifts, that He will enable us to enter more fully into this and many other mysteries of His government, which I understand most imperfectly, but which have helped me to understand myself.

ESSAY XIII.

ON INSPIRATION.

Any Clergyman who ventures to write on Inspiration, will be asked whether he is prepared to defend the popular views on that subject. If not, all his more judicious friends will advise him to be silent. He may injure his own reputation; he may do what is much worse,—he may injure the faith of his countrymen and countrywomen.

I cannot undertake to defend the popular views upon this or any other subject. First, I find it very difficult to ascertain what they are. What is called a popular view expands or contracts at the pleasure of writers in newspapers and reviews. It appears to be exceedingly definite; you approach it, it has almost vanished. Popular notions have a considerable vigour for purposes of attack. They can be used with great effect against a supposed enemy of the faith. They only fail when you want them for use and comfort. They are full of warmth and fervour on the platform, in the closet they are as cold as ice. They stir up all the elements of strife and bitterness in the natural heart; I do not find that they stir the spirit to any energetic action for God or man. Next, what are called popular notions answer, it seems to me, very ill to their name. They do not come from the people, they do not touch the hearts of the people. They are not like old, racy, homely proverbs, which embody so much of common, and therefore so much of genuine, feeling. They do not call forth any hearty, intelligent response when they are proclaimed among simple men who work with their hands. There is a sickly perfume about them, which denotes them not to have been nursed in the open air, but in flower-pots. The seeds of them may have been sown in the study, but they have ripened in the boudoir; their greatest exposure has been in crowds, in which there is breath enough of some kind, but which the breath of heaven is not suffered to visit. And lastly, adherence to these popular notions is, I think, incompatible with a strict adherence to those Creeds which we solemnly confess, still more incompatible with a continual and direct appeal to the Bible, as a guide and an authority. I have explained why I think so in other cases; some of the popular notions about Inspiration, instead of being an exception to either remark, offer, I suspect, the most striking illustrations of both

What is said about the danger to reputation is perfectly true; every one should consider it for himself. A man trembles for his wealth in proportion to the insecurity of his investment; the miser, who has been afraid to deposit it anywhere but in some chest or cupboard within his reach, has the best reason of all for trembling. The religious world has a painful feeling that it has been hoarding up treasures for itself, and has not been rich towards God; therefore it is continually in dread of burglars and pickpockets. Let it use all precautions; let it prove how free it is from the maxims of the ordinary world, by banishing trust and cultivating universal suspicion. All of us like its smiles, dread its frowns. We shall take great pains to secure one, and avert the other, if there is no smile that we care for more, no frown which we count more terrible. But many of us persuade ourselves, all of us have probably at one time yielded to the opinion, that reputation is necessary for the sake of *usefulness.* Every hour, I think, will show us more and more that the concern about reputation is the great hindrance to usefulness; that if we desire to be useful, we must struggle against it night and day.

That thought suggests the really great argument against meddling with this subject of Inspiration; we may injure the faith of our brothers and sisters. A most potent reason for taking *some* course in reference to it; whether silence is that course, they may be able to decide who know something of the present feeling of different classes of Englishmen. Can you prevent any set of men, nay, any man or woman, from knowing that this question has been stirred? Do not those who lay down theories of Inspiration, and denounce others for not acquiescing in them, proclaim that fact aloud? Is it not true, as these persons affirm so constantly, that the faith of our countrymen, as well as of other Europeans, in the Bible, is shaken already? Are there not very clear evidences in their restless eagerness to get all objections put down, that their own faith is feeble and tottering? Is it not a duty which we owe to those who confess their doubts, which we owe quite as much to those who are trying to hush their doubts by making a noise, *not* to avoid the subject, but to face it, and to express ourselves upon it with as much frankness, as little ambiguity, as possible? To avoid the *charge* of ambiguity, of wilfully concealing some opinion which it would be inconvenient to express, is impossible. No one who has had the slightest experience will expect to do that. The most vehement champion of modern theories about the Inspiration of the Bible,—the most passionate denier of its Inspiration,—will agree in declaring that any person who refuses the shibboleths of either is tampering with his conscience, and does not mean what he says. They are perfectly entitled to their opinion; their harmony upon one point, while they agree on no other, will be a decisive proof with many that they are right. Those who try to disturb so fixed a conviction, will always repent of their pains, and will find that the argument,—probably, which is much more precious, the temper—they have expended, has brought no calculable return. The utmost any one can dream of or should desire is, that his sincerity should be tried by his peers; that is to say, by those who have felt these difficulties, and have sought, or still seek, a solution of them; not by men of another and altogether superior race, who are quite above human dangers and human sympathies, and are able to look down upon us from a region of self-satisfied, untroubled orthodoxy, or from a region which, being exactly antipodal to this, resembles it in temperature, the region of self-satisfied, untroubled unbelief.

The only legitimate reason which can deter a person who has spoken or written much on theological subjects, from entering on this, is, that he must almost necessarily have handled it before. The question of Inspiration touches so nearly upon all the thoughts with which men in this day are occupied, that at whatever point one comes into contact with those thoughts, it must be encountered. The fear of repeating the same propositions again and again, besets every one who tries to express convictions which are very sacred to him, and which he thinks his contemporaries have as much right in as he has. As he knows only common-places, and cares for nothing else, he cannot deal in novelties. But he must be conscious how much common-places lose their force, and are mistaken for the idiosyncrasies of a particular mind, when they come forth frequently clothed in the phrases and forms which education or circumstances have made habitual to him. The dread of giving them merely a personal character, grows with his belief that they are truths for mankind. But however justifiable this feeling is, it must often yield to other considerations. A man will not understand what your convictions are, till you have put them in various lights; till you have given him an opportunity of applying various tests to them. It is not enough to treat of any great subject which an age is busy with, collaterally; you must speak of it directly, must grapple with the very words and forms in which people are wont to see it exhibited; else they will fancy that you and they are not intending the same thing. It is better to run the risk of a hundred repetitions, (which, after all, not fifty or twenty persons may be aware of,) than to omit an opportunity when it offers, of relieving the conscience of a fellow-creature from some distressing bondage, or of protesting against some unrighteous attempt to keep it in prison.*

* Not at all that I may oblige any reader (which I could not do if I would) to look into books which he may never have heard of, but simply that any one who pleases may have an opportunity of proving either that I have merely said again here what I have said before, or that I have said something altogether inconsistent with that, I would mention that I have alluded to the subject of Inspiration in a chapter on the Bible, in a book called 'The Kingdom of Christ,' which was published many years ago; more recently in a Sermon on the Psalms, contained in a volume on the Prayer Book; and in a Sermon on the

I shall therefore fix my thoughts on the word *Inspiration:* our disputes are emphatically about the word. They are not less real for that. They point to facts and to substances; but the best way of getting at these, and of coming to understand what we mean ourselves and what others mean, is to examine our uses of the name which we feel to be so sacred.

1. We find the singers of the old world asking some divine power to inspire them. In the last age this language of theirs was not much heeded. It had been so much abused by the vulgarest writers who adopted classical *fashions* (I should be scarcely correct in saying classical forms), that it was supposed never to have had any signification. We have learnt to do more justice to the men whom we profess to admire. We feel that they would be worthy of no admiration, that they could not have won any, if they had not been simple and sincere. If they were merely using a trade phrase when they asked a Muse or a God to teach them, they must have had the fate of similar traders in later times. The rest of their speech is genuine and transparent; this part of

character of Balaam, in a volume on the Old Testament. I should not have spoken of some still more casual references to it, in a book on the Prophets and Kings of the Old Testament, published this year, if a particularly kind critic in the Nonconformist, for whose commendations, and still more for whose friendly reproofs, I desire to express my gratitude, had not called upon me to develop more clearly my hints, and to state my whole mind on the subject of Inspiration. I would request him to accept this Essay as an answer to that courteous challenge.

it cannot be less so. It must express, not their loosest convictions, but their strongest.

2. But whatever force we allow to this sense of the word, are we to suppose it has any even the slightest relation to the sense in which religious men speak of the Inspiration of the Bible? A number of voices all around us are saying, 'There is no real distinction 'between these books and any others. Inspiration is 'predicable of both, in the same sense. It can be 'but a question of degree, and therefore if you feel 'yourselves at liberty to exercise all kinds of criticism 'upon the methods, principles, and authority of the one, 'you cannot fairly debar yourself or any one else from 'the same liberty in respect of the other.' We hear again a number of voices saying, 'You exercise that 'liberty at your peril. The Bible must be looked upon 'as *the* inspired book. To put it on the same ground 'with any other, is to deprive us of all foundation for 'our faith now, for our hopes in the world to come.'

3. But again: religious men, the most earnestly religious men, speak of themselves as taught, actuated, inhabited by a Divine Spirit. They declare that they could know nothing of the Scriptures except they were under this guidance. Is *this* the Inspiration which we attribute to the writers of the Old and New Testament, or is that different from it in kind?

4. A number of religious teachers actually claim to be inspired men, and circles of admiring disciples

believe them; nay, crowds run after them, in the faith that they have a divine commission. Here is another fact which well deserves to be examined, a very serious fact indeed. It is one which the peremptory decrees of our schools have certainly not cleared up. They have not prevented the fanatics from appearing by their maxim respecting inspiration. They have not done much to weaken or to explain their influence. If fanaticism is to be checked, we must understand ourselves a little better about its nature and cause.

5. But the Church of England, which many religious people say is not spiritual enough, whose sons boast that it is expressly opposed to fanaticism, has used this very word 'Inspiration,' and has claimed it for these sons, apparently in a fuller, larger sense than either of the classes to which I have last referred. On the Fifth Sunday after Easter, we ask 'Him from whom all good 'things do come, that by His holy *inspiration* we may 'think those things that be good, and by His merciful 'guiding may perform the same.' Every Sunday morning, and on every Festival-day, we ask, in our Communion Service, that 'the thoughts of our hearts may be 'cleansed by the *inspiration* of the Holy Spirit, so that 'we may perfectly love God, and worthily magnify His 'name.' Here are petitions which concern not a few specially religious men or some illuminated teachers, but the whole flock; to say the least, all the miscellaneous people who are gathered together in a particular con-

gregation. Are we paltering with words in a double sense? When we speak of Inspiration do we mean Inspiration? When we refer to the Inspiration of the Scriptures in our sermons, ought we to say, 'Brethren, 'we beseech you not to suppose that *this* Inspiration at 'all resembles that for which we have been praying. 'They are generically, essentially unlike. It is blas- 'phemous to connect them in our minds; the Church is 'very guilty for having suggested the association.' These are the questions we have to discuss; let us not shrink from them, or dispose of them lightly and frivolously, as if the hearts of tens of thousands were not interested in them.

1. When St. Paul came into the different cities of Greece, he found men whose traditions told them of an Inspiration, which poets, prophets, priestesses, received from some divine source. These traditions had facts for their basis. Men were actually seen to be carried far above the level of their ordinary thoughts; they spoke as they did not speak when they were buying and selling; their words entered into other men's minds and worked mightily there. There was no denying this; the experience of men established it beyond all controversy. And I think the conscience of men, expressed in these traditions, was entitled to bear its testimony as well as their experience. That conscience said, 'This power is something which we cannot measure 'and reduce under rules. It works in us, but it is above

'us. We may in some sort control its exercises, but 'we are the subjects of it. It must come from some 'higher source. A God must have imparted it to us.'

The next and more awful question was, '*What* God, 'what is his *name?*' When they tried to consider this question, a number of new facts forced themselves upon their observation. A man under the influence of some extraordinary *afflatus*, might be raised to a higher and nobler state, might be an inventor of arts, might overcome his inclinations to pleasure, might do heroic acts for the benefit of the world, might have intuitions of the future. Or he might be merely inebriated, maddened, might exhibit wild contentions, might, in the worst and grossest sense, lose the mastery of himself. The theory of a divine Inspirer must, they thought, explain both these discordant experiences. Every one who reflects upon the legends which cluster about the name of Dionysus, and the various grotesque forms which embodied them for the eye, will understand how the heart and imagination of the Greek were exercised by this problem.

How might we suppose that St. Paul would act,—how do we know that he *did* act,—when he brought his Gospel to a people with these notions and traditions? If he had told them that all the thoughts of their ancestors were unmeaning and ridiculous, he would have found a willing and prepared audience in Athens and Corinth. Their sophists had told them so before; the inclination of their minds was to accept the statement.

They would indeed have continued to bow down to all manner of idols; why not? they were beautiful objects; worship might do them some good; who could tell? 'The people certainly needed such images; it was 'philosophical to humour the vulgar taste; a very high 'philosophy might see a meaning in it.' But St. Paul did not take this course. The one which he did take must have tended to awaken that old faith out of its sleep; not to smother it in its sleep. For he spoke of gifts of healing; gifts of speech; gifts of government. He spoke of these gifts as proceeding from a Person. He spoke of His presence as the great gift of all. He spoke of that gift as coming to men, because a Man had appeared in the world, and had ascended on high, who was the Son of God. Such language could not but associate itself with all the thoughts which they had before of Inspirations and an Inspirer. We know that it did, for most of the confusions in the Corinthian Church arose from the old dreams of a Dionysiac inspiration. And how are the two distinguished? There would have been nothing to distinguish them, there would have been *no* witness against idol worship or demon worship, if St. Paul had said, 'Those powers which you referred to Dionysus, or 'Apollo, or Æsculapius, are not what we are permitted 'and enabled to exercise;' for the understanding would still have demanded, 'What then *is* the origin of *those?*' But if he was able to say, 'What you have attributed 'to a demon, to a being whom you have fashioned out 'of a set of phænomena which you could not account for, 'I come to vindicate for the Father of Spirits, for the 'Father of our Lord Jesus Christ;' this would indeed have been the most triumphant testimony he could bear, that the reign of the old Gods was over, and that the one Lord who had spoken to a poor band of exiles from Egypt, was now asserting His dominion over the world. And so—and only so—it would be apparent, why He who lifted men into a nobler and freer life, could not mean man to be the victim of a frenzy, or of mere animal impulses. The history which the Apostle told was the history of the gradual discovery of man's relation to God, and consequently of man's spiritual condition. That a Divine Spirit should come to meet and raise a spirit hard pressed with animal inclinations, to give it the power of maintaining its own position, of looking up to Him in whose likeness it was made, apart from whom it had no life, was so reasonable, was so necessary a corollary from the previous part of the message, that the heart of the hearers anticipated it, was eager to recognise it. But then whatever counteracted this influence, whatever led the animal to assert that supremacy to which it had been proved to have no claim, must be either the turbulent and rebellious movement of the lower nature, or the action of some evil power, speaking directly to the spirit and aiming to destroy it.

The opposition between the divine and either the animal or the devilish, which had been confounded with it in the old mythology, was manifested just in proportion as those very powers and gifts, which man had felt before he could not ascribe to himself, were ascribed to the Spirit of God, the Spirit of Order and Truth. But it is equally evident that there was another great and broad distinction between the old and new belief. The first had been partial, narrow, peculiar. It had tried to explain how extraordinary men, or men in some extraordinary crisis of their lives, were able to do strange acts, to speak unusual words. St. Paul's Gospel was human and universal. It explained indeed the influence of seers and prophets; it asserted the existence of special endowments; it put all honour upon distinct callings. But first, it asserted that the Spirit was necessary for all human beings, and was intended for all. And this human gift it did not degrade below the other, as being a secondary, inferior exhibition of that which the great man obtained in its highest form. The Divine Spirit, the Spirit of Love, who was promised to all, was described as the source and spring of those peculiar endowments which were given to this and that man as He willed. They were to esteem their gifts mainly as witnesses of His presence.

2. But if St. Paul asserted that the inspiration which the Greeks had attributed to false Gods was derived only from the true, what kind of dignity did he claim for the inspiration of his own seers and prophets? I apprehend that he could say nothing more glorious for

them than this, that they had spoken as they were moved by the Holy Ghost; that they had consistently disclaimed all wisdom and power for themselves; that they had been, in the most orderly and divine manner, preparing the way for that manifestation of Him which had been promised to their children, and had at length been granted. Inspiration was not the first idea in the mind of a Jew, as it was perhaps in that of a Greek. The Law took precedence of the Prophets; the Covenant was before either. The Lord had said to Abram, '*Get thee out of thy father's house, to a land that I will show thee,*'—had promised '*that in him and his seed the families of the earth should be blessed.*' The Lord had declared to Moses His great name, had sent him to be the deliverer of His people, had given them through him commandments, and statutes, and ordinances. The Righteous King and Judge, who claims men as His servants, who teaches them to judge between right and wrong, is revealed first. The prophet who speaks in His name is still mainly the witness of Unchangeable Right, and of judgments that shall distinguish between it and the wrong. And the Word, who comes to him, and speaks to him, makes him aware how he and his people are related to that Lord God whom the heaven of heavens cannot contain; makes him understand that there is a King on the holy hill of Zion, One whom he can call *his* Lord, and to whom *the* Lord is saying, '*Sit Thou on my right hand, till I make Thine enemies Thy footstool.*' The revelation of this mysterious Teacher, this Divine King, is what he looks for; he gains glimpses of the steps and method of His manifestation through his own sorrows and the trials of his country; he is confident that some day God will be fully declared, and that in that day man, His image, will attain his proper glory.

But how is it that the prophet is able to enter into these divine communications? What is there in him different from other men which makes him capable of them? What mean these stirrings within him, this sense of a power which seems at times more than he can bear, this mighty influence to which he must yield, which does not suffer him to speak till it has humbled and crushed him; which, when he does speak, makes him know that his words, though they have come out of the depths of his own heart, are the Lord's, and that they belong as much to all his countrymen as to him? This is surely *Inspiration.* But who is the Inspirer? How can He be so near to him, to his own very self? For this power is not merely or chiefly one which elevates and transports. It does not merely take hold of some faculty or impart some energy. It carries on the most searching, intimate, terrible converse with him who uses the faculty, who wields the energies.

The answer to this demand came gradually, slowly, like the answer to the other. St. Paul believed that it had come at last most effectually. John the Baptist preached of repentance for the remission of sins. But he preached of One coming after him, that was before him, who should baptize with the Holy Ghost and with fire. Jesus (so Paul's companion tells us) had received the Holy Ghost in His baptism, when He was proclaimed to be the Son of God. In the power of that Holy Ghost, he resisted the Tempter, healed the broken-hearted, preached deliverance to the captives, proclaimed the Jubilee of the Lord. Then when He was going away, He spoke of a Spirit of Truth whom He would send to His disciples from the Father, who would abide with them, who would bring all things to their remembrance, who would show them plainly of the Father. He had spoken continually in his earlier discourses of a Father who was both His and theirs; all these words seemed intended to receive their interpretation from what He said to them now of a Comforter. The disciples were perplexed. How could they have another to supply His place? How could He be with His Father, and yet manifest Himself to them? What could He mean by saying that He and His Father would come to them, and abide with them? He told them to wait for the promise of the Father; then they would know what was now dark to them. When He had ascended, and had led them, by that strange discipline I spoke of in a former Essay, to believe that in some wonderful way they were even then to ascend with Him, and be with Him where He was, He again told them to wait; He could not satisfy their desire to know whether the kingdom would be at that time restored to Israel; He could only assure them that they should be endued with powers from on high. On the Festival day, St. Luke says, the sound of the mighty rushing wind was heard; the cloven tongues sat upon the Apostles; they spoke as the Spirit gave them utterance; the multitude heard them in their own tongues proclaiming the wonderful works of God. Herein St. Paul saw the revelation of Him who had inspired the Prophets; the fulfilment of the divine promise; the assurance that the Father of all was indeed claiming the sons of men, Jews, Greeks, barbarians, as His children. So soon as he learnt this truth, he became the herald of a new dispensation. This manifestation of the Spirit was that which the world had been waiting for so long. He had taught prophets to speak, He had enabled them to suffer, He had given them glimpses of a glory which their children should see, in which they themselves should be sharers. Now it might be proclaimed aloud. 'The Baptism which John foretold is 'for you all. *Because ye are sons, God hath sent forth 'the Spirit of His Son into your hearts, crying, Abba, 'Father.*' All gifts ever bestowed upon prophets, were the gifts of a Father to His children, the foretastes of that adoption and emancipation which were awaiting men, when their schooling under the elements of the world should be completed.

What a magnificent idea, then, must St. Paul have

had of those books, which, in his Pharisaical days, had seemed to him merely objects of fear, and of a kind of worship; excuses for Jewish self-exaltation! How every old teacher will have started into life, when he contemplated him no longer as a mere utterer of dark sentences, which the Scribes copied out and made darker by their expositions, but as endued with that same Divine Spirit which was enabling him to be a teacher of the Gentiles; of whom he could dare to say to each Church, 'He dwells with you;' to each member of a Church, 'He has made your body His habitation!' What a grand procession those old teachers formed, each one of whom was leading men onwards to that discovery of the Inspirer! What was there in all the rest of the world together that could compare with them, not in their distinct worth alone or chiefly, but in their continuity, their orderly succession, their harmony; their worth as witnesses to the divine method of government in their own day, a method which must be the same in all after generations; their worth as foreseers of that which had now come to pass! What would the history of the rest of the world be but a collection of inexplicable fragments, if there were not this revelation to unite them and make them a whole!

But if this was the effect of his New Testament wisdom, how must he have feared any relapse into that state of mind from which he had emerged; how must he have dreaded it for his converts, and for those who should come after them! Can we conceive any view of the Holy Scriptures,—either of those he had known from a child, or those he was contributing to form,—which would have seemed to him more dreadful, than one which, under colour of exalting them, should set aside their own express testimony concerning the unspeakable gift which God had conferred on His creatures? If he would have turned with indignation from those in later days who, pretending to honour the Bible, forbid men to read it, lest it should awaken the questionings in their hearts, which it is meant to awaken, and which a Church instead of stifling should encounter, and satisfy; would he have felt less indignant with those who, talking of the Bible as their only religion, and only rule of life, prevent it from being either, by saying that its Inspiration has no relation to that of the writers whose dark sayings it illuminates, to that of the human beings it is intended to educate and console?

3. This Scribe notion of the Bible was stoutly resisted by the Evangelical teachers of the last age. Francke and Spener have been referred to again and again by their admirers in this country, as faithful witnesses against the hard German doctors of their day, who looked upon the Bible as a mere collection of dry facts and dogmas, and who supposed that it could be understood without the aid of such a Spirit as dwelt in the writers of it. Our own Venns and Newtons took up the same language; the orthodoxy as well as

the liberalism of their contemporaries was offensive to them, precisely because both seemed equally to separate the Bible from the conflicts and experiences of Christian men. The testimony which they bore, I hope, is not extinct,—has not merely given birth to a set of phrases about 'head knowledge,' or to charges of 'want of 'vital and experimental acquaintance with divine things,' —phrases which any one can learn by heart, and which may often be used most glibly by those who are half conscious that they have a very near and personal application. In solitary chambers, among bedridden sufferers, the words of the old men have still a living force. The Bible is read there truly as an inspired book; as a book which does not stand aloof from human life, but meets it; which proves itself not to be the work of a different Spirit from that which is reproving and comforting the sinner, but of the same. It is of quite infinite importance that the confidence in which these humble students read, should not be set at nought and contradicted by decisions and conclusions of ours. It is absolutely necessary that we should be able to say, that they are not practising a delusion upon themselves; that they are not amiable enthusiasts; that they are believing a truth and acting upon it. But we cannot say this if we must adopt the formulas, which some people would force upon us. Either we must set at nought the faith of those who have clung to the Bible, and found a meaning in it when the doctors could not interpret it, or we must forego the demand which we make on the consciences of young men, when we compel them to declare that they regard the Inspiration of the Bible as generically unlike that which God bestows on His children in this day.

I know well how this last remark will be met. 'Do 'you not know,' some one will say, 'that the simple 'Christians you speak of have the most unfeigned, un-'questioning reverence for the Bible? do you not know, 'also, that those young men of whose consciences you 'are so tender, avoid explicit statements respecting the 'Inspiration of the Bible, precisely because they are full 'of neological doubts and theories about it, which never 'entered into the heads of the others, and would utterly 'shock them if they did? What folly or dishonesty to 'compare cases so dissimilar!' Now I am perfectly ready to admit, that, in a great many cases, perhaps in most, scruples, which may be called neological, are at the bottom of the objections which the younger members of Evangelical families make to the doctrines respecting the Inspiration of the Bible, which their elders require them to accept. But I venture to think, first, that it is neither foolish nor dishonest to protest against the invention of tests to meet a particular case, which—supposing they do accomplish their particular object, and supposing *that* is a good one—also may promote another which is decidedly and evidently bad. I should have thought that the history of heresies might have taught us that, whenever a dogma has been devised merely to fit and contradict some denial which is prevalent, it has almost always been the parent of some other denial quite as dangerous. But secondly, I should like to be informed how these neological tendencies have arisen in persons apparently so well secured by their education against them. It seems to me that this is generally the history of their growth. These young men were informed early that no true knowledge of the Bible could be had, unless God's Spirit illuminated the page and their hearts. It was intimated to them also, (or this was what they gathered from the lessons they received,) that they did not at present possess this illumination. In the meantime they were instructed in what was called the external evidence, which proved that these records were of divine authority. Some of this evidence might be good, such as would pass muster in any English court of justice; some might be tolerable, such as would be listened to if there were nothing to overweigh it on the other side; some was decidedly weak and worthless. But the best could not put in the least claim to authority; it would have abandoned all its peculiar boast if it had. All was therefore open to legitimate examination and criticism; that which could not hold water must give way; that which was worthy would often be suspected for its sake. Very soon the book itself, the merits and dignity of which had been staked upon this issue,—which the youth had been distinctly *told* that he was not to receive, merely because his parents or his country received it, which he had been told also that he could not yet receive upon any distinct witness of his own spirit, sank nearly—never quite—to the level of the arguments by which it had been recommended to him. He discloses his perplexities, he asks whether this or that passage in the book is not less tenable than the rest: he is told that he must take all or none: the whole is inspired; to doubt it is to renounce the word of God, —to renounce God himself. This course I hold to be inhuman and ungodly, one which will infallibly make the doubter what you accuse him of being. It is possible to pursue quite a different method, one that may make your children feel that the Bible is their book as it was their fathers', and that no modern wisdom will supply the place of it. You may show them that there is divinity here and inspiration there; you may lead them to confess that there are passages which speak to the heart within them, which awaken a heart that was asleep; you may make them know,—if you believe it yourself,—that there is a Divine Word who is enlightening them, that there is a Divine Spirit who is seeking to inspire them. You may then bring them gradually, with many tears and much joy, to trace that Word and that Spirit not only here and there, but connecting, reconciling those various documents which seemed to them so inconsistent with themselves, explaining the facts of the universe with which they appeared to be at war. Be sure, however, that before you can take one step in this course, you must give up the attempt to impose a theory of Inspiration upon them, nay, you must very gravely consider whether the one which you hold is compatible with that *belief* in Inspiration which belonged to prophets and apostles.

I foresee that some critic will say to me, 'It is a 'cunning method to put forward these young men, and 'to pretend so much sympathy with them. Every one 'can see that you are really pleading your own cause. 'You have some secret unbelief about the books of the 'Bible, which makes you shrink from this tenet of 'Inspiration. We are glad to know it. The screw 'should always be applied where there are any symptoms 'of tenderness or wincing.'

I wish my friend the critic could look me as steadily in the face, while he is making these observations, as, if he stood before me, I would look him in the face while I replied to them. I would tell him that I am conscious of just as much unbelief about the books of the Bible, as I am about the facts of nature and of my own existence. I *am* conscious of unbelief about those facts; oftentimes they seem to me quite incredible. I overcome this unbelief, and acquire what I think is a truer state of mind, when I turn to the Bible as the interpretation of them. The more difficulties I have found in myself and in the world, the more help has it been to me. The Bible is not the cause of my perplexities, but the resolver of them. Of course there are a multitude of things in it which I do not understand; a multitude more in myself which I do not understand. But this has been my experience hitherto, and each year, almost each day, that experience is strengthened. Instead, therefore, of wishing to get rid of those documents which the traditions of my country teach me to hold divine, because they belong to some bygone condition of things with which modern civilization has nothing to do, I feel the necessity of them increasing with every step which civilization takes, with every new complication of feelings and circumstances in which I am myself involved. Books of the Bible which were lying in shadow for me, in which I could see little meaning, have come forth into clearness, because I met with hard passages in myself or in society which I could not construe without their help. And I have found this to be the case more and more in proportion as I have rested my faith on the God whom the Bible declares to me, and not upon my conclusions respecting the authenticity of different books. These conclusions may be sound,—I hope they are; but they may not be sound. My understanding is very liable to error; and how can those who require me to consider the Bible as alone free from error, encourage me, at the same moment, to transfer that immunity to myself? This they must do, if they will not let me first of all accept the canon of Scripture as given to me, and secondly, rise gradually to believe, not on the authority of any Samaritan woman or Church doctor, but because I have heard Christ for myself, speaking to me out of this book, and speaking to me in my heart, and therefore know that He is indeed that Saviour who should come into the world.*

* A distinction is often hinted at, sometimes formally taken, between Facts and Doctrines. 'You may,' it is said, 'believe that the 'Spirit guides a man into a knowledge of principles. But do you accept 'the facts of the Bible? Do you look upon them as divinely com'municated to the seer?' Any one who considers doctrines as I have considered them in these Essays, finds it exceedingly hard to separate them from facts; doctrines and principles he supposes to be the meaning of facts. If, then, I am asked whether I receive the *transcendent* facts of Scripture, those which offer most occasion to disbelief, I appeal to what I have written here. If I am asked whether I believe the ordinary facts of Scripture, *e. g.* that such a city was taken at such a time? I answer, that when I find a man so free from biblical prepossessions as Niebuhr assuming Isaiah and Jeremiah to be better authorities about such facts than any he knew of, I am surprised that *our* divines and religious people should be so very eager to get confirmation of the testimonies in sacred books from profane authorities, as if they felt insecure of them till then,—a sentiment I cannot the least understand or share in; that, believing the writers of the Bible to have been possessed by the Spirit of Truth, I am sure they will have more shrunk from fictions, and have been more careful to avoid mixing them with facts, than other men; that it seems to me far safer, more scriptural, more godly, to suppose they did *take pains*, and that the Spirit taught them to take pains, in sifting facts, than to suppose that they were merely told the facts; that I most assuredly should *not* give up the faith in God which they have cherished in me, if I found they had made mistakes; and that I have too much respect and honour for those who use the strongest expressions about the certainty of every word in the Scriptures, to suppose that *they* would. I will not believe any Christian man, even upon his own testimony, who tells me that he should cease to trust in the Son of God, because he found chronological or historical misstatements in the Scriptures, as great as ever have been charged against them by their bitterest opponents. If I did suspect him of such hollowness, I should pray

On his way to this discovery, a man may have to pass, as numbers have passed before him, through terrible struggles and contradictions of mind. But you believe it is true, do you not? You think God has revealed it, do you not? You believe He lives, do you not? If so, He can perhaps take about as good care of His truth, His book, His creatures and the universe, as you or I can. He can teach us without a theory of Inspiration, which is taking the place, it is to be feared, in very many minds, not only of faith in Inspiration, but of faith in Him.

For the different forms in which this theory expresses itself, I care little. If any one likes to talk of a *verbal* Inspiration, if that phrase conveys some substantial meaning to his mind, by all means let him keep it. He cannot go further than I should, in calling for a laborious and reverent attention to the very words of Scripture, and in denouncing the unreasonable notion, that thoughts and words can be separated; that the life which is in one must not penetrate the other. If any one likes to speak of *plenary* Inspiration, I would not complain; I object to the Inspiration which people talk of, for being too empty, not for being too full. These forms of speech are pretty toys for those who have leisure to play with

for him that he might never meet with any travellers or philologers who confirmed the statements of Scripture; none but such as denied them or mocked at them; because the sooner such a foundation as this is shaken, the better it will be for him.

them, and if they are not made so hard as to do mischief, the use of them should never be checked. But they do not belong to business. They are not for those who are struggling with life and death; such persons want, not a plenary Inspiration or a verbal Inspiration, but a book of Life; and they will know that they have such a book when you have courage to tell them that there is a Spirit with them, who will guide them into the truth of it.

4. 'But if these words are openly proclaimed, what a 'plentiful crop of ranters and fanatics shall we have! 'What crowds will run after them; for who then will 'have a right to deny their inspiration?' A dreadful prospect! But is it a prospect? Have we not the fanatics and ranters already? Do they not draw disciples after them? You have tried to weaken their influence by telling them that the Bible was the Inspired book; that it is utterly absurd and extravagant for men in these days to call themselves inspired; that the same course has been tried in former times, and has always led to ruin. There is great apparent justification for this method; it has been used often by very ingenious and sagacious men, with whom it ought to have succeeded, if it was to succeed. But it has not succeeded. It has not cured the immediate evil which it was meant to cure; it has left the seeds which produced that evil always ready for fresh germination. And what is worse, this kind of treatment has destroyed precious seeds, which God has planted in men's hearts, and which they

cannot afford to lose. You long to expose the impostor, the mountebank, who is deceiving a number of poor simple souls. But do you desire that the earnest, cordial faith, which has been called forth in them, while they are following him, should be taken from them? Do you desire that those fervent hopes, kindled for the first time in men who have been crawling all their days on the earth and eating dust, should be put out for ever? Do you think nothing of the desolation which they will feel, when they find that he in whom they trusted has failed them utterly, and that what looked the most real of all things, was but a dream? Oh! is there nothing dreadful in the unbelief, the prostration of soul, the wretchlessness of unclean living, which follows such disappointments and discoveries?

'But they must come,' you say, 'how can we help it?' We could have done this. We could have told the deceiver that he was not exaggerating in the least the blessings of which a man is capable, and which God is willing to bestow on him. We could have told him that instead of a mere power of utterance, which it is evident he possesses, and for which he will have to give an account, the Spirit who has endued him with that power is near him, claiming him as a servant; near him, and near every one of those too whom he is making his tools. We might say to him, 'If you believe this, 'there will come into your mind such an awe, such a 'sense of the fearfulness of trifling with this gift and 'blessing,—there will come such a desire to learn, such 'a fear of the responsibility of ruling over other men, 'such a conviction that you can only do it without a 'crime, when you give up yourself to the Spirit of 'Truth,—that nothing will seem to you so great a 'reason for penitence and shame, as that you have dared 'to exalt yourself on the plea of possessing that, which 'if you had possessed it rightly, would have entirely 'humbled you.' And if with this, we teach the people that the Spirit of God has come down, not on the great prophet only, but for the whole flock of Christ, to keep them from pride and self-conceit and delusion, and to guide them into all truth, I believe we shall do our best that the chaff in their minds may be separated from the wheat, and may be burned up.

5. For this principle, we of the Church of England are, I conceive, specially bound to bear testimony. The collects I have quoted, and the tenour of our prayers, which is in conformity with them, lay us under this obligation. The function which our orthodox men in the last century claimed for us, of being witnesses against fanaticism, is a most honourable function. God grant that we may be able to fulfil it! But we cannot fulfil it in the way they dreamed of,—by setting at nought all belief in spiritual operations, by referring all that is spoken of them in Scripture to the age of the Apostles. That plan has been tried; none ever failed so completely and shamefully. We cannot do it by the course which our

modern evangelical school, renouncing the maxims of their forefathers, seem inclined to recommend,—the course of setting up the Bible as a book which encloses all that may lawfully be called Inspiration. That plan is under trial, and, if we may judge by present indications, it is likely to produce a general alienation from the Bible, a widely spread unbelief in Christianity. There is another method: may we have faith to follow it out! It is that of saying to our countrymen, of every order and degree, 'The Father of all has sent forth His 'Son, made of a woman, that you may receive the 'adoption of sons. He has baptized you with the Spirit 'of His Son: and that Spirit would be crying in your 'hearts, Abba, Father. That Spirit would be leading 'you into fellowship with all your brethren. That Spirit 'would be making you humble, teachable, courageous, 'free. That Spirit would claim all things for you; 'common books and the chief book, Nature and Grace, 'Earth and Heaven.'

It may seem to some Unitarian listener, who had hoped that I was going to join him in cursing several of his enemies, that I have blessed them these three times. He might expect from me some more rational theory about Inspiration than that which is current among our Evangelical and High Church teachers. He might think my apparent indifference to their opinions, promising. But I have at last come to a conclusion which will strike him as far more distant from his own than theirs is. I have appeared to protest against current theories of Inspiration, because they *fail* to assert the actual presence of that Spirit, whom it has been one of the standing articles of his creed *not* to confess.

I cannot deny this charge. I do think that our theories of Inspiration, however little they may accord with Unitarian notions, have a semi-Unitarian character; that they are derived from that unbelief in the Holy Ghost which is latent in us all, but which was developed and embodied in the Unitarianism of the last century. I have not been able to conceal this opinion in the present case or in other cases. I have not tried to conceal it; for I am persuaded that we must go further from Unitarianism, if we would embrace Unitarians; that we shall never know them as brothers, or love them as brothers, till we bring out our own faith more fully, and disengage it from some of the elements of distrust which we, in imitation of them, have allowed to mingle with it. Especially do I look forward to this result, however distant and improbable it may seem, from a full assertion of that portion of our creed which refers to the Person of the Comforter. I do see in that, such a bond of loving fellowship for all men,—such a breaking down of sect-barriers,—that I long to speak of it, even if it be with the most stammering tongue, to those who have been divided from us. I have not entered upon that subject here. Till the question of

Inspiration had been fairly considered, I saw no hope of being able to express my thoughts fully and clearly upon it: for nothing seems to me so dangerous, as that the Bible should be used to hinder the reception of a truth which can alone make its words intelligible, and, apart from which, its Inspiration, and all inspiration, is the dream of a shadow.

But as the subject of this Essay is not merely inspiration but the inspiration of the Bible, I should like to say one word on a method of treating that book which is characteristic of the new Unitarian school. The members of that school readily recognise the inspiration of Apostles and of Prophets. Where their fathers honoured the letter, they perceive a divine mind in the old seers. But they do not half so much accept them as *teachers.* It seems to me that the last writer of an article in one of their newspapers or reviews looks upon himself as a much more enlightened man than St. Paul or St. John, as one who can afford to compliment them upon the approximations which they often made to the wisdom which he has attained. I discover this tendency in men who I think really wish to be modest and self-distrusting; who are driven into what must strike us as insufferable arrogance, not willingly, but by the necessity of their position. They defend that position as being the only one which it is possible for men of science and men of progress to occupy. If earnest search is always rewarded with new discoveries, how can we acquiesce in the decrees of the past? If the world is always advancing, is not a third-rate man of this day wiser than the greatest of ages gone by? Such questions are not in general fairly met. The understanding is staggered by them; though I believe the conscience in every man revolts at the conclusion to which they lead.

The process of thought by which I have myself been delivered from them is something of this kind. Physical science, it has seemed to me, presumes a world which exists and which we did not create. Science was impossible while men glorified their own thoughts and speculations more than that which nature presented to them. It has become firm and safe since they have humbled themselves into the condition of learners. This has been the secret of discovery, this has been the security for progress. Is it altogether otherwise, I have asked myself, in moral science? Is self-worship the posture of mind which is most favourable to that, as self-abnegation is the great pre-requisite in the other? Shall we discover because we believe in our powers of discovery? Will the ages to come learn from us if we teach them that all wisdom is concentrated in us? I have not the least reason to think so. I do not meet with any man who does think so consistently. I often see those who ought to hold this opinion, if their other statements were true, clinging to the past with great affection and reverence, nay, not seldom disposed to appeal to it with even a fond idolatry, when they find themselves pressed down and tormented by the maxims of their own age. And so I have been forced by the inconsistencies of these modern teachers when I liked them best, by the vanity which made me despair of all good from them when they were following their theory to its consequences, to inquire whether that old notion of a Bible, a book of books, a book which sets forth a revelation that has been made of God and His relations to man, a revelation that is complete and cannot receive additions from our researches,—is unfavourable to science, to discovery, to progress; nay, may not be the necessary protection of all three. If Science concerns that which is fixed and absolute, *that which is*, then to believe that God has declared Himself, that He has withdrawn the veil which hides Him from His creatures, that He has in a wonderful and orderly history enabled us to see what He is, and what He is to us, what those eternal laws and principles are which dwell in Himself and which determine His dealings with us, is to believe that there is a divine and human *Science*, that we are not left to the anticipations or guesses of one age or of another. If He who thus reveals Himself is light, there must be perpetual openings for *Discovery* the more we meditate upon His revelation, the more we compare it with our own experiences and the experiences of the world. Instead of being cut off from such discoveries by acknowledging that we are not the authors of them, we enter upon just such a steady and gradual method for arriving at them as the physical student entered on when he exchanged the syllogisms of the study for the induction of the laboratory. If all Progress consists in the advancing further into light and the scattering of mists which had obstructed it, the Bible contains the promise of such *Progress*, a promise which has been most fulfilled when it has been most reverently listened to, when men have gone to it with the greatest confidence and hope. I complain of our modern religious world, not for cherishing this confidence or this hope, but for abandoning it and robbing others of it. If we come to the Bible as learners, it has more to teach us yet than we can ask or think. If we believe that we know all that is in it and merely resort to it for sentences and watchwords to confirm our own notions and to condemn our brethren, God will show us,—He is showing us,—how great the punishment to us and to our children must be, for abusing the unspeakably precious treasure with which He has endowed us.

ESSAY XIV.

ON THE PERSONALITY AND TEACHING OF THE HOLY SPIRIT.

I SUPPOSE there is nothing which is causing so much unbelief here and everywhere, as a comparison of the hopes which Scripture seems to hold out of the effects that should follow the revelation of Christ, with the history of the world since He appeared in it. I apprehend this difficulty is felt much more strongly in our day than in former days. There are several reasons why it must be so. We have been led to consider the different portions of history more in relation to each other than our fathers did. The records of the old Pagan world have been brought side by side with those of the Christian Church. Great differences have been observed in them, no doubt; more differences than were perceived formerly. But though all new inquiries may show us more clearly what crimes, what contradiction of moral principles, what superstition existed in the countries whose literature we have been most taught to prize, they show us also, that our ancestors were not mistaken in speaking of the patriotism and nobleness of particular men in those countries, of the ideal which they set before themselves, nay, of the homage which was paid to that ideal by the body of their countrymen,—proving it to be national, not individual. 'What other 'conclusion does the history of the later world suggest? 'There, too, is crime, contradiction of moral principles, 'fearful superstition. There, too, are facts which show 'that many have set before themselves a high standard, 'and have done various acts in conformity with it; 'there, too, we see that their contemporaries, who often 'persecuted them and cast out their names as evil, yet 'confessed that their aim was the right aim; there we 'find proofs that they were not creating a rule for 'themselves, but following one which would have been 'good for all men. Where is the great alteration? Are 'not all things much as they were from the beginning? 'In some respects, is there not a change for the worse? 'Does not Christendom confess, by the pains which it has 'taken that its sons should study the lore of the old 'Pagan world, that something is to be gained from that 'lore which is not to be found among its own treasures? 'Have not some crimes, against which the old world 'protested, been canonized by what has been called the 'faith of the new? Have not some of the old virtues 'been disparaged, even trampled under foot, by the pro-'fessors of the same faith?'

There is another cause for the new strength which these reflections have gained in our time. If we thought, as many divines in the last century thought, that the appearance of an illustrious Teacher, a great Messiah, in the world, who promulgated a sublime code of morals, and did certain extraordinary acts to illustrate its truth, is all that was signified by the New Testament Dispensation and the name 'Christianity,' we might not be under any great obligation to explain why that Teacher had not been much more heeded than those who preceded Him, why the announcement of His code has not ensured obedience to it, why His miracles may be acknowledged as singular occurrences for the time which witnessed them, and yet may have left no distinct practical impression upon human life. But we have abandoned,—I think, have been compelled to abandon,—this apparently secure position. The hearts of suffering men have demanded from the book which we told them contained the charter of their inheritance,—have found in it,—information which these statements did not convey. They have asked whether God had merely laid down rules for them, without giving them any power to follow the rules; whether He had bidden them love Him and their neighbours, without taking account of the tremendous inclination they had to care only for themselves, or supplying them with any means to overcome it. They have craved for some influence over themselves, a quickening, transforming influence. And they have thought that the Bible very distinctly met these necessities of theirs. In the New Testament especially, they have discovered continual reference to a Spirit who should work in men to do those acts which they were least able of themselves to do, who should help their infirmities, who should teach them what they wanted, and how they might ask for it; who should knit together those whom place, time, jealousies had divided. They have perceived that the promise of this Spirit is put forth as the most obvious and characteristic promise of the Christian dispensation. The very name of Christ, they have learnt, indicates that He was Himself endowed or anointed with a Spirit; the preaching of His forerunner and all His own preaching declared that He had received it Himself, to the end that He might bestow it upon His disciples then and in ages to come. Churchmen have discovered that the language of our formularies, as well as of the Scriptures, is in accordance with these convictions. We have learned to speak habitually of a dispensation of *the Spirit;* we have said that our Lord's coming in the flesh would have effected very little, that His moral teaching would have been necessarily inoperative, if He had not carried out His own assurance, and sent His Spirit to enlighten and renew hearts which would have been otherwise dark and lifeless.

But if we adopt this language, we ought to understand that we give every one a right to ask us some searching questions. They will take this form :—

'A Divine Spirit,' you tell us, 'has been given to men, 'given for the very purpose of moulding their lives into 'conformity with the law which has been proclaimed to 'them. Surely, then, you are bound to show some evi-'dence of that conformity. It cannot suffice merely to 'complain of men's disobedience or incredulity. Do 'you mean there has not been a power which could 'overcome these? It cannot avail to talk of a world, or 'flesh, or Devil. Do you mean that these are stronger 'than God?'

There are several ways of evading this difficulty, of which Christian teachers and students have not failed to avail themselves. 'We can point you,' they have said, 'to fruits of faith and love, which can only have been 'produced by a divine influence; we can show you that 'those who have done the best deeds and cherished the 'best thoughts have traced them to this influence. More 'than this we are not bound to do. Nay, we *are* bound 'to draw a broad line between these and the multitude 'who do not confess any spiritual influence, who are not 'the subjects of any.'

To a reader of the New Testament this statement must be most unsatisfactory. The Apostles speak of the holy men of old as moved by the Holy Ghost; no one who reads the words of those men can doubt that they referred every true thing in themselves to a divine source. Yet the Apostles teach us, and they teach us, that they were looking forward to a blessing which had not been given them, and which later ages should inherit. This expectation, as I showed in my last Essay, pointed not merely to the manifestation of a great king, but also to the manifestation of Him from whom their thoughts and impulses had proceeded.

The Christian kingdom cannot be described as a dispensation of the Spirit if these anticipations were not fulfilled. The Apostles must have deceived their hearers if the condition of those who lived after Christ's glorification, was not better in this respect than that of those who waited for His coming. The story of the descent of the Spirit on the day of Pentecost, and of the signs which accompanied it, and of the preaching which followed it, must be thrown aside altogether, if no great blessing was then vouchsafed to *mankind*,—if a few here and there may vindicate and appropriate to themselves a treasure, which the true men who understood its nature best were impatient to acknowledge as universal.

Some of those who could not acquiesce in so limited a view of the language of the Gospels and the Acts of the Apostles as this, have suggested that since the holy Scriptures are the work of the Divine Spirit, the complete Bible may perhaps be that common possession which distinguishes the new world from the old. To possess a divine history which was growing for centuries, in its order and fulness, so that all the steps of it may be traced, and the issue to which it was leading distinctly apprehended, is no doubt an incalculable advantage. But, if what I said in the last Essay is true, we lose altogether the sense and symmetry of this history unless we look upon the revelation of the Divine Spirit to men as that which explains the past to us and binds it to the future. Nay, according to its own showing, we have not the capacity of judging of its particular passages, and of their relation to each other, unless we partake of the Spirit by which its writers were guided. So that to put the book as the substitute for the gift of which it testifies, or as including it, is as flagrant a contradiction as we can possibly fall into.

A popular ecclesiastical historian of the last century, quite alive to this inconsistency, and, at the same time, aware of the wretched divisions and horrible atrocities which he should have to record, has resorted to the hypothesis that there have been certain 'lapses' of the Spirit in different periods, like in their principle, though not in their outward tokens, to that of which Whitsuntide reminds us. Such lapses he thought would account for the revival of moral light and life after long ages of superstition and degeneracy; for such events as the Reformation in the sixteenth century, and for others nearer to his own day, to which he attached a similar, and almost equal, significance. I shall not now inquire whether his theory will account for these facts, or, if it does, whether there are not others equally demanding interpretation, for which it does not account. I would only remark that the phrase, occasional 'lapses' of the

Spirit, cannot be an exact counterpart of that which our Lord uses when He speaks of a Spirit who shall abide with His disciples for ever, and that what we have to consider is whether such a description corresponds with the experience of Christendom, or contradicts it.

Finally, in our own day, a number of persons fancy they have discovered a sufficient equivalent for the doctrine of Scripture respecting a divine Spirit imparted to man, in the belief that man himself has a spiritual nature,—that all his powers, energies, affections show him to be more than a creature of flesh and blood. The doctrine of the Creed, they say, is only an old theocratic mode of enunciating a truth which belongs to the consciousness of all men, and of which some races have had a much keener intuition than the Jews. As I have already maintained that the Gospels and Epistles assert not merely that man has a spiritual nature, but that he is a spiritual being, as I have spoken of our Lord's ascension according to the ordinary view of it, as being the practical vindication of our spiritual position and spiritual capacities, I certainly cannot refuse to *connect* the doctrine of the coming of a divine Comforter with that human principle. St. John connects them; for he says, '*The Spirit was not yet given, because that Jesus was not yet glorified.*' But both he and St. Paul take the greatest possible pains to distinguish them. A mighty gift, according to the one, was bestowed upon God's creature as soon as that creature was capable of receiving it. '*The Spirit*,' according to the other, '*witnesseth with our spirit that we are the sons of God.*'

It would have been obviously unfitting that I should reckon amongst these methods of explaining the words of our Lord and His Apostles that to which a Phrygian heretic of the second century resorted, when he affirmed that the Comforter whom our Lord promised was a bodily teacher, who was to fill up the gaps in His doctrine. But since that proposition, even accompanied with the assertion that Montanus himself was the fulfiller of the promise, had plausibility enough to secure the support of so able a man as Tertullian, and since it has reappeared in various shapes ever since, and was never more likely to appear than now, I think it is worth while to consider why it has seemed to those who entertained it, to answer more exactly to our Lord's language than any mere notion of an invisible influence.

Such an influence is continually spoken of in Scripture. The symbols of 'rain' and 'dew' serve beautifully to describe its silent, penetrating, life-giving, orderly nature. But what is there in such symbols which corresponds to these words?—

'*And when He is come, He will reprove the world of sin, and of righteousness, and of judgment: of Sin, because they believe not on me; of Righteousness, because I go to my Father, and ye see me no more; of Judgment, because the Prince of this world is judged.*'

All here is personal in the strictest sense. I will send *Him*, *He* shall come, *He* shall reprove. Is a Teacher, a Helper, a Sustainer, like moisture or vapour? I apprehend, then, that if a man has been much vexed, as Tertullian with his fierce African nature was, by Gnostical Teachers, who have no associations with Spirit, except these,—who do habitually confound it with vapour, and do not even attach to vapour that sense of power which the sight of a locomotive engine suggests to us,—he is very likely to adopt a coarse material counterpart of reality, and as the punishment of his intemperate folly, to become the victim of some feeble impostor. A great lesson lies, I think, in that painful experience. If Christ has shown that the body which He took did not constitute His personality, but that, because He was a Person, because He was the Son of God, he could raise, redeem, and glorify His body; if He has shown a man not to be a person because he has a body, but that he only claims and realizes his personality then when he maintains his relation to God, and holds his body as a subject; if the Evil Spirit is not less personal because he comes to us and came to Christ in no bodily shape; if we can only worship the living and true God as a Person and a Father;—then I believe we shall accept the words which I have quoted in the most literal sense when we take them in their most spiritual sense. There is indeed a deep question growing out of this concerning the relation of the Person of the Comforter to the Son, who says He will send Him,—to the Father, from whom He is said to proceed. That question I reserve for a future Essay. In this I propose only to inquire whether, if we acknowledge this Spirit as a Person, and if we accept our Lord's account of His work, we shall not have a solution of the difficulty with which I started—the only interpretation of the dark as well as of the bright passages in the History of Christendom.

1. I suppose no one doubts that the feelings about Sin in the modern world have been very different from any which can be traced in the old. I have little need to make out a proof of this fact, because it will be rather eagerly accepted as a concession by those who hold that Christianity has operated injuriously on the welfare of mankind. They will say, 'It is certainly true that there has been a terror in the minds of 'men respecting a number of practices and habits which 'seemed very innocent to Pagans, comparatively inno'cent even to Jews. There has been a fear of teaching, 'tasting, handling, which belonged in an immeasurably 'less degree to Greeks and Romans. A dark shadow 'has been cast over the face of nature, and over social 'life.' I shall not now inquire to what extent these charges are true, because I have considered the subject in my second Essay; and I have had occasion in every succeeding one to make use of the conclusions at which I arrived in the course of it. I spoke of an evil which lies beneath the transgression for which laws affix

punishment, beneath the habits and temperament to which the mere ethical philosopher confines himself. This evil lies close to myself; I become conscious of it when I think of myself; I cannot refer it to the operation of outward circumstances; I am rather obliged to confess it as the cause of anything wrong which affects me in them. I said that undoubtedly this sense of personal evil had set men upon devising a multitude of schemes for avoiding its present anguish, for escaping from the terrors of which it seemed pregnant in the future, for conciliating the Power whom it might have offended. If then it is true that this sense of personal evil did not exist to at all the same extent before the coming of Christ as it has existed since; that though we may trace clear anticipations of it in some of the great thinkers of the old world, as well as in the popular belief, yet that for the most part both are occupied with the less radical and inward forms of evil, it is quite to be expected that the superstitions of the latter time should have had oftentimes a worse character than those of the former, that the wickedness should be of a more conscious kind, that the man should be in more direct open war with himself, with his fellows, and with his Creator. All this sounds very shocking, and very confirmatory of that which the objector urges. And yet I maintained that it is good for a man thus to know what is going on within him; thus to see himself stript bare of appearances and plausibilities; thus to be prevented from transferring to accidents, which he cannot remedy, what may be cured when he sees it and confesses it as his own. And I urged that all the mischief of those contrivances which the man himself has imagined, or his priest suggested, for the sake of soothing his pain, lies in this, that they throw him back into a region of phantoms and shadows, out of which this dreadful experience is intended to lead him; that they hinder him from seeking the moral freedom which is awaiting him if he will receive it.

For there is another set of facts, as we have seen, in the history of Christendom to which, also, there is only a most imperfect parallel in the ancient world. We find men emerging out of darkness into a marvellous light, coming to understand what that strife in themselves meant, and how and why they had fallen into it, coming to see that their true state is that of union with One higher than themselves, their King and their Deliverer, in whom they were created, apart from whom they cannot subsist, in trusting whom they lose that feverish self-consciousness which has been their death, and acquire a pure, and true, and common life.

Now, what is it that one wants to make these two sets of facts, which comprise so much of what is most dismal and most blessed in the individual and in the social experience of eighteen centuries, intelligible to us? Is it not the belief that some Person has been leading men, in spite of all struggles and reluctance on their parts, in spite of all efforts to escape from the reality of things, in spite of all the soothing or irritating prescriptions of earthly doctors, to a knowledge of what they are according to that separate, unnatural, immoral condition which they have imagined for themselves, and of what they are according to the true and blessed order which God has established for them? And is not this precisely what is expressed in the words, '*The Comforter shall reprove*' (or *convict*) '*the world of sin, because they believe not on me?*'

Nothing in those words determines how this or that man shall receive the influence which is exerted upon him. The '*world*' is said to be the subject of the conviction; the whole of Society will be acted upon by the divine Spirit. And yet it is not to the outside world that He will speak. A conviction of *Sin* must be addressed to the conscience, the inner man, the person from whom thoughts, words and acts flow. There will, it is said, be this silent mysterious operation. It will produce results. These results may be merely fear, cowardice, horror of God, contrivances to escape from Him. They may be trust in Him as a Friend and Deliverer, a renunciation of all self-seeking experiments, rest in the Son of Man. They may be any condition of feeling between these two extremes. On this subject we have no information; we require none. We want to know who is speaking to us; what He is saying, to what issue He would lead us, what there is in us which may yield to Him or resist Him. On these points we have all the light we require; all that can help us to obedience and peace. If we wish to limit the movements of that Spirit which bloweth where it listeth, that we may prove ourselves to be within the circle of His influence, we offer a sad evidence that we *are* resisting Him.

2. If the conscience of sin is characteristic of the new world as distinguished from the old, I do not think any one can doubt that there has been also a higher standard of Righteousness than any which can be traced in the best men and the best nations that classical history introduces to us. I make this remark with a full recollection of the apparent objections to it which I noticed before, and with the greatest desire to admit their reasonableness. I acknowledge that the elevation of the Christian standard has been a plea for treating the love of city and country which the Greek and Roman heroes exhibited as mundane and heathenish. I acknowledge that this feeling has prevailed among Protestants as well as Romanists, and that whenever and wherever it has prevailed, there has been the best excuse for exclaiming against the popular religious doctrines and doctors as immoral and anti-social, for declaring that the patriotism which they despised was better and truer than any thing which they put in its place. I admit, as I did in my Essay on Regeneration, that spiritual or ecclesiastical maxims of life have proved, not only hostile to civil life, but to domestic; to those relations

upon which God, in the Jewish dispensation, put such high honour, which He takes as the very instruments of revealing himself, which St. Paul connects with the life and substance of the Church. And this being the case, it has followed, of course, that the ideal Righteousness has sunk into a meaner and more degrading form of Self-righteousness than any which can be found beyond the circle of Christendom. Nay, it would seem as if the self-righteous practices which have tormented the world elsewhere have their centre and explanation in Christian Society.

Above all, the fearful contradictions which have gathered about the idea of Sacrifice, and have made the giving up of Self the plea for the most intense calculating Selfishness, have received their fullest illustration from the acts and conceptions of Christian men. Among them, too, the horrible notion of making the safety of the soul a motive for violations of Truth, nay of making Truth merely a means to safety, has led to such intricacies of deception and of cruelty, as it would be hard to find examples of in the countries where it has never been proclaimed that the Lord God is a God of Truth and without iniquity, one who hateth robbery for burnt-offering.

I do not want to conceal one of these terrible observations; we have need to meditate them more and more deeply. I only want you to dwell as earnestly, on another class of observations, which appear utterly opposed to them, and yet which cannot be separated from them. That wicked contempt for national and domestic life to which I alluded, is connected with such an idea of a universal fellowship, of a union with men as men, of duties owing to all men everywhere, with such evidences that this idea is not a barren one, not a mere maxim or theory, but a mighty operative principle,—as you can scarcely perceive the faintest foreshadowing of among the greatest citizens of the old republics. That grovelling notion of men practising acts of devotion that they may avert some penalty or buy some prize, has been associated with such a resolute casting away of life, reputation, hope, everything, when other men were to be blessed, and the love of God to them was to be declared,—with such an overpowering belief in a charity that is mightier than Sin, Death, the Devil, which can penetrate the being of man, and utterly destroy the selfishness there,—as you can only hear the feeblest prophecy of in the highest raptures of ancient poets and philosophers; and yet the realization of it has been among peasants and feeble women. That blasphemous notion of lying for God, which has defiled the morality of Romanists and Protestants, has been accompanied in the minds of both, with a persuasion that Truth is higher than Heaven and deeper than Hell, that God Himself is the Truth; that everything is to be parted with for the sake of that. I do not say that the best men in the old world had not a conviction that this must be so, or that we do not owe them gratitude unspeakable, for having testified that man's business in life is to seek for that which is, to believe in it that he may find it, and to strip himself of all phantoms and shadows which interfere with the apprehension of it. God be thanked for having raised up such witnesses to Himself! What I say is, that the witness has been found to be real and substantial, by tens of thousands who have known nothing of dialectics, whose only training has been that of poverty, sickness, the prison, the rack. These were their schoolmasters; by these they were lifted up to feel that there was a perfect Righteousness, a universal self-sacrificing Love, an eternal Truth, of which they were inheritors.

And here is the solution of the mystery. '*When He cometh He shall convince the world of Righteousness, because I go to my Father, and ye see me no more.*' There had been a standard of eternal righteousness, love, self-sacrifice, exhibited in the world, exhibited by a man carrying mortal flesh, dying a death which we die. And that man had gone out of sight, had seemed to leave no traces of Himself on earth. But a voice was ever whispering at men's hearts, 'He is ascended 'on high to His Father and your Father. That 'Righteousness which was seen here, is now yours; it 'is for one and all of you. You are participators in 'that sacrifice which He has offered for all, and which 'He is presenting as your Intercessor to His Father.

'You may know that Truth, and that Truth may make 'you free, of which He came into the world, and died, 'and has ascended, to testify.'

How otherwise we could bring these different warring experiences into harmony, I cannot conceive. The wisdom of Church teachers will not explain them; they have been often the great agents in corruption, and when they have been otherwise the secret must be accounted for. The innate nobleness of man will not explain them, for we have to interpret proofs of his debasement. His innate evil will not explain them, for we have to interpret high thoughts and glorious deeds. If we believed that there had been a Spirit of Truth, not acting upon the surface of men's minds, but carrying on a controversy with them in their inmost being, encountering all the rebellions of the cowardly, reluctant Will, all its desires to become a mere Self-will, bringing out its darkness, as light always must, into fuller and stronger relief, making the devilish apparent because it was confronted with the divine; if we could believe that this was a Comforter, a divine Person, stronger than His enemies, able to strengthen man to all fixed resolutions and noble purposes,—to bring the objects which he perceives dimly and at a distance, within the sphere of his vision; able to inspire longings and hopes when the spirit of man is most bent and cowed; able to point him upwards to a Father in Heaven when he is most ready to call himself merely a son of earth; able at the same time to make him understand his work on earth, and to endow him with powers for performing it; able to support him in suffering, to give him glimpses of the substantial glory into which Christ has entered through suffering; able to make him perceive that everything which is merely his own is perishable, that what is most divine is common to him with his fellows;—then I think we need not choose the bright spots of modern history and conceal its horrors; the more courageously we face the one, the more hope will come to us from the contemplation of the other.

3. For assuredly there has been, and is, a conviction working in the minds of men, the most various and unlike each other, that this kind of conflict is not to go on for ever. There is a sense of Judgment, of some great decision, that is to settle for ever which of these is the stronger, the Evil, or the Good with which the Evil has been so intricately combined. This thought of Judgment has been itself as perplexed as either of the others. Men have fancied they were to prepare for judgment by eschewing their common duties,—by devoting themselves to the work of saving their own souls. They have fancied that if, by any means, they could escape from judgment, it would be an unspeakable blessing. They have fancied that Christ came, not as He said, to save the *world*, but to save *them*, that they might not be judged like their fellows. The strangest results, doctrinal and practical, have followed from these habits

of mind, and from the encouragement which Christian teachers have given to them; some of them I pointed out in my twelfth Essay. But in the midst of these we perceive a deep and settled *desire* for judgment, a longing that there should not be a perpetual confusion of Sin and Righteousness, of Truth and Falsehood,—a certainty that if Christ is King, there cannot be. While there has been, and is, such a dread of judgment as there never was in the old world, there has been, and is, such a passionate craving for judgment as the heroes of it may have now and then felt in hopeful moments when the contradictions of the world became very oppressive; but such as certainly never became a part of their abiding convictions. For it is evident that the feelings respecting Judgment must correspond to those respecting Sin and Righteousness. If our thoughts of these are superficial, our thoughts of that will be; if we connect them with the very substance of our being, the judgment will bear reference to that. The awfulness of the thoughts of Judgment which we in Christendom have entertained has been the inevitable consequence of Sin coming out in such close tremendous connexion with our own selves, of the Righteousness which opposes it being brought so close to us. The hopefulness of our thoughts respecting Judgment has arisen in like manner from the sense of a mighty struggle in the inmost region of our thoughts and consciences between the powers of good and evil, from the certainty that the good is mightier even there, and that God, being absolutely righteous, is on the side of the good against the evil. But what external doctrine about the righteousness of God could have kept this faith alive in any single heart, far more in the heart of Christendom, for eighteen centuries? What confidence that Christ had come and preached of good being mightier than ill, nay, had shewn it in His own person to be mightier, could have kept it alive; or how could that confidence have been itself preserved? '*When He cometh He shall convince the world of judgment, because the Prince of this world is judged.*' Yes! The Spirit has been saying to every generation, He is saying very emphatically to ours,—'It is not uncertain what the issue of the battle 'between right and wrong, truth and lies, will be. It 'is known; you may know it. The evil power seems 'to have a mighty ascendency. If you look at the outside of history, if you merely dwell upon statistics, 'you will come to the conclusion that the good is very 'weak indeed. But examine the inner life of the world, 'search into the principles and causes of its peace and 'order, of its misery and confusion; above all, look into 'the principles and causes of the right and truth you 'have sought and done, of the wrong and falsehood to 'which you have yielded, and you will find in the one 'the pledges of endurance and eternity, in the other of 'swift and sudden destruction. It is true for you; it is 'true for mankind; Christ has proved it; and though 'heaven and earth pass away, His words, His acts, His 'triumphs, do not pass away. He will bring forth right'eousness to judgment.'

To speak of this conviction merely as some gracious influence which steals into certain gentle, prepared, believing hearts, is altogether to misinterpret its nature, and to make such influences unintelligible to the persons who receive them. They are worth nothing to any one who calls them his own. They soon become occasions of pride and self-glorification, or else of despondency, because the feelings which were so serene and pleasant yesterday are turbulent and gloomy to-day; unless they are traced to One whose presence does not depend upon any of our changeable moods. No doubt it is a paradox that we have the Comforter, and ask for the Comforter; that we pray for Him, and could not pray without Him. No doubt it is a paradox that He is with those who feel His presence least; that when we seem for a moment to feel He is ours, He is gone. These are paradoxes; for everything which has relation to our internal being, puts on a strange shape when it takes the form of a proposition. Every man finds this out for himself, when he begins to think and suffer. The difficulty is not increased by referring our thoughts and feelings to One who overlooks them, and knows them, and sympathises with them. It is saved from being intolerable. If we were forced to think that all which Scripture tells us of One who grieves with us, and for us, and whom we may grieve, is mere fiction, the burden of existence would have nothing to lighten it. Few as there may be who attach a distinct meaning to those words, all would find an infinite loss if they were taken away. For they belong to all, and we cheat ourselves of the blessing they might afford us, and the light they throw upon God's ways, by denying them to any.

Again, it cannot be that this Teacher is merely speaking to us out of the Bible. To have Him speaking there in broad common words; to have Him setting before us thoughts that were thought, and feelings that were felt, ages ago, and which we may, nevertheless, assert as ours to have Him there, unfolding the steps of a world-drama which has reached a divine catastrophe, and yet which is moving on to another catastrophe,—we being persons in it now, and able to understand the passing scenes of it by those which are presented to us in the book,—and to be sure that the same Divine Person who appeared at the opening of it, has been present throughout, and will gather all round Himself, at the end; this is wonderful: this is a sign to us that we are not to control the Spirit, or make Him the mere minister of our experiences. But the Comforter is not in the book if He is not convincing the world.

And therefore it cannot be that He descends now and then, at distant intervals, in uncertain lapses, like the Angel into the pool of Bethesda. There may be great crises in the education of the world, times when it starts up after years or centuries of paralysis, into a more vigorous and healthy life; when buried truths come forth out of their caves, and cast away their grave-clothes; when there seems to be a new heaven and a new earth, because the clouds which hid the face of one, and hindered the quickening processes of the other, have passed away. But such moments, however surprising they may seem to us, obey some fixed law, and are connected by close, however invisible, links, and denote the action and inspiration of One who is dwelling in the midst of us.

But oh, how melancholy if we must resolve this Spirit into the spiritual movements, affections, powers of the creatures whom He came to guide and animate! Thanks be to God for the witness which is borne in our day for the spirituality, not of a few men, but of man as man. It is His teaching, His way of declaring His Son to us, the battle of His Spirit with our pettishness and vanity. But if we substitute the lesson for the Teacher, if man falls down and worships his own faculties of worship, if he determines to be a God because he has the capacity of knowing God, what a tyranny of particular spiritual men is he preparing for himself, what a slavery to mere gifts, what a rivalry of impostors, each pretending to be *the* spiritual and divine man who can guide the rest; ultimately what an abyss of materialism! We shall not have one Montanus claiming to be the Comforter, but each little neighbourhood and sect will have its own Montanus, its petty prophet, to take the place of the Spirit *who guideth into all truth.*

'After all, how easy it has been for the Unitarian 'to deny the Personality of the Holy Spirit, and even to 'find Scriptural excuses for his denial!' It is most easy for him, and for all of us. I could find a thousand excuses if I wanted them; I should not despair of bringing any texts by skilful processes to vote on my side; after a time I might convince myself that that was their most natural meaning. But I cannot find that it is an object for which I ought to spend this labour. I cannot find that I should be much the gainer if I persuaded myself that I had not this Friend, and Teacher, and Comforter with me. I do not mean in ease, or satisfaction, or peace of mind. These, one is never to keep at the expense of truth. In fact, I have never discovered how one can keep them, if one prefers them to truth. But it seems to me that I shall not love the truth better, if I feel I have not a Spirit of Truth guiding me towards it. I think I should give up the pursuit altogether, I should take up with any appearances or falsehoods that looked plausible.

'It is not, however,' some Unitarian will say, 'a 'proof of our having a gift, that we have a need 'of it. Locke's argument against the Papists has 'always passed muster with us. You say there is an 'infallible authority, because we should be the better for 'having one; how much better we should be off if we 'were all infallible, and yet we are not.' I am bold enough to differ both with Locke and the Papists. I do not think we should be better for having an infallible mortal guide, or for being infallible ourselves. If either state were good for us, I believe it would have been appointed for us. I think we have an infallible, immortal Guide, and that this is what we need. But do not accept the evidence of your wishes or necessities, if you think that unsatisfactory. Try whether you can solve the problems of the world without the belief in this personal Teacher. Or if you do not care for the problems of the world, try whether you can solve the problems of your own heart. I speak boldly to you on this point, for I am satisfied that you have this Comforter with you as I have; that He is convincing you of sin, of righteousness, and of judgment, as well as me. I am sure there is a Spirit of lies who is always striving to lead me into all falsehood, and to separate me from you and from all men. I believe we shall understand one another when we know that his adversary is with us, to make us true and to make us one. The unity of the Spirit, however, and what is involved in it, I reserve for my next subject.

ESSAY XV.

ON THE UNITY OF THE CHURCH.

'SUPPOSING those facts which you dwelt upon in 'your last Essay do imply the presence of Him whom our 'Lord calls the Comforter, the great difficulty for those 'who compare the promises of the New Testament with 'the History of Christendom still remains. The Apostles 'speak, or have always been supposed to speak, of a '*Church*, a one Catholic Church, as established, or about 'to be established, on this earth. They connect that 'Church with the gift of a Spirit, who is called the Holy 'Spirit, who, it was said, should dwell in the Church as 'He did not in the world,—who was to purify the hearts 'of its members. Where is this Church? What does 'History say of it? What do our eyes tell us about it? 'Answer these questions, or the deepest anxieties of our 'age are still unsatisfied.'

I feel the truth of these remarks. The subject which I discussed in the last Essay approaches so closely to this, that I could not always avoid allusion to it. But I passed it by as much as I could; the words of our Lord on which I commented enabled me to do so. They speak of a *World*, not of a *Church*. They speak of the Comforter as convicting the world of Sin, of Righteousness, of Judgment,—not of Him as a Sanctifier, or Reconciler. I desired to follow His guidance: but I did not wish to shrink from the other examination, however appalling it may seem. I allow that there is a very distinct obligation laid upon us all to explain what we understand by the language of Scripture respecting the gift of the Spirit and the foundation of the Church, and how we suppose the records of the world, and the world which we see, can be explained in accordance with it.

I cannot make this task easier to myself by maintaining that the New Testament promises certain spiritual blessings to individuals, but that it does not connect the gift of the Spirit with a Society. Every passage in the Bible—the construction of the Bible—refutes that supposition. The earlier records speak of a nation called out by God to be the witness of His presence and government; the later records have no connexion with these,—have no distinct meaning of their own,—if they do not describe the expansion of a national Society into a human and universal Society. The expectations of the Apostles, awakened and sustained by their Lord's teachings, pointed to this issue:—they were to be the ministers of a kingdom; they were to preach of a kingdom to

Israelites; finally, they were to baptize all nations. They were told they had not yet power to fulfil that work. They knew that they had not. They had a mysterious assurance that they were united still to the Lord who had been with them on earth; they felt they might call upon His Father as their Father. But they could not realize their relation to that invisible world into which their Master had entered—entered, He said, for them. He had chosen them as a body to work under Him. He had told them that they were to work together after He had gone away. He had said that all men would know they were His disciples by the love they had to each other. But they were conscious of jealousies and rivalries; each might soon again be trying to live and act for himself. Unless their Lord could bind them together by that power which bound Him to them, fellowship among such naturally unsociable elements was impossible. And surely such a power was needed if they were ever to break through the fetters of their Jewish exclusiveness; to have any communion with men of other kindreds and tongues. The events said to have occurred on the day of Pentecost, exactly corresponded to these anticipations. A power is said to have taken possession of them,—a power which governed their thought and speech. But it was the power of a Spirit who made them feel they were one, and proclaim their oneness with the crowd which was assembled at that feast, because He who established it, and whose mighty works were commemorated in it, was declaring them to be one with Him. The story follows of the baptism of the three thousand, who were to receive the same gift as the Apostles had received, and of the new Society at Jerusalem,—which is not noted for the exercise of the gift of tongues, but for the continuance of its members in the Apostles' doctrine and fellowship, for the joy and singleness of heart with which they ate their bread, for their not counting the things they had as their own, for the distribution which they made to those who had need, for their courage before the Sanhedrim, for the confidence with which they prayed that they might speak with all boldness of the King against whom Jews and Gentiles had gathered together.

The Apostles do indeed exercise powers of healing, and they are especially careful to assert that no cure was wrought in their own name, but in the name of the ascended Son of God. But what the historian chiefly dwells on, is the order of the Society which was established in that Name, its unity and holiness while it confessed the Spirit to be with it,—the punishment of those (for there were such in that infant community) who lied against the Holy Ghost,—the new organization which was suggested by the quarrels (for there were those in that infant community) between Hebrews and Hellenists.

When St. Paul goes with his Gospel into the cities of Asia Minor, of Macedonia, of Greece Proper, it is still to form Societies. Each of these is named an Ecclesia; the members of it are said to be called or chosen, or to be in God the Father and His Son Jesus Christ. They are said to be baptized by one Spirit into one body. These distinct bodies are portions of a universal body.

Everything, then, in the Old and New Testament, speaks of fellowship and organization. And to suppose that the latest birth in the universe so solemnly announced, so long waited for, was an abortion, or that the child was not to come to the use of its limbs and vital energies for centuries, is to suppose the Apostles at once deceived and deceivers. They told their disciples, as their Lord had told them, that a crisis to be witnessed by some of them, would show that a kingdom had come forth, which, however apparently insignificant, was instinct with a Spirit that would enable it to rule the nations.

Admitting this, how can I dare to face the problems which the world, as we see it, presents to us? Must I not save the credit of Inspiration by resorting to fictions which have not done men much good hitherto, and which will certainly not save them now? By assuming, for instance, that forms and professions constitute a Church,—that external badges mean the same thing as an indwelling Spirit? I hope I shall be preserved from any such wicked trifling; if I fall into it, the falsehood will soon make itself evident.

I. First then; we find a body which affirms itself to be

the one Holy Catholic Church of the world. Its members form the bulk of the population of Western Europe: its claims to be what it represents itself to be, are publicly recognised by many of the most conspicuous and civilized states. This body boasts that it is the heir of that which was established in Jerusalem on the day of Pentecost: whatever rights and powers resided in that Church, it says, have descended upon it. If that Church was able to do wonderful works, this Church declares that it can do the same; the gift, it says, has never been withdrawn, has been exercised at intervals in all generations, makes itself manifest now. This sign of continuance and identity it is inclined to dwell upon most; still others are not wanting. 'There has been no break,' it declares, 'in the line of Church ministers, from the time 'of the Apostles downwards. The character of the 'organization is the same. The Apostles were regarded 'as the fathers of a family; the idea of paternity has 'been strictly preserved; it has even unfolded itself; it 'is more completely realized now than it was at first. 'The capital of the Church,' it is admitted, 'has been 'changed; but that change came to pass, first, by a 'divine ordinance expressly depriving Jerusalem of its 'honour; secondly, by a series of events,—equally 'attesting the divine purpose,—which have deposed the 'old Cæsars from their seat, and have established the 'successors of St. Peter upon it. And this circumstance 'has, it is said, produced an unity which would other-

'wise have been wanting to Christendom. The wild 'Gothic tribes, full of their separate strifes, impatient of 'fellowship, have been brought to confess a general 'spiritual head, and a community of faith higher than 'any differences of race or any national disagreements. 'In defiance of the tendencies of each nation to find a 'separate language for itself, a common *language* has 'established itself as an organ of devotion. In defiance, 'again, of the tendency of each nation to set up for itself 'a separate *worship*—a tendency equally evident in the 'Old world and the New,—a common creed and a com'mon worship have succeeded in keeping their ground 'for many centuries, the head of the Society being 'always able to interpret what has been misunderstood, 'to put down the inventors of new opinions, to provide 'for fresh emergencies. For, there being such a person, 'whose authority all the different members of this So'ciety acknowledge as infallible and past appeal, the 'Church,' it is said, 'can combine the greatest fixedness 'with the greatest elasticity. It has maintained the 'faith once delivered to the saints without wavering; 'it has ever been giving birth to new opinions and 'practices, where they were needful to develope and 'complete the old,—to new orders of men when it was 'requisite to encounter diseases or necessities in the body 'politic, that had previously not existed or not been 'observed.

'This Church,' it is further declared, 'is not only

'spread over the whole surface of modern European so-'ciety; not only are its priests to be seen at the corners 'of every street; not only are they performing services 'continually in every Church, which establish a commu-'nion between angels and men, the living and the 'departed; not only is the Sacrifice continually offered 'up which reconciles the offending creatures to their 'Creator, and brings down blessings on the earth; not 'only is that Sacrifice lifted before the eyes of men, that 'they may believe and adore,—but the influence of the 'Church affects the politics of all kingdoms, penetrates 'into the recesses of all families. Every individual is 'within the reach of its guidance and blessing. Every 'burdened conscience knows where it may go that it 'may lay down its burden,—who can set it free. 'Nothing in the arrangements of this Society,' it is said, 'is merely distant and abstract; it meets each peculiar 'case, provides a remedy for every ailment, a satisfaction 'for every craving. And it proves,'—so its champions triumphantly continue,—'its title to be the one Catholic 'Church, since all who rebel against it or separate from 'it necessarily become divided, since no body besides 'it can put forth the least pretension to universality. 'And it proves itself to be holy, because no other 'can show such an array of devoted, self-sacrificing 'saints.'

It is at this point, I suspect, that the ordinary observer, the simple layman, the European traveller,—for it is to such a man, and not to some adverse divine, that these statements are likely to be addressed,—will step in with an objection. 'All your arguments,' he will answer, 'may be true enough; at all events, I cannot 'refute them. You may have the miraculous powers 'you speak of, the uninterrupted descent, the infallible 'authority, the fixed dogmas, the adaptation to circum-'stances, the band of saints. But when you talk of a '*holy* society, do tell me what your words mean, for 'they utterly bewilder me. Do you call this society, in 'which I am dwelling, a holy society? Do you call this 'country, for instance, which is nearest the centre of 'holiness, a holy country? I will not press you too 'much. I will suppose that though you have miraculous 'powers, the power does not always exert itself in this 'way. That it can make statues wink more easily than 'it can make human beings abandon their habits of 'revenge or lying,—I can understand. But when the 'power *is* exerted, when you are doing a work for men, 'I want to know whether *that* is for good or for ill? 'I cannot make up my mind that it is for good. I 'cannot help perceiving, not that you do not reclaim 'men from being false, but that you continually *make* 'them false; not that you sometimes fail in *preventing* 'moral corruption, but that you are working very hard, 'by some of your most potent and most vaunted agen-'cies, to *promote* it; not that evil and debasing habits 'have defied all the energies of preachers, confessors, 'and absolvers; but that preachers, confessors, and 'absolvers, are very often helping more to strengthen 'these habits, and make them invincible, than all other 'men together.'

This kind of conviction,—Romanists should understand it, and we for our humiliation should understand it too,—is doing immeasurably more to make their arguments fall lifeless upon practical men, whose minds are not blinded to the distinction of right and wrong, than all our elaborate reasonings. And when a man has gone so far in his examination of the phrase, 'One Holy 'Catholic Church,' his observation, without any help from divinity, or much from ecclesiastical history, may carry him a little further. He may demur to a unity which is compatible with the infinite *contrarieties*, not diversities, of belief, which he will himself have met with in Roman Catholic countries; with the wild immoral heathenish superstitions, which an intelligent priest will at once disclaim, yet which exist in the very classes that most acknowledge the influence of priests; with the contemptuous infidelity which they themselves impute to the classes that are out of their reach; with the discontent that is muttered by better men. All this,—with the modifications of faith which exist in the sacerdotal order itself, touching all points from the most unquestioning orthodoxy to absolute atheism,—may co-exist, no doubt, with something that is *called* unity; nay, these differences may be alleged as proofs how vigorous the system must be which can enforce a uniformity in spite of them. But they may somewhat puzzle a person who is inquiring whether this is that Church which began when a *Spirit* of unity took possession of a body of men, allowing them to retain their *external* differences, because they had that *within* which made them one. And a similar difficulty will beset him when he considers that the symbol of the descent of that Spirit was, that men could hear, in their *different* tongues, the wonderful works of God, and when he observes that the *one* tongue which is the symbol of modern Catholicism is a sentence of exclusion to the whole body of Greeks, seeing that they boast of a somewhat older and more sacred dialect. And generally it will strike him, I fancy, that the boasts of Romanists themselves establish the inference which he would have deduced from his own experience, that the preservation of a vast machinery, of a surface uniformity, of an artificial holiness, is what they understand by the preservation of a Church in which the Holy Spirit of Unity has made His habitation.

II. An impartial observer who has arrived at this mournful conclusion may turn, with some pleasure, to another class of facts which the modern European world offers to him. He may hear with satisfaction that several nations have raised their protest against the attempt to crush all distinct thoughts and languages, under one general name. He will rejoice to find that their rulers are considered responsible to God, for their conduct to their subjects and to other lands; and to no earthly superior, whatever claims of infallibility or divinity he may allege. He may find that in such countries there is a recognition of the dignity of civil life, of the duty of nations to maintain their independence, of the inviolability of the domestic hearth, of the worth which belongs to the ordinary virtues of plain dealing and truth-speaking, which he has sought for in vain among those who only breathe a sacerdotal atmosphere. He may be pleased to observe that nevertheless in these countries there is an acknowledgment of the importance and necessity of a spiritual influence; that the priest, though he cannot claim to be a king, has his own recognised and lawful position.

At first such discoveries may be very cheering; possibly they will not cease to be so. But he will soon hear, not only from Romanists, not only from those who suppose that the Romanist is somewhere near the truth in his conception of the Church, but also from those who regard him as hopelessly and fatally astray, that these protesting nations are altogether unspiritual and secular. These hard names will not be bestowed without some startling evidence to show that they are deserved. 'Look,' he will be told, 'at the lower classes 'in these nations. They may be less flagrantly super-'stitious than those in Romish countries. Are they less 'debased, less animal, less ignorant? What spiritual 'influence has been exerted over them?'—'Look,' it will be said again, 'at the upper classes. The priests are 'less obnoxious to them than the Romish priests are to 'those among whom they dwell. Is not this because it 'is more clearly understood that they shall be left to 'themselves, that their vices and their wrong doings to 'those who are under their influence shall not be noticed; 'that the priest shall abdicate his functions as a spiritual 'reprover, and shall be content to be reckoned a safety-'valve of the social machine, or as some insignificant 'accessory to it, which no one will disturb until it begins 'to move? Certain doctrines he is to believe, certain 'words he is to repeat, certain acts he is to go through; 'what have those doctrines, words, acts, to do with men 'not of his profession;—often, what have they to do with 'him? They are charms to keep the different classes of 'a country in those positions to each other, which the 'laws and conventions of the land have assigned them. 'And whither,' it is asked, 'are these nations tending? 'Are not material gratifications becoming more and more 'the only prizes which they are setting before them-'selves? Is not the pursuit of wealth the one great 'means of winning that prize? Are not art, science, 'religion, valued just so far as they contribute to make 'the possession of money more agreeable, or the search 'for it more secure? Is it here that we are to look for a 'Holy Catholic Church; can we find tokens here that a 'Spirit of Holiness and Love is dwelling among men?'

What use can there be in shutting one's ears to such words as these? Is it not better to take in the full force of them, and to meditate on them silently? For so we may in due time discover, not the secret of acquiescence in the evils which press upon us, but the secret of deliverance from them. Those who are flying to Rome expect that a miraculous illumination will some day enable them to see the anomalies which now shock them in its system, quite differently. It is probable that a blindness, (which may be also miraculous), will by degrees save them from the unhappiness of seeing these anomalies at all. We should wish and pray, in proportion as we love our country, that we may not shrink from contemplating one of its sins which are our own, but that God's light may show them to us just as they are.

III. Perhaps the student may find some relief in turning from both these spectacles to a number of particular societies, which declare that the so-called Catholic body, and the bodies which pretend to be National Churches, have equally mistaken the foundation on which a Church ought to rest. He must needs be attracted by their statements, not only because they point out evils which he has himself noticed in their opponents, but because they affirm that the true spiritual principle is with them. 'The Church,' they say, 'cannot be a mere world. It must 'be a body of men chosen out of the world. It cannot be 'a body merely held together by certain external profes- 'sions. It must consist of those who are drawn by a Divine

'Spirit to confess a Divine Lord.' What data can sound more hopeful than these? How likely it seems that here at last the feet of weary pilgrims will find some resting-place; that here we have arrived at the secret which has escaped anxious and earnest men for so many generations! There is much in the early history of all sects to favour this opinion. Who can deny the fervent zeal against injustice and evil which possessed the leaders; the hearty affection, genial sympathy, passionate self-devotion of the followers? Who can say that they were only denouncing other men, and not uttering the deepest conviction of their own hearts? If they were sometimes unjust and violent, their fierce language was often the indication of a loving rather than of a hating spirit; a wise man who was the object of it would have liked it much better than the smooth and civil speeches of less cordial foes. A Spirit—yes, the Spirit of Truth—there must have been among these men; their sect would not have survived them for a century, or even a year, if it had been merely gathered for a purpose of spite or faction.

A person who has arrived at this conviction will not be driven from it by any criticisms or denunciations of those who oppose these sects. But what if he should hear deep groans arising from the midst of them, from the very persons who have been educated in them, from those who have learnt to despise, and have continued to despise, the bodies whence they have gone out? What if the complaints of them should be of this kind,—that they are not spiritual bodies at all, but formal and worldly; not assertors of moral freedom, but great restrainers of it; that they are bitter against each other, seldom at peace within; that the best praise which can be bestowed upon the best man in any one of these bodies,—the praise which his admirers always dwell upon,—is that he has emancipated himself from the ordinary habits and temper of it? Such is the testimony, not of hard judges, but of sufferers. And if so, can we find among these sects the resemblance of that Church of which St. Paul spoke as being one Body, into which all had been baptized by one Spirit?

But if no one of these separate inquiries has led to any satisfactory result, how much more unsatisfactory would the comparison of them seem to be! What an impression that must leave upon every mind of conflict, strife, contradiction, in those who bear the name of the one Lord! What utter despair it must awaken in him of all Unity, unless, indeed, men can agree that they are *not* spiritual beings; that they are *not* connected with an invisible world at all; that they are *not* children of a Father in Heaven; that they have no ties to each other except such as are produced by outward animal necessities, which one man cannot satisfy without the assistance of his neighbour. Were it possible to arrive at *that* state of feeling, some difficulties might no doubt be removed. But does experience show that it is possible? Would perfect unity or unbroken discord—a war of elements, without the hope or chance of peace,—be the consequence, if it were?

To one revolving that frightful possibility, and asking whether there must not be some way out of this labyrinth, the thought, I am sure, will at last present itself, that those facts which he has been pondering, offer the most decisive witness for, not against, the law which was proclaimed on the day of Pentecost; for, not against, the assertion that it is the law of human Society,—the one by which Society *is* governed,—however much men may be denying it or rebelling against it. Look once again at that Church which boasts to be One, Holy, Catholic. Is her boast too grand a one? Has she believed too firmly that a Church has been established of which all her sons have a right to call themselves members, that a Spirit has been given of which they all have a right to be partakers? Would to God she did hold that belief! What a different picture her history would present if she had held it steadfastly! If she had been convinced that Heaven and Earth were brought into one,—that a real fellowship exists, and has been manifested, between them,—what a mass of contrivances to produce that fellowship, to fill up the chasm between the visible and the invisible world, would be swept away! What portentous superstitions, what dark idolatries, would vanish if once that faith,—not the faith of her enemies, but her own,—was really accepted, honestly carried out!

I pressed this point in my Essay on Regeneration; but I could not then speak of the faith which the Romish Church professes to have in an in-dwelling Spirit, a Spirit of truth, and love, and power, which is to bind all together in one and enable her to rule the nations. I could not then point out what the contradiction was between this profession and her adoption of those practices of the conjuror, which the miracles of the Gospel were intended to explode; of the practices of the diplomatist, from which she ought to have delivered the nations, instead of setting the vilest example of them; of the practices of the hard-hearted worldly oppressor, crushing the spirit under the flesh, the conscience under casuistry, the reason under decrees, when she was sent to teach men of a Father who had claimed them as His sons, of a Son who was at His right hand for them, of a Spirit who was within them to make them inheritors of His glory. I could not then show how great the sin was which she had committed in assuming that St. Peter, or any successor of his, could be *the* Father of the Church, how necessarily such a fiction divides earth from heaven, and makes the Church into a world.

Like the Angelo of our great dramatist, the deputy of a true ruler has played his tyrannical and hypocritical tricks, punishing others for the crimes which he commits himself, often betraying the innocence which he is commissioned to protect. But, as that same story teaches us, the Duke is not really absent from his government, but is watching, counteracting, bringing to an altogether different issue, the plots of his agent. See how the Papal history in its most palmy moment bears witness of that fact. The policy of Innocent III. was so mysterious and so perfect, that a modern German historian, through admiration of it, is said to have abandoned the faith of his childhood. 'What but a divine power,' he and others have argued, 'could have enabled a man 'to rule the world as Innocent did; to guide at the 'same moment the Latin kingdom in Greece, which he 'did not assist in establishing, but which he knew so 'well how to use when it was established; to nurse a 'young monarch for Germany, who might hereafter 'make the Empire the tool of the Papacy; to set his foot 'on the prostrate monarch of England?' A wonderful spectacle assuredly; but there is another as well worthy of our study. Is it not as clear an evidence of a divine government in the world, that all these exquisite plots came to nothing; that the reviving energies of Greece so soon shattered the Latin kingdom in pieces; that Frederic II. became, not the instrument of Popes, but their most hated enemy and scourge; that Stephen Langton, forced into his see by interdicts and excommunications, became the assertor of English independence, the punisher of the monarch who betrayed his trust, the author of the Charter? Is it not as great a proof of a spiritual power in the world, that the feeble Francis of Assisi, by the one thought that Christ is the friend of the poor, did so much more to preserve and extend the Church,—even to support the Papacy itself,—than the hundred-handed Pope, with all his resources of outward strength and unrivalled craft? Is it nothing that Louis IX., because he was a faithful national sovereign who loved justice, was felt to be such a saint as no Pope had ever been?

Thus, then, every oppression and crime that has been rightly imputed to Rome, has arisen from her not confessing in deed, as she has confessed in words, that a Spirit has appeared to build up a one Holy Catholic Church. Every healthful influence she has ever exercised,—or Christian men and women have ever exercised in her name,—has proceeded from that belief.

And may not all the sins, which, with no less truth, have been imputed to Protestant National Churches, be traced to the same unbelief; all that has been good to the same faith? Have they erred from their too great patriotism, their too zealous determination not to give it up for emperor or pope, for man or devil; from their fixed purpose that no religion whatever should rob them of their common morality, or persuade them to do evil for the sake of pleasing God? No; but they have erred in not thinking that the Spirit of God was with them, to enable them to maintain their national steadfastness, to fulfil their common duties, to support their love of truth against the temptations which are continually overpowering it; to purify their patriotism of exclusiveness, their zeal for the plain and the practical, of sordidness; to enable them to feel that all citizens of the same commonwealth, however different their ranks and civil positions, are, in the highest sense, equal; to give them the freedom, the manliness, the sympathy with those of other races, which selfishness is taking from them.

And why have those sects I spoke of become so partial, so hard, so cruel? Is it because their forefathers were wrong in telling them that the Spirit was seeking to bind them in one, and that no mere external bond could bind them? Surely not; this lesson taken home to the heart, makes men first true, in due time Catholic, leading them to cling mightily to the special conviction God has wrought in them, afterwards enabling them to feel the necessity of other convictions to sustain that. It is the *loss* of this faith, it is the substitution of some petty external badge and symbol of theirs, for the belief and confession of a Divine Spirit, which is making them impatient of dogmas, yet fiercely dogmatic; eager to rob other men of their treasures; feeble in their hold upon their own. It is this which tempts their sons to ask whether the earth has no other foundations than those which the sects have laid, often to arrive at the miserable conclusion that its foundations are built on rottenness.

But it is not so! however much excuse they may have for suspecting it. There has no promise of Scripture been proved nugatory; there is none which has not been fulfilled more than men dreamed of, which will not be fulfilled to the very letter. I have said there were liars and murmurers in the Church at Jerusalem. The promise was not, that there should not be these in the time to come. Every form of corruption and heresy was discovered by St. Paul in the Churches to which he wrote. There was no pledge given, that these should not appear in the later time. St. John said there were many Antichrists in his day. It is no stumbling-block to our faith, if there are many in ours. But it would be the utter uprooting of our faith if we found that there was no such body as the Apostles told us there should be, with which all lying and contention should be at war; if there was no Spirit dwelling in that body against which these heresies and corruptions and Antichrists are fighting, and which will at last prevail against them. Romanists, Protestant nations, all sects, declare that there is such a body, and that there is such a Spirit. Their words bear witness of it; their crimes, which outrage those words, bear witness of it still more.

And thus we are enabled to understand better than by all artificial definitions, how a Church differs from a world. '*The Comforter*,' our Lord says, '*shall convince the world.*' When He speaks to the disciples, He says, '*He shall come and dwell in you.*' The world contains the elements of which the Church is composed. In the Church, these elements are penetrated by a uniting, reconciling power. The Church is, therefore, human society in its normal state; the World, that same society irregular and abnormal. The world is the Church without God; the Church is the world restored to its relation with God, taken back by Him into the state for which He created it. Deprive the Church of its Centre, and you make it into a world. If you give it a false Centre, as the Romanists have done, still preserving the sacraments, forms, creeds, which speak of the true Centre, there necessarily comes out that grotesque hybrid which we witness, a world assuming all the dignity and authority of a Church,—a Church practising all the worst fictions of a world; the world assuming to be heavenly,—a Church confessing itself to be of the earth, earthly.

From this contradiction a number of others proceed: I will take one which will serve as the specimen of a whole class. The doctrine, *Nulla salus extra Ecclesiam*, sounds the cruellest of all doctrines; it has become so in fact. But consider the origin of it. A man possessed with the conviction that human beings are not meant to live in a world where every one is divided from his neighbour,—in which there is no uniting, fusing principle, in which each lives to himself, and for himself,—bids them fly from that chaos. For he cries, 'There is 'a universe for you! Nay, more, there is a Father's 'house open to you. God is not the frowning, distant 'tyrant the world takes Him to be; not split up into a 'multitude of broken forms and images; not One to 'whom we are to offer a cold civil lip service, by way 'of conciliating Him or doing Him honour. He is the 'Head of a family; His Son has proved you to be 'members of it; His Spirit is given you that you may 'know Him as He is, not as your hard material hearts 'represent Him to you. Come into this Ark! Take 'up your place in this Family! Here is deliverance and 'health! *Nulla salus extra Ecclesiam.* No comfort, 'no health, no peace, while you count yourselves exiles 'from God, strangers to your brethren.'

Is this a hard saying? Is it not full of gentleness, benignity, love? But the Church becomes a world-Church; a Church that speaks of a Father in Heaven, and sets up a Father on earth; that introduces earthly mediators because the Mediator has gone away, and it is needful to make Him propitious; that boasts itself to be endued with a Spirit of truth, and can only exhibit the powers of the Spirit in doing untrue acts: then the phrase necessarily assumes, not a different meaning from this, but one that is directly opposite to it. '*Nulla salus extra Ecclesiam!* God is ready to 'destroy you. We can save you from Him. Think 'what a risk you are incurring. You may be wrong! 'Then perdition is certain.' Oh, doctrine of devils, if such is to be found in earth or in hell! Surely, Salvation and Damnation become identical, if the soul is saved by the loss of its trust in God, by conceiving Him to be like those demons from whom the Apostles said that Christ came to deliver mankind, as unlike as possible to the perfect image which was shown forth in Him!

We cannot, however, cast stones at the Romanists, for adopting this notion of safety. We have fallen into it almost as much as they have. It belongs especially to our money-getting habits. If some wander from our Church to Rome, because they believe that, on the whole, they have a better chance of escaping destruction there, we have ourselves to blame; we have sown the wind of selfishness, and we must reap the whirlwind of desertion. But it would be a great mistake and injustice, to suppose that the selfish motive is the exclusive one, even in the worst cases, or the predominant one in any better men. Love and Selfishness are strangely, inextricably blended. The true idea of Safety is mixed with its accursed counterfeit. They long for a larger fellowship, a Father's house, a Spirit who can make them brothers with all men, Greeks, Romanists, Protestants. The wish may be shrivelled and contracted by a thousand causes; but it is there; and if we cannot gratify it,—if we cannot tell them that they are inheritors of Christ's kingdom in earth and heaven, and that the Spirit of the Father and Son is with them—in order that the inheritance may not be a nominal, but a real one,—

we shall not keep them, we ought not to keep them. They will try whether that blessing which our creeds and prayers assure them is theirs, can be obtained elsewhere; and if they meet with bitter disappointment, or take up with a wretched substitute for the infinite good which God has taught them to feel necessary, is not our unbelief the cause? And is not the only way of preserving our National Church, to declare solemnly, habitually, perseveringly, that it does bear this witness not for itself alone, but on behalf of the Romanist and the Protestant Sectarian? yes! that it is ready to make any sacrifices if it can but bear that witness effectually?

I do not indeed say that this witness must come from us alone, perhaps not from us chiefly. Let it come from where it will, God must be the author of it. He may see fit to bring this truth with mighty power to the heart of some Italian monk, who has been seeking in vain to make himself holy, and discovers that holiness must come from a Spirit of Holiness, who is also a Spirit of Unity. It may come to some Romish Bishop as he listens to the *Veni Creator Spiritus*, and believes that the sevenfold gifts are intended for him. It may come to some earnest member of a Protestant sect, feeling that the Spirit of Truth cannot be the Spirit of narrowness. It may come to some man lying outside of all churches and sects, and asking whether he can be intended to be only a part of an unsympathising, forlorn world. To whichever it comes first, the faith will pass rapidly, as by an electrical chain, from one to another. It will break through all barriers of opinion and circumstance. None will know how he has received it, because all will have received it from that Spirit who bloweth where He listeth, and of whom you cannot say whence He cometh or whither He goeth.

But seeing that what appear to us the most irregular currents obey a fixed and eternal law, we may be sure that that Spirit will work as He has always worked; that He will change nothing and yet will make all things new. That mighty wonder which we behold every year when the self-same roots and stems, which were the symbols of all that is hard, and dry, and separate, become clothed with verdure, full of life, and joy, and music, will be exhibited in the moral world. No form will be cast away, no ordinance will be treated as worthless, nothing which has expressed the thought or belief of any man will be found unmeaning, because the Spirit of the living God will call forth every sleeping and latent power into activity, everything that has been dead into life, all that has been divided into harmony. Only the miserable counterfeits will pass away. Whatever has been true, if it has been ever so weak and broken, will find its place in that creation which God has declared to be very good.

But have I not spoken again and again in this Essay of a Father, a Son, and a Spirit? Has not all my comfort in the past, my hope for the future, been connected with the revelation of that Name, with the full acknowledgment of it? Even so, my Unitarian brother. And all the longings you have for fellowship, and freedom, and unity, for the breaking down of barriers, for a universal comprehension, point the same way. I have not deceived you by pretending to agree with you where I cannot. I am more entirely at issue with you in your denials than those who denounce you most. I have come now to the root of all your denials, to that Name which *I* believe to be the ground of human life, and of human society. If you have borne with me so far—considering many of my words, no doubt, enthusiastical, antiquated, obscure, foolish, yet still I hope now and then detecting a sense in them which answers to a sense in you,—will you listen while I tell you why I could not believe that a Trinity in Unity is a foundation for myself to rest upon, if I did not also regard it as a foundation for you and for all men?

ESSAY XVI.

ON THE TRINITY IN UNITY.

My first Essay was on *Charity;* this will also be on Charity. I could not find that a charity which believed all things, hoped all things, endured all things, had its root on this earth, or in the heart of any man who dwells on this earth. Yet it seemed to me that such a Charity was needed to make this earth what it ought to be, and that human hearts have a profound sense of its necessity for them, an infinite craving to possess it, and be filled with it. Something stood in the way of the good which the earth sighs for, and which man sighs for. A vision of *Sin* rose up before us confronting the vision of Charity. It was portentous, for it seemed part of the very creature who had the dream of a perfect good. But he disclaimed it, he tried to account for it by some accidents of his position, or by some essential error in his constitution; at last he said, I have yielded to an oppressor; an *Evil Spirit* has withdrawn me from my true Lord. Then arose the question, Who is this true Lord?

where is He to be found? *Righteousness* was felt to be even more closely intertwined with the being of the man than Evil; for awhile he was disposed to claim it as his own; suffering, and the sense of an infinite contradiction, did not deliver him from that belief. But some one there was who led him to cry for a *Redeemer*, to be sure that He lived, to be sure that Righteousness was in Him, and therefore was Man's.

Was this Redeemer, so near to man, so inseparable from man, of earthly race? The vision of a *Son of God* rose upon us; a thousand different traditions pointed to it; it took the most various forms; but the heart of man said, 'There must be one in whom all these meet; there 'must be One who did not rise from manhood into God-'head, but who can exhibit the perfection of manhood, 'because he has the perfection of Godhead.' Is the perfection of manhood then compatible with the infirmities and corruptions of which men have become heirs? The mythologies of the world said, 'It must be so, we 'need *Incarnations;* our deliverers must share our flesh, 'our sorrows;' yes! they could not stop there—'our 'sins.' The philosophers said, 'It cannot be so; the 'Divine Nature must be free from the contact of that 'which debases us, of that from which we ourselves need 'emancipation.' They could show how men, forming the Gods after their own images, had glorified and deified what was most immoral and base. The Scripture spoke to us of the Son of God taking the flesh of man, entering into all the infirmities of man, bearing the sins of man, so showing forth the purity, compassion, love, of His Father.

But the sense in men of a separation from the God to whom they were meant to be united, had, we found, produced innumerable schemes for bringing about a reconciliation. The Scriptures told us of an *Atonement*, originating with God; made with men in His Son; who entirely trusted and entirely obeyed His Father; who willingly entered into the death of man; who made the perfect Sacrifice which took away Sin; whose death was the satisfaction to the Divine Love of the Father; the expression of that wrath against Evil which is a part of Love; the satisfaction of man's yearnings for reconciliation with God. Yet *Death, the Grave, the Abyss beyond*, are the dark contradictions for human beings; He could not be a perfect deliverer who had not entered into them, or who remained under their power. The idea of a bodily *Resurrection*, we found, had been accepted by men, not as a fact to be attested by a great amount of evidence, but as the inevitable issue of the previous revelation. If there is a Son of God, a Lord of man, He *must* rise. What did such a Resurrection imply? The Scripture speaks of it as implying a *Justification* of Gentile as well as of Jew; that is, of every man, who might therefore believe in Christ and acquire His Righteousness. We saw how Christians had evaded this declaration, and the evidence of it which their baptism offered, limiting the blessing by certain rules and measures of theirs, even using the witness of it as an excuse for doubt, and for new efforts of their own to make themselves righteous; then, at last, discovering that faith in God's Justification is the only condition of doing any good acts. But this faith of each individual man, that God had justified him by the Resurrection of Christ, and was inviting him to habitual trust, implied something more. We discovered in the belief of Christians the acknowledgment of a *Regeneration*, effected not for individual men merely, but for human society in the true Lord and Head of it.

This belief, however feebly and imperfectly held by the Church, had nevertheless vindicated itself by the experience of history, and enabled us to reconcile the doctrines of eminent moralists respecting the constitution of man, with the fullest admission of actual departures from it. For, if the Resurrection of Christ declared that men, in spite of all that seemed to put them at a distance from God, were recognised by him as his children on earth, the *Ascension* of Christ in their nature proclaimed that they did not belong to earth; that they were spiritual beings, capable of holding converse with Him who is a Spirit; able to do so, because that Son who had taken their flesh, and had offered it up to God, and had glorified it, had said that His body and blood should be their food and nourishment. This belief of the Ascension as the great triumph for man, was greatly shaken by a prevalent notion that Christ, being absent now and not exercising the functions of royalty or judgment, will assume them at some distant day; and be subject again to earthly limitations. It was therefore needful to show, that the *Judgment* spoken of in the Bible and the Creed, implied the continual presence of Christ, the daily exposure of men and nations to His cognisance and censure, the assurance that He will be manifested, not in some humbler condition, but as He is, to the consciences and eyes of men; for the putting down of all evil, and the establishment of righteousness. But though the minds of men had always felt that they must look upwards to some Ruler above them, they had equally confessed the presence of an Inspirer within them. The Christian revelation, we found, corresponded as much to these anticipations, as to any which we had considered before. It explained to us whence all *Inspirations* had proceeded, who was the Author of them, how they are to be received, how they may be abused. The full Revelation, with that which was the preparation for it, had been recorded to us in a book which had been the treasure of the Church, the witness of the emancipation of mankind, the assurance of a *Comforter* who should come to the ages following Christ's Ascension, in a way He had not come to those which preceded it. I inquired whether events have justified this assurance. I endeavoured to show that there had been such a sense of sin, of righteousness, and of judgment in the later periods of the world's history, as cannot be traced in the earlier, and as could only have proceeded from the teaching of a *Person*, such as our Lord describes to us. But finally, we were told this Person would not only convince a world, but be the establisher of a *One Holy Catholic Church.* The difficulty of accepting this statement was very great. A certain body had claimed to be the one Catholic Church, a number of bodies had claimed to be Churches; they had denounced each other; there had been that in all which contradicted the idea the Scripture sets forth of holiness, unity, universality. But this contradiction showed that the Scripture had revealed the true law of human society; for that one body and these different bodies had not become partial, tyrannical, godless by maintaining too strongly that Earth and Heaven had been reconciled, and that the Spirit had come down from the Father and the Son to establish that reconciliation; but by acting as if Heaven and Earth were still separated, as if we had still to effect for ourselves that which the Scripture declares that God has effected, as if there were no Spirit to unite us with the Father and the Son, and with each other. To this cause,—no other was adequate,—we could trace the want of holiness, catholicity, unity in the Church. This unbelief being removed, all that man has dreamed of, all that God has promised, must be accomplished.

I have not, then, to enter upon a new subject in this Essay. I am not speaking for the first time, of the

Trinity in Unity. I have been speaking of it throughout. Each consciousness that we have discovered in man, each fact of Revelation that has answered to it, has been a step in the discovery and demonstration of this truth. I should be abandoning the method to which I have endeavoured strictly to adhere, if I admitted that now, at last, I have come upon a mere dogma, which had no support but tradition, or inferences from texts of Scripture; or, on the other hand, upon a great philosophical tenet which wise men may deduce from reason or find latent in nature, but with which the poor wayfarer has nothing to do. We may owe much to tradition for giving expression to the faith in a Trinity; texts of Scripture may confirm it; the context of Scripture may bring it out in beautiful harmony with all the divine discoveries to man. Philosophy may have seen indications of a Trinity in the forms and principles of the universe, in the constitution of man himself. But unless we are utterly inconsistent with all that has been said hitherto, these can be but indexes and guides to a Name which is implied in our thoughts, acts, words, in our fellowship with each other; without which we cannot explain the utterances of the poorest peasant, or of the greatest sage; which makes thoughts real, prayers possible; which brings distinctness out of vagueness, unity out of division; which shows us how in fact, and not merely in imagination, the charity of God may find its reflex and expression in the charity of man, and the charity of man its substance as well as its fruition in the charity of God. What I have to do in this Essay, then, is certainly not to bring forward arguments against those who impugn this doctrine, but only to show how each portion of that Name into which we are baptized, answers to some apprehension and anticipation of human beings; how the setting up of one part of the Name against another has been the cause of strife, unrighteousness, superstition; why, therefore, the acknowledgment of that Name in its fulness and Unity, is Eternal Life.

I. It often seems to us a great contradiction in Greek Mythology, that the chief of the Gods should be represented as himself subject to Fate. We do not enough consider what a real and deep comfort the Polytheist found in this thought. A ruler of the Elements might have in himself all the vicissitudes which nature exhibits. If he were like a human sovereign, he might have all the caprices of a human sovereign. This faith in Necessity told the Greek that the Universe was not after all, dependent on those natural vicissitudes or human caprices, that a law fixed and unchangeable was beneath them all. At times, it seemed to him as if Jove, the king of earth, was chaining down all the aspirations of man, was fastening to a rock, and tormenting with a vulture, the champions who sought to do him good, to make him freer and wiser. What a relief to think that Destiny had determined the period of this captivity, and of the tyranny which had imposed it! And yet there were times when the sense of a hard, dry, iron rule,—an irresistible necessity,—became more intolerable than the government of the most uncertain king; when the heart fled from that as a horrible oppression, to this as human and sympathetic. Especially these words, 'Father of Gods and men,' touched chords which at once responded to them. There was the hint of something not only more friendly than Fate, but more mighty. The will in man leaps up to acknowledge a Will that is akin to its own, and that may govern it.

Through all the Jewish History, fixed law, grounded on the name of the I AM, had been coming forth in conjunction with a course of discipline which the God of Abraham, Isaac, and Jacob was declared by prophets and holy men to be carrying on for the children of His Covenant. The Law asserted that which was right; nothing could alter it; to violate it was death. The Judge of the whole earth was doing right; His design was to make His people right. Christ on the Mountain announced the Will of which that law was the expression. He said it was the Will of a Father. Here is the root and substance of His revelation. He does not proclaim a Will which dispenses with law or changes it, but that absolutely righteous and true Will of which it affirms the existence, but which it cannot make effectual. And this Will is the Will of the Father. Beneath the name of the God of Abraham, this was concealed. The sound of it was from time to time caught, not only by holy men in their closets, but by the ordinary worshipper. The Greek heard the echo of it from his Thessalian hill. Christ uttered it.

For those who receive His message, the two conceptions which were always fighting with each other, always trying to be one, are actually united. There is the perfect rest which comes from the thought that there can be no caprice in the order of the Universe,—that right can never become wrong, or wrong right; there is the comfort that no hard fate controls caprice, that the Divine Will excludes it. The fixed and the absolute which man craves for as the support of his being, and of all creation, is there. It is bound inseparably with a name which speaks of Relation, which tells him what he was sure must be; that his own Will has an author; that he is not merely a creature of the highest God, but a child.

All is peace if we accept this as a Revelation,—as a Gospel from God. Reduce it again into the conceptions of your own mind,—make your anticipations, not the *test*, *that* they must be, but the *measure* of the Revelation,—and all becomes war again. An iron necessity for the nineteenth century after Christ, as much as for all before it, becomes that to which you refer the world's life and your own. It is your best comfort to do so. And yet it is such miserable comfort that you will be continually seeking a refuge from it. The vision of some present helper,—some one to whom you can address cries and litanies,—rises up whether your philosophy has taught you to banish it or not. To such a one you will give the name of Father; it will seem the most natural name; you will feel that you must use it, or that your words die in the utterance. But that name will be associated, as it was among old Polytheists, with thoughts of the clouds and the changes of Nature; if your heart insists upon more human associations, then with the turbulence and irregularity you find in yourself. Deal honestly with your own experiences,—it is all I ask,—and then say whether the old name, the *given* name, is not that which you need, and which you are trying to spell out. You are sure it is there: it must be very near to you. But speculaion does not bring it nearer. The child must confess its Father, and confess itself to Him; then it knows whose Will rules it, and with what Will it has been striving.

All our past inquiries into the superstitions of the Christian world have brought us to the same conclusion. From whatever quarter they have proceeded, their tendency has been the same. The notion of a sovereign Necessity has taken the place of a Will of absolute truth and goodness; the notion of a capricious Power to be made placable by some agency of ours has superseded the belief in a Father, whose will Christ came on earth to manifest and to fulfil. Each opinion gives birth to the other as a deliverance from it; one is supposed to be more philosophical, the other more practical, than our Baptismal Faith; that remains as a refuge for those who have found the first utterly offensive to their reason, the second subversive of their morality. The more simply it is proclaimed, the less pains we take to sustain it by our proofs,—the more it will commend itself to the hearts that are needing it. If we substitute for a belief in a Father a belief in a notion of ours about a Father, we shall turn a confession which should be the greatest witness that the Kingdom of Heaven has been opened to all, into a means of excluding our brethren as well as ourselves from it.

II. There can be no Mediator between a man and a mere Fate or Necessity. A multitude of mediators will be conceived between a man and the capricious Power who seems to be dealing with him at his pleasure. These mediators will be all, more or less distinctly, felt to be the helpers of the creatures against their Creator; they may be regarded as having some natural relationship to him, or as having by some merit obtained an influence or a right over him; but they will be always the benignant patrons of those whom he is disposed, for some reason, to injure. When the word 'Father' has taken any strong hold of a man anywhere, when it has displaced the notion of a mere sovereign, there will be a counteraction to this feeling. Those who plead for man with Him, must be felt *in some sense* to express His mind; they will be acknowledged as His sons. But this counteraction, though great, will be inadequate till we have learnt the lesson of which I was speaking just now,—the lesson that the Will of this Father is as steadfast as any Fate can be; that its steadfastness consists in its righteousness; that there cannot be variableness in it, because it is good, and can only seek to do good. This Will demands that which the Necessity excludes. It must speak, it must utter itself. A Will cannot be without a *Word*. A Will that is, and lives, must utter itself by a living Word. This is what St. John, in his divine theology, declares to us. But if he speaks in one sentence of a Word, he speaks in the next of a Son. The names are used interchangeably; but we should, I believe, lose more than we know, if either had been used exclusively. Experience has shown that those who determinately prefer the first, soon fall into that notion of a mere emanation from some mysterious abyss of Divinity, which haunted the oriental mystics and the early heretics, or else into the notion of a mere principle indwelling in man. The Word becomes impersonal: the Will becomes impersonal: very soon the man forgets that he is a person himself, and becomes a mere dreamer or speculator. The blessed name of Son, which connects itself with all human sympathies and relationships, is the deliverance from this phantom region. While we cleave to it, we can never forget that only a Person can express the Will of the Absolute Being; that only in a Person He can see His own image. But the Son of God will soon be merged for us in the Son of Man,—we shall refer His relationship to ours, not ours to His,—if we do not recur to that other name, if we do not, by meditating upon it, save ourselves from the unspeakable dangers into which those fall who think of the Son only as their Saviour, and not as the brightness of His Father's glory. Both these perils are besetting us now as much as they beset any former age. I think they are besetting us more; often when we are not conscious of either as a theological tendency, it is affecting our moral and social feelings, and our ordinary acts, in innumerable ways.

There is an abstract way of thinking about the Son of God which is hurrying some of us into Pantheism, and multitudes partake of the effect who are not in the least alive to the cause. There is a popular way of thinking about the Son of God, which is hurrying us into idolatry; and parents are startled at seeing their children fall over a precipice, to the edge of which they have walked under their guidance. Nor do I see how either evil can be averted if we do not more earnestly consider what is involved in the faith of little children; whether the name of the Son into which we are baptized is not our redemption from all vagueness, and from all partial, separate, self-seeking worship, a witness that we are adopted into Him as members of His body, and must therefore seek the things that are above, where He sitteth at the right hand of God. This faith is not notional, but practical; not for this and that man, but for mankind. If we were forced to form conceptions about a Son of God, or Son of Man, there would be a perpetual strife of intellects; there could be no consent; each man must think differently from his neighbour, must try to establish his own thought against his neighbour's. If He is revealed to us as the ground of our intellects,—the creative Word of God from whom they derive their light: as the centre of our fellowship, the only-begotten Son of God, in whom we are made sons of God; the weary effort is over; our thoughts may travel to the ends of the earth, but here is their home; apart from Him men have infinite disagreements; in Him they have peace.

III. A mere Fate or Necessity of course communicates no life or energy to those who are the subjects of it. Life and energy are excluded from the very idea of Necessity. A Ruler or Lord of Nature may impart powers or energies to particular men. It will be the great sign of his favouring them, above others, that he does so. A free and imaginative people like the Greeks would account it a much greater proof of a man's being dear to the Gods, that he was able to perform rare achievements, and exhibit unusual wit and prowess, than that he possessed houses and land, and an outward good fortune. High gifts were felt, as I showed before, to indicate an Inspirer, and that Inspirer was acknowledged to have descended from the highest God. Here, again, the name of Father greatly modified the previous belief. The gift of Inspiration was generally taken as an evidence that the man who received it stood in some real relation to the Divine Power; it was not *merely* bestowed from choice or favouritism, it was a kind of inheritance.

The moment a Will drives out a Fate, an absolute will to good, mere irresistible decrees, the belief that this Will must seek to make other wills like its own, forces itself upon us. '*This is the will of God, even your sanctification*,' becomes the deepest conviction of the reason.

At first these words may be reflected on with much inward satisfaction, without any great awe. But when a man remembers that holiness, in its fullest sense, holiness as involving truth and love by involving separation from what is false and unlovely, must be the innermost nature of God, he may well wonder and tremble while he hears that of this, it is the will of God to make him partaker. This gift is so amazing, so essential, that he is utterly baffled when he tries to meditate how he can ever be possessed of it. Can he become a God? While he dreamed of God as a being of mere power, he might dream also of measuring his own power with His. But as soon as the belief of God's holiness has at all entered into him, his desire is to sink rather than to rise. The consciousness of his pride is that which alarms him most. And that pride haunts him perpetually. If he became the most abject of men, he feels as if he should be proud of that abjectness,—more proud than he had ever been before. This is a perplexity concerning himself; there is another concerning God. It is wonderful that the inmost life of God should be communicated; but it would be a contradiction that it should not be communicated. We cannot think of a Being of perfect love as wrapt up in Himself, as dwelling in the contemplation of His own excellence and perfection; we can as little think of His being satisfied with any lower excellence or perfection. The belief of a Spirit proceeding from the Father and the Son, meets both the human and the divine difficulty. To think of the Father resting in the Son, in the deepest sense knowing the Son, and of the Son knowing the Father, we must think of a uniting Spirit. And if there is such a Spirit, it must be capable of being imparted; that must be the way in which holiness is imparted. And if this gift comes to men through the Son, we are sure that the Spirit which they receive must be the Spirit of lowliness, and meekness, and obedience. We are sure that it cannot be a Spirit which exalts any one man above his fellow. It must bring all to a level. In so far as they confess it to be the Spirit of a Father, they must confess that it is meant to make them Sons of God; in so far as they confess that it is the Spirit of Christ, they confess that it is meant to make them brothers. But the more this Spirit quickens them, the more they will delight to own it as distinct from them; the more our Lord's words respecting a Comforter will seem to them the truest and fullest of all; the more they will be compelled to feel that there is a Divine Person with them to whom they owe reverence and worship.

So wonderfully,—if our baptismal faith is true,—are Divinity and Humanity blended; so awfully are they distinguished. Each step in the revelation of the distinct Persons comes out to meet and satisfy some infinite need of man; some witness which has been awakened within him of his own grandeur, and of his own weakness; of his belonging to a society, and of his being an individual; of his dwelling in a world, subject to all the accidents of time; of his right to a state that is free from these accidents. The more near he is brought to God, the greater he feels is the necessity for adoration and worship; while he contemplates Him at a distance there is terror, but not reverence or awe.

And it is equally true that while he beholds Him at a distance from himself, as the heathen did, and as we are always prone to do, there can be no acknowledgment of His Unity. As long as a Jove, or some Lord of Nature is worshipped, he must be divided into a multitude of forms. The conception of such a being shows what a need the heart and reason have of Unity, but also how impossible it is for them to find it, or create it for themselves. The multitude of forms which we behold in the world will make, in spite of all reasonings and theories, a multitude of world-gods; it is only when we ask in wonder whence we ourselves are; to what law we are subject; in whom it is that we are living, and moving, and having our being; who is guiding us; whither he would lead us; that we begin to escape from darkness into light, from division into Unity. When the Gospel was preached, when the name of the Father, the Son, and the Holy Ghost, was uttered, when men had been baptized into it, idols fell down; the worship of the visible became intolerable; the sense of Unity profound. The separation of that name has been in all ages since, the secret of division, the commencement of idolatry. If we watched our own minds more we should find that it is so with them. We have sometimes fancied we could dwell simply on the thought of a Father; all others should be discarded as unnecessary. But soon it has not been a Father we have contemplated, it has been a mere substratum of the things we saw, a name under which we collected them. How rejoiced is the heart to pass from such a cold void to the thought of a Son filled with all human sympathies! But how soon does the sin-sick soul frame a thousand images and pictures of its own as a substitute for the perfect Image; dream of Mediators closer and more gracious than the One who died for all! What a relief to fly from these fancies to a Divine Spirit! How we wonder that we should ever have thought that God could be anywhere but in the contrite heart and pure! Alas, the heart does not long remain contrite and pure! Its holiness disappears: then the Object of its worship disappears; for that Object was becoming more and more itself. And the man either is content with that miserable condition, and amuses himself with high phrases about humanity to hide the facts of it from his own conscience; or he asks for some mortal to tell him what he should believe, because he discovers that he has come to believe nothing.

He will find many ready to meet that craving. He will hear voices saying to him, 'To what a condition 'you have reduced yourself by forsaking the one safe 'guide, the only teacher who can enable you to obtain 'Eternal Life! For does not Christ say that we can 'only obtain eternal life by knowing God and Him? 'And what knowledge, what *certainty*, have you on 'these subjects? How can you get that certainty unless 'there is an infallible guide who will say to you, This 'is true, believe it?' What a powerful, almost irresistible, argument to one who fancied that he believed everything, and is beginning to find that he scarcely believes in a God! And if the new teacher could restore him *that* belief, what else does he want, what might he not sacrifice for such a gift? But can that be, when he begins with assuming our Lord to have uttered words which He never did utter, and which directly set at nought His actual words? He did not say, 'Men 'obtain eternal life by knowing God;' but, '*This is life eternal, that they may know Thee, the only true God, and Jesus Christ whom thou hast sent.*' The knowledge does not procure the life, but the knowledge constitutes the life.

We fancy we attach a distinct meaning to these words,

Eternal Life; they are such precious words, that every one tries to form some notion of them. But surely if there is any subject on which we want a guide, an infallible guide, it is on this. We feel that we are under a law of change and succession, that we live in days, and months, and years. We feel also that we have to do with that which is not changeable, which cannot be represented by any divisions of time. A long life, the poet says, may be curdled into an hour. Every great and serious event of our lives has taught us that this is so. We experience the utter vanity and emptiness of chronology as a measure of suffering, of thought, of hope, of love. All these belong to another state of things. We perceive that Scripture is speaking to us of that state of things; that it is educating us into the apprehension of it. The more we attend to the New Testament, the more we find to confirm the witness of our reason, that eternity is not a lengthening out or continuation of time; that they are generically different; as St. Paul so beautifully expresses it, '*that which we see is temporal; that which we do not see is eternal.*' The spiritual world,—we are obliged to confess it in a thousand ways,—is not subject to temporal conditions. This is no discovery of philosophers. Every peasant knows it as well as Newton. If you have listened with earnestness to the questions of a child, you may often think that it knows more of eternity than of time. The succession of years confounds it; it mixes the dates which it has been instructed in most strangely; but its intuition of something which is beyond all dates makes you marvel. Scripture, in like manner, illustrates and makes clear our own thoughts about Life and Death. It teaches us to think that the healthy activity of all our powers and perceptions, and their direction to their right object, is the living state; that the torpor of these, or their concentration on themselves, is a state of Death.

With these hints, which every day's reading of the Scriptures, by an earnest student, will multiply and expand, what need we have of some direct words to bring together the two thoughts of Eternity and of Life. If I spoke of *defining* Eternal Life, I should feel, and I think all would feel, that I was using an improper word; for how can we define that which is out of the limits of time? But in the depth of prayer and communion with His Father, our Lord gives us that which corresponds to the most accurate and divine definition, an exposition which we are bound henceforth, if we reverence His authority, to apply on all occasions, and to use as the correction of our loose and vague conceptions. Instead of picturing to ourselves some future bliss, calling that eternal life, and determining the worth of it by a number of years, or centuries, or millenniums, we are bound to say once for all: 'This is the eternal life, that which Christ has 'brought with Him, that which we have in Him, the 'knowledge of God; the entering into His mind and 'character, the knowing Him as we only can know any 'person, by sympathy, fellowship, love.' And so the meaning and order of the Divine revelation become evident to us; God has been declaring Himself to us that we might know Him, because He would have us partakers of this eternal life. And the final Revelation, that which is expressed in our Baptismal name, tells us what all the experience of ourselves and of the world tells us also, that unless the Spirit of the Father and the Son were with us, we could not break loose from the fetters of Time, the confusions of Sense, the narrowness of Selfishness; that if we yield to that Spirit we can have fellowship with those who are nigh and those who are far off; with men of every habit, colour, opinion; with those whom the veil of flesh divides from us; with Him who is the Perfect Charity; with the Father and the Son who dwell in the Unity of one blessed and eternal Spirit.

Many Unitarians still think as their fathers did, that the idea of a Trinity involves an utter contradiction,—that every rational man must reject it. Many of them are aware that some of the deepest minds in the world have felt that the acknowledgment of a Trinity was necessary to their reason. But they are careful to observe that *this* is not the Trinity of which we speak; if they should ever come to accept *a* Trinity as a portion of their belief they would still, they say, not be stooping to a creed. That act would be a sign of Progress, not of retrogression; they would welcome a discovery of philosophy, not surrender themselves to a religious tradition.

Such language is lofty; I would beseech every earnest Unitarian to consider whether it is wise. Does he mean by a discovery of philosophy, the discovery of a verbal formula? If he does, I must leave him to any advantage he may get from it, only reminding him that *he* has now become the worshipper of formulas; that he cannot henceforth cast that charge upon us. But if it is a *truth* he discovers, may it not be a truth for mankind? And may not a living and true God have taken some way of making that truth known to the creatures whom He has made capable of knowing it? When we speak of a Creed which may be taught and believed, we say that He has done this. We say that in Christ the Trinity is revealed substantially. It is not a doctrine, unless it is more than a doctrine. Either real Persons are declared to us, or nothing is declared about those Persons. Either a real Unity is declared, or nothing is made known to us about a Unity. Supposing philosophy to have perceived a Trinity, or the shadow, or the hint of one, it cannot appropriate this perception to itself,—any more than Gravitation is a truth which Newton could appropriate to himself. The philosopher must ask to what reality the perception or intuition corresponds; of what substance that which he sees is the shadow. No one is bound to assume the position of a philosopher; few have any call to assume it; but supposing a man becomes one, this must be the condition of his work:—he must seek for that which is human and universal; for Truth itself, not for some image of it or some logical expression of it. And he must ask how truth in this sense,—truth as the equivalent of substance or being,—can be made known, so that all shall be partakers of it. I leave that thought to the modern Unitarian philosopher. I would not have him abandon his task, if he thinks that he is appointed to it. I would have him pursue it steadily. For I believe he will find that the philosopher must ascend to knowledge by the same steps as the man; that if he is to find truth, God must reveal Himself to him.

These last words suggest a subject upon which I should like to say a few words. I have used the phrase that a belief in the Trinity makes 'Prayer possible.' Do I mean that it is *impossible* to every person who has not received our Creed,—that the Unitarian cannot pray? I mean no such thing. My great desire has been to show that we are dwelling in a Mystery deeper than any of our plummets can fathom, a Mystery of Love. Our prayers are not measured by our conceptions; they do not spring from us. He who knows us, teaches us what we should pray for, and how to pray. Therefore, of all transgressors of our Lord's command 'not to judge,' they are the greatest who pretend to pronounce upon the depth or sincerity of their neighbour's prayer, who think they can ascertain it by the professions which he makes, by his apparent pride or humility.

But the more I have seen of Unitarians, or have read of their books, the more have I been convinced that this was the great difficulty of their Creed—that in which its other difficulties begin and terminate. 'Is God's Will 'good,—then why attempt to move it by petitions and 'intercessions? Is it not good? then how hopeless 'the effort must be, seeing that He is omnipotent!' These logical icebergs continually move away for human sufferers who are trying to force a passage between them. They pray because they cannot help it. Whether the effort is a reasonable one or not, they must make it. When the necessity has passed away, the understanding finds a justification for the violence which has been put upon it, and for the habitual repetition of such violence, by saying that though our prayers cannot move God, they are useful for their action upon our minds. But conscience then comes in with its protest: 'What, 'practise a pious fraud in order to effect an improve-'ment in your moral condition! Pretend that you are 'praying to some Being beyond yourself, when you are, 'in fact, your own object! What charms, what Budd-'hist praying-machine can be more insincere than such a 'process? Can the adoption of it make us more serious 'and truthful? If not, what is that reaction upon our 'own characters, which is urged as a defence of it?'

I do not think the Unitarian has ever been able to answer these objections, and yet I am nearly sure that many Unitarians would sooner die than give up the act of prayer, and that they believe it not to be the falsest, but the truest of all acts, that which is necessary to make them sincere, and keep them sincere. I do not doubt that the greater part of Unitarians, even those who retain Dr. Priestley's dogma of Necessity in their speculative creed, contrive to separate the idea of Him they call Father, from that Necessity. They confess a Will; they do not worship a mere God of Nature. And they can believe that this Will may govern *them*, in some different way from that in which He governs the trees, and flowers, and streams. This belief implies the possibility of some *intercourse;* yes! they must use that name, however much it savours of what they have been wont to call fanaticism; no other will avail. But again the doubt occurs. 'How can this intercourse take 'place? Am I sure that I have any relation to this 'mysterious Will? Are the words "speech and hear- 'ing" applicable to this subject?' Consider these questions in all ways. You are afraid of traditions. I do not ask you to receive mine. You long to be rational. Use your reason upon this subject. And see whether the doctrine of a Mediator, one with the Father, one with you, does not meet it,—whether anything else can.

But think again; some anguish drove you to prayer. I do not ask what it was. It might be the loss of reputation; it might be the loss of a friend or child. Whatever it was, I am certain a sense of wrong, of remorse, of repentance, mingled with your sorrow: you had been hardly treated, but you were not quite blameless; the friend was very dear, but you might have done more for him. That misery drove you *to* God; but did it not also keep you *from* Him? There was a feeling of separation, not merely from the human being that was gone, but from Him. Was it overcome? I do not say that it was not, for I believe that God has given the Son in whom He sees us, and in whom we may see Him, *to be a ransom for all, to be testified in due time.* But if you acknowledged that ransom,—if you accepted Christ's Sacrifice, as the assurance of His reconciliation with you,—would not that explain the sense of strife; the union which is mightier than it; the possibility, the infinite truth of prayer? And will not the thought, 'Such an one is ever presenting His 'Sacrifice not for me, but for the whole family; it is 'binding me to men as well as to God,'—put an end to the struggle and selfishness of your prayers in time to come, without making them less earnest, less individual? For you must know, then, that you are not striving to get something which God is unwilling to give; that you are crying out for the victory of His Will over your own and over all others. And if you believe this Will is that all should be saved, and should come to the knowledge of the truth, and that Christ has fulfilled this Will on earth, and is fulfilling it now, is it not an infinite comfort that your wishes are but the feeble echoes of His?

Yet there is something more wanted still to make your prayers real, and to explain that 'reaction on your own minds' which you have talked of. Are not you conscious very often of utter powerlessness, of a mind anything but disposed to good, anything but disposed to love or aid your fellow-men as you think God is loving and aiding them? Would it not be a satisfaction,—not to your feelings only but to your sincerity,—to believe that there is a Spirit who is urging us to those higher impulses to which we are so indisposed, who is lifting us above ourselves, who is drawing us to the Father of our Spirits? I ask you to ponder these thoughts. If you entered into them you would not at all be adopting the doctrines of this book. You might be leaving them and me, far behind you. You might be entering into a knowledge of God which I have never attained; might be contemplating Christ's sacrifice as I have been unable to contemplate it; might be seeing the future condition of the world and God's judgment of it under aspects altogether different from mine. But you would be realizing all that I desire for myself, for you, for my brethren, because you would be committing us and yourselves to God.

I should, indeed, be contradicting all I have said hitherto, and the deepest testimony of my soul, if I persuaded any Unitarian to pray as if that was true which as yet he does not believe to be true. Let him cling to his belief in a One God; let him hold fast to the name of Father. I do not dread his zeal, but his indifference; not his grasp of his own convictions, but his inclination to use them as weapons against other men. While *we* use the doctrine of the Trinity in that way, I am certain we shall not believe it, whatever we may pretend. While *they* think they know what that awful name 'Father' means, because they can pronounce it, or what that wonderful word 'Unity' means, because they can fight for it, they will not only not enlarge the circle of their convictions, but they will lose those that they have. Let them pray the Lord's prayer, determining that the first words of it shall not be mere words to them,—that they shall be such as sick people want who sigh for the morning; as poor men want who toil in mines; as captives want who are chained together in loathsome prisons; and I have no fear of their coming to acknowledge the whole name which we confess. Let them sigh for that Unity which all the strifes and divisions of the world are rending, and I have no doubt they will learn to pray *to* as well as *for* a Spirit of Unity, or that their prayer will take the form of the old hymn of which we have this simple and noble version:—

Teach us to know the Father, Son,
And Thee of both, to be but one;
That through the ages all along
This may be our endless song,—
Praise to thy eternal merit,
Father, Son, and Holy Spirit.

Note.—As the remark in this passage on Romanist arguers applies directly to some Sermons of Mr. Manning's, on John, c. 17, v. 3, I cannot let it go forth without saying, that I entirely acquit him of that which would be a great sin, the *intention* of interpolating our Lord's words. I can quite conceive that vehement opponents of Rome have read his Sermons without discovering *that* flaw in them. For the truth is, that we adopt this paraphrase as much as the Romanists do. Mr. Manning probably learnt it among English divines, and is making fair use of it against them now. What I hoped and believed was, that he had risen out of such a low notion of orthodoxy, to whatever society it belongs. In the fourth volume of his Sermons, published shortly before he left the English Church, there was such a vein of true Catholicity, such an assertion of the highest Theology as the possession for all men, such a vindication of the truth that the knowledge of God *is* Eternal Life, as it did one's heart good to meet with anywhere. Though there were sufficient indications in that volume, that the writer might not stay very long amongst us, I could not help hailing it as a far nobler addition to the stores of English divinity, than those very exquisite, probably more popular, but it seemed to me less masculine, discourses which Mr. Manning had put forth previously. I ventured to hope,—almost to prophecy,—that he might only be breaking the fetters of our Anglican system, and that even the new fetters of Romanism would not hinder him from being Catholic. Nor will I abandon that hope now. In a still more recent Sermon he has asserted the doctrine which I have maintained in these Essays, that Love is the groundwork of all Divinity, with a breadth and fulness which I should rejoice to find in the Discourses of those whom he has forsaken. I trust that he believes himself, and will teach others, that the Spirit of Love is also the Spirit of Truth, and that *no lie is of the Truth:* when he and we are possessed by that conviction, we cannot long be separate.

In Illustration of what I have said on the generical distinction between Time and Eternity, I should wish my readers to meditate these lines of Milton.

"Fly, envious Time, till thou run out thy race;
Call on the lazy, leaden-stepping hours,
Whose speed is but the heavy plummet's pace;
And glut thyself with what thy womb devours,
Which is no more than what is false and vain,
And merely mortal dross :
So little is our loss,
So little is thy gain.

For when, as each thing bad thou hast intomb'd,
And last of all thy greedy self consumed,
Then long Eternity shall greet our bliss
With an individual kiss;
And joy shall overtake us as a flood,
When everything that is sincerely good
And perfectly divine,
With Truth, and Peace, and Love shall ever shine
About the supreme throne
Of Him to whose happy-making sight alone
When once our heavenly-guided soul shall climb
Then, all this earthly grossness quit,
Attired with stars we shall for ever sit
Triumphing over Death, and Chance, and thee, O Time."

CONCLUDING ESSAY.

ETERNAL LIFE AND ETERNAL DEATH.

Here I might stop; for the Trinity is, as I believe, the ground on which the Church stands and on which Humanity stands; Prayer and Sacrifice are, I believe, the means whereby the Trinity is made known to us: in the Trinity I find the Love for which I have been seeking; in Prayer and Sacrifice I hold that we may become partakers of it. But here I cannot stop, for the Unitarians and multitudes who are not Unitarians, declare that all I have said is futile, for that there is another doctrine which contradicts the principle of my whole book, and yet which is as much an article of my faith as the Trinity itself. 'Your Church,' they say, 'maintains the notion of everlasting punishment after death. 'Consider what is included in that notion. You cannot 'thrust it into a corner as you might naturally wish to 'do. You cannot mention it as something by the way. 'If it is anything, it is fundamental. Theologians and 'popular preachers treat it as such. They start from it; 'they put it forth as the ground of their exhortations,

'The world, according to them, lies under a sentence 'of condemnation. An immense—an incalculable—'majority of all that have been born into it, must, if 'their statements mean anything, if they are not merely 'idle frivolous rhetoric, be hopelessly doomed. Their 'object is to point out how a few, a very few, may be 'saved from the sentence. All their doctrines there-'fore have this centre. Let them speak of Atone-'ment, Justification, Regeneration;—these are only 'different names to denote the methods by which certain 'men may have the comfort of feeling that they are not 'sharers in the condition to which God has consigned 'our race.'

'What is most appalling,' the objector continues, 'to a 'person who takes the words of Scripture literally, is 'that the passages from which the proofs of this doctrine 'are derived, are found in the New Testament, in the 'discourses of Christ himself. Dr. John Owen espe-'cially draws the attention of his readers to the fact, 'that here, and not in the Old Testament, which is 'supposed to contain the severer and sterner religion 'of the Law, the sentences concerning eternal perdition 'occur. There can be no doubt, that his observation is 'true, whatever reason may be given for it. Our fathers 'used to think that they could explain away such 'passages by giving a different force to the word '*Eternal*, when it is connected with blessedness, and 'when it is connected with punishment. But such 'philological tricks will not answer in our day. We 'feel the necessity of giving up the passages, of supposing 'that they were not spoken by Him to whom they are 'attributed, or that He was mistaken. But you dare 'not take that course.'

'It is a discouraging circumstance also,' they say, 'that in respect of this tenet, theology has not gained 'by the Reformation, but has lost considerably. The 'belief in hopeless punishment belongs, no doubt, as 'much to Romanism as to Protestantism. But how 'much are its extreme horrors mitigated by the admis-'sion of a Purgatory for a great multitude of human 'souls! To whatever abuses that notion may have been 'subjected by superstition or cupidity, it is surely milder 'and more humane than the decree which goes forth 'from so many pulpits in our land; *Understand, sinners,* '*whatever be your offences, whatever your temptations,* '*the same irremediable anguish is prepared for you* '*all.* Even in the Inferno of the Florentine poet, 'though all hope was to forsake those who entered it, 'what traces there are of recollection and affection, what 'hints of a moral improvement through suffering! With 'us, there is only one dark abyss of torment and sin for 'all who, in the course of threescore years and ten, 'have not been brought to believe things which they 'could not believe or have never learnt, who have not 'abstained from acts which they have been taught from 'their youth up to commit.'

'Once more;' they proceed, 'experience, which is said 'to teach individuals a little—nations almost nothing—'has taught theologians, it seems, to be *more* outrageous, '*more* contemptuous to human sympathies and con-'science, than they used to be when all men bowed 'the neck to their yoke. This tenet must be accepted 'with *greater* precision now than in the days gone by. 'The Evangelical Alliance, longing to embrace all 'Protestant schools and parties, makes it one of its nine 'articles of faith, one of those first principles which are 'involved in the very nature of a comprehensive Christi-'anity. It is clear, that they are not solitary in their 'wish to give the doctrine of everlasting punishment 'this character. Your orthodox English Churchmen, 'though they may dissent from some of their opinions 'as too wide, will join heart and soul with them, when-'ever they are narrow and exclusive. They may suffer 'doubts and modifications in some points ; on this, be 'sure, they will demand simple unqualified acquiescence.'

These statements may be heard in all circles, from young and old, from men and women, from persons longing to believe, from those who are settled down into indifference. Those who know, say that they are producing infidelity in the highest classes ;—hard-working clergymen in the Metropolis can bear witness that they supply the most staple arguments to those who are preaching infidelity among the lowest. How impossible it is that I can pass them by, every one must perceive. They affect not one, but each of the principles which I have been discussing. If *all* these assertions are true, all that I have written is false. I am bound, therefore, to examine which of them have a foundation and which have not. For no one can doubt that there is a truth in some of them which cannot be gainsaid.

I. I admit, without the slightest hesitation, that there is very much more about Eternity and eternal punishment in the Gospel than in the Law, in the words of Christ than in the books of Moses and the Prophets. Let that point be well recollected and carefully reflected upon, in connexion with the opinion which all in some way or other entertain, in some language or other express, that the New Testament is more completely a revelation of the Love of God than the Old is. The two assertions must be reconciled. We cannot go on repeating them both, dwelling upon them both, drawing arguments from them both, while yet we feel them to be incompatible or contradictory. Let it be further conceded at once, that we cannot honestly get rid of this contradiction by attaching two different meanings to the word *αἰώνιος* in different applications. The subjects which it qualifies cannot affect the sense we put upon it. If we turn it the least awry to meet our convenience, we deal unfaithfully with the book which we profess to take as our guide.

Starting from these premises, let us consider why it is

that the New Testament has more to do with Eternity than the Old. I think no Christian will differ very widely from me when I answer, 'it is because the living 'and eternal God is more fully and perfectly revealed in 'the one than in the other.' In both He is discovering Himself to men; in both He is piercing through the mists which conceal Him from them. But in the one He is making Himself known chiefly in His relations to the visible economy of the world; in the other He is exhibiting His own inward nature, and is declaring Himself as He is in Him who is the brightness of His glory, the express image of His person. Whenever the word *Eternal* is used, then, in the New Testament, it ought first, by all rules of reason, to be considered in reference to God. Its use when it is applied to Him, must determine all its other uses. There must be no shrinking from this rule, no efforts to evade the force of it; for this is what we agreed to condemn in the Unitarians and Universalists of the last age, that they changed the force of the adjective at their pleasure, so that it might not mean the same in reference to punishment as to life. How can we carry out this rule? Shall we say that Eternal means, in reference to God, 'without beginning or end'? How then can we affix that meaning to Eternal, when we are speaking of man's bliss or misery? Is that without beginning as well as without end? 'Oh 'no! you must leave out the beginning. That of course 'has nothing to do with this case.' Who told you so?

How dare you play thus fast and loose with God's word? How dare you fix the standard by which the signification of a word is to be judged, and reject that very standard a moment after?

But are there no better reasons why we should not affix this meaning, 'without beginning and end,' to the word *αἰώνιος* when it is applied in the New Testament to God? I quite agree that such a meaning might have seemed very natural to an ordinary Greek. The word might have been used in that sense by a classical author, or in colloquial language, without the least impropriety. But just *the* lesson which God had been teaching men by the revelation of Himself was, that mere negatives are utterly unfit to express His being, His substance. From the very first, He had taught His chosen people to look upon Him as the *righteous* Being, to believe that all their righteousness was grounded on His. He had promised them a more complete knowledge of His righteousness. Every true Israelite had looked to this knowledge as His reward, as the deliverance from his enemies, as the satisfaction of his inmost longings, as the great blessing to his nation and to mankind, as well as to himself. His Righteousness, His Truth, His Love, the Jew came more and more to perceive, were the substantial and eternal things, by seeking which he was delivered from the worship of Gods of Time and Sense, as well as from the more miserable philosophical abstraction of a God who is merely a negative of time; *without* beginning and *without* end. Therefore, when the Son was revealed, this is the language in which the beloved disciple speaks, '*The life* '*was manifested, and we have seen it, and we declare unto* '*you that eternal life which was with the Father, and* '*which has been manifested unto us.*' This is but a specimen of his uniform language. Yes, and I will be bold to say that his language interprets all the language of the New Testament. The eternal life is the righteousness, and truth, and love of God which are manifested in Christ Jesus; manifested to men that they may be partakers of them, that they may have fellowship with the Father and with the Son. This is held out as the eternal blessedness of those who seek God and love Him. This it is, of which our Lord must have spoken in His last prayer, if he who reports that prayer did not misinterpret His meaning.

Is it inconsistent, then, with the general object and character of the New Testament, as the manifestation of His love, that Eternity in all its aspects should come before us there as it does nowhere else, that there we should be taught what it means? Is it inconsistent with its scope and object that there, too, we should be taught what the horror and awfulness is, of being without this love, of setting ourselves in opposition to it? Those who would not own Christ in His brethren, who did not visit Him when they were sick and in prison, go away, He said, into eternal or everlasting punishment. Are we affixing a new meaning to these words, or the very meaning which the context demands, the only meaning which is consistent with the force that is given to the adjective by our Lord and His apostles elsewhere, if we say that the eternal punishment is the punishment of being without the knowledge of God, who is love, and of Jesus Christ who has manifested it; even as eternal life is declared to be the having the knowledge of God and of Jesus Christ? If it is right, if it is a duty, to say that Eternity in relation to God has nothing to do with time or duration, are we not bound to say that also in reference to life or to punishment, it has nothing to do with time or duration?

II. What I have said respecting the New Testament will explain some phenomena, which have puzzled observers, in the opinions of the early Church upon this subject. Uniformity is not to be looked for. If any one expects to find that, he will be woefully disappointed. He will probably discover in all the Fathers a very strange, almost overwhelming, feeling that Christ had revealed eternity, the eternal world, the eternal God, as they had never been revealed before, that a quite new blessedness had been disclosed to men, that there was a tremendous disclosure of evil correspondent to that. But as in every case the wisest teachers of these centuries were but trying to catch the meaning of our Lord and His Apostles, some seeing it on one side, some on another;—some through the refracting medium of a heathen education, some through the Jewish Scriptures, some through their own conflicts and the conflicts of their time; — so was it here. One caught at *this* aspect of eternity, one at *that*. *Here* was an eloquent preacher who drew pictures of miseries to come, and mixed together material images with spiritual ideas. *There* was a Universalist who dwelt on the possibility of men being restored after ages of suffering to the favour of God. There was one who dreamed of alternations of misery and blessedness. There were those who learnt in the dreadful strife with Manicheism the real distinction of time and eternity, of life and death. There were those who, troubling themselves less with questions respecting the future state of men, dwelt on the eternity of the Father and the co-eternity of the Son, and showed how needful it was that no notions of time or duration should intrude themselves into such mysteries. The influence of these last men upon the Church was great; so far as fixing the language of her formularies in questions respecting the distinction of temporal and eternal things, it was paramount. Even their anathemas against opponents, however reckless, as they pointed to a disbelief which concerned the knowledge of God, kept up the feeling in the Church that that knowledge constitutes Eternal Life, and that the loss of it is Eternal Death. But the practical teachers naturally gave the form to the popular divinity. It is only wonderful that that divinity should have preserved so spiritual a tone as it did; that a preacher like Chrysostom, for instance, should have spoken of the second death as the death of Sin, the loss of the moral being, when he must have been continually tempted to think that the coarse reprobates of Antioch and Constantinople needed only, and could only understand, threats of material brimstone. But God did not suffer the champion whom He had educated to be the opposer of courts and empresses, habitually to adopt the low policy which is so suitable to them, so shameful in the minister of Truth.

Very different was the behaviour of the bishops in the city which he ruled so righteously, a century and a half after his death. Yielding to the intrigues of a successor of Eudoxia,—in comparison with whom she was an angel, —a woman who had the greatest interest, one would have thought, in believing that the love of God might convert even the lowest victims of lust and hatred into His servants and children,—these reverend Fathers consigned Origen to endless perdition because he had held the opinion that his fellow-beings were not intended for it. This example how far morality was interested in such decrees,—how much of grovelling submission on the part of ecclesiastics to civil rulers was the cause of them,—might have led the Western Church, which had other reasons for not esteeming very highly the orthodoxy of Justinian and Theodora, to pause before they advanced in the same course. But barbarians were crowding into the fold of Christ, who brought with them all the dreams of a Walhalla. To govern was the function of the Latin Church; theology was to be used as an instrument of government. Distinctions, once established, were to be carefully defended and enforced. But where none existed, the Church was to prove its capacity of embracing the nations, by adapting herself, with wonderful facility, to the superstitions which she found among them, by incorporating them into her own body of doctrine, by stooping to material influences and artifices, for the sake of moving those who were supposed to have little or nothing in them which could respond to a spiritual message. To a superficial and yet an honest observer, the whole course of Papal history looks merely like a series of these politic appeals to the appetites of the lower nature, for the sake of bribing them not to instigate crimes, or of enlisting them in the service of the Church,—nothing but a series of testimonies what crimes must be the result of such bribery, what a service that must be which secures the aid of such mercenaries. The efforts to materialize the terrors of the future world, and to make those terrors the great motives to obedience,—with the obedience which was actually produced by them,—at once suggest themselves as the most startling and decisive points in the evidence. The vision of a purgatory from which men might be delivered by prayers or by money, coming so much more near to the conscience, suggesting so much more practical methods of proceeding than the mere distant background of hopeless torment, offers itself as the natural product of a scheme, devised to act upon the fears and hopes of man, not drawn from the word of God. But a more careful student is not satisfied with this statement of the case, though he is forced to confess that it is true. He perceives that there were words belonging to the popular language of the Latins, not derived from the Greek, which showed that the doctrine of the New Testament respecting eternal life and death, had still a hold upon the conscience of the Western Church.

What is Perdition but a loss? What is eternal damnation, but the loss of a good which God had revealed to His creatures, of which He had put them in possession? What a witness there lay in these words, even when thrown about by the most random rhetorician, against the notion of a mere future prize to be won by men who could purchase it by sacrifices, of a future misery which God had designed for His creatures! And the witness was not inoperative. The noblest Doctors of the Middle Ages did believe this to be the meaning of all which they dreaded for themselves and for mankind. They did believe that Love was at the root of all things, and that to lose Love, was to lose all things. This was the ground of their most passionate exhortations, whatever forms they might take. Whatever were the crudities of their intellects, this was the undoubting testimony of their hearts. It was this inward conviction which made them tolerant of the idea of Purgatory—which allowed them to wink with a dangerous 'œconomy' at what they must have known were the abominations connected with it. They were afraid to limit the love which they felt had been so mighty for them and for the world. They did not dare to measure the sacrifice of Christ and His intercession by their notions. The deep conviction which they had of Evil as opposed to the nature of God, made them shudder as they looked down into that abyss. They would rather think of material punishments which might, elsewhere as here, be God's instruments of acting upon the spirit to awaken it out of death. The great poem of the Florentine brings out this deeper theology of the Middle Ages, in connexion with all the forms in which it was hidden. The loss of intellectual life, of the vision of God, is with him the infinite horror of hell. Men are in eternal misery, because they are still covetous, proud, loveless. The evil priest or pope is in the worst circle of all, because he has been brought most closely into contact with spiritual and eternal things. Even here, there are all varieties of evil, approximations to penitence and good. The purgatory is the ascent, not out of material torments, but out of moral evil, into a higher moral state. The Paradise is the consummation of that state in the vision of perfect truth and love. Those who dwell there, are ever looking down upon the poor wanderers below, aware of their strifes, choosing guides for them,—it may be some poet of the old world,—who shall be helpers in their perplexity, who shall enable them to have a clearer vision of the order which lies beneath the confusions of the world, of the divine government to which all human governments must submit, and by which they must be judged. There may be all material accidents about the poem, derived from the age in which it was written; but that this is its theological substance, I do not think any considerate reader has ever doubted.

But whatever right we have to detect that theology, through its external coverings, in the writings of divines or of patriots, the two were inextricably blended in the popular as well as the scholastical teaching, and the darkness was endeavouring more and more to draw down the light into itself. In the period between Dante and the Reformation, there were many in Germany, in England, in France,—one noble Dominican at least in his own Florence,—who were labouring to disentangle the threads, and to teach Christendom that moral evil is the eternal misery from which they need to be delivered, the righteousness of God the good which they have to attain. But dilettanti popes, who believed nothing and therefore were desirous that the world which they ruled should believe everything, who promoted letters by denying all knowledge to the people, who built churches to him who they said was the rock of the Church, by the help of missionaries who proved that it stood upon no rock but money,—these popes were consummating all the confusions that had been in the theology of the Church before; were establishing, once for all, the doctrine that the thing men have to dread is punishment and not sin, and that the greatest reward which the highest power in the Church can hold out is deliverance from punishment, not deliverance from sin. Let us understand it well; it was against this doctrine that Luther protested in his theses at Wittenberg. Everything in these theses, everything in his subsequent career, turns upon the assertion that a man requires and desires punishment, not indulgence, when he has done evil; that, if you cannot free him from evil you do him no service; that Tetzel had therefore not only been robbing people of their money, had not only been uttering wild and blasphemous words about his own powers and the powers of those who sent him, but that he had been promising that which it is not good for a man to have, which a man should most earnestly pray not to have, but to escape from, if it could be given him for nothing. That which we call the great proclamation of the Reformation, that a man is justified by faith alone, becomes intelligible through this principle, and is not intelligible without it. Luther declared that what man wants is freedom from sin and not freedom from punishment, that righteousness is the reward we crave for. And then he said, 'This freedom, which no pope can 'give you, this reward which you can acquire by no 'efforts and labours of yours, God has given you freely 'in Christ. Believing in Christ, the righteous One, 'you rise out of your own sins, you become righteous 'men, you are able to do righteous acts.' And this doctrine, which we are told in our days is so fine and abstract, that no men can listen to it or care for it, except some people of delicate and tender consciences, went through the length and breadth of Europe, spoke to the hearts of the commonest handicraftsmen and labourers, was recognised by them as the message which they were waiting to hear, because it enabled them to obtain a moral standing-ground and a moral life, which threats of future punishments and hopes of outward rewards had never won for them.

The consequence of this doctrine where it was believed, was unquestionably to bring out the contrast between the good and evil state so distinctly and sharply, that the notion of any intermediate state between these, was vehemently rejected. Hell as the state of unrighteousness, Heaven as the state of righteousness, Earth as the battle-field between the two, filled and possessed the mind. Even if purgatory had not been so connected with the system of indulgences, it could scarcely have found its place among the thoughts which were then driving all others before them. In the great Jesuit reaction of the sixteenth century, it recovered its hold upon numbers who had been dispossessed of it, because the social feelings and sympathies of men, and their sense of an intimate connexion between the visible and the invisible world, for which the Middle Age theology, amidst all its confusions, had borne witness, had met with a very inadequate recognition in the different schools of the Reformation. But though this was the case, it is not true that Protestantism has pronounced more positively than Romanism did upon the future condition of men. So far as our own Church is concerned, the assertion is not only wide of the truth, but is directly in opposition to it.

In the first draft of our Articles, in the reign of Edward VI., one was introduced, the forty-second, which contained a decree upon this subject. It was expressed in the most moderate terms. It merely declared that 'They also are worthy of condemnation who endeavour 'at this time to restore the dangerous opinion, that all 'men, be they never so ungodly, shall at length be 'saved, when they have suffered pain for their sins 'a certain time appointed by God's justice.'

After what I have said of the character of the Reformation, it cannot be wonderful that those who had entered most into the spirit of it, should be most anxious to show that pain did not make amends for sin, and that the misery of sin does not consist in an arbitrary penalty affixed to it by God, who has sent His Son to make men righteous. On these grounds the Divines of Edward VI.'s reign might easily have excused themselves to their contemporaries, and even to their successors, for adopting an Article which had already been sanctioned at Augsburg. Nevertheless it has been contended, with great reasonableness, from the expression 'at this time,' and from two other Articles which are found in the same draft, that this sentence was devised to meet a special emergency. The Anabaptists, among a number of other tenets, all of which had taken a sensual and a revolutionary form, had propounded some theory like that which the Reformers here denounced. Every one knows how eager Lutherans, Calvinists, and English Reformers were to disclaim sympathy with those who had done so much to make the new doctrines odious in the eyes of Europe. It was very likely indeed that this eagerness should be exhibited in any careful digest of their own doctrines. But the dread of the danger had subsided in the time of Queen Elizabeth. It had not, indeed, so subsided that the framers of the Articles in that reign thought it safe to omit a special denunciation of the doctrine of community of goods. But they could venture, and they seized the privilege, to strike out the forty-second Article.

This statement is not mine. It is the justification which is offered for the compilers of our Articles, by those who would have wished them to dogmatize most peremptorily on the subject. Taking their explanation, the evidence that the members of the Church of England have perfect freedom on this subject, is irresistible. It is scarcely possible to invent a case in one's mind, which would be equally strong. Mere silence might be accounted for. But here is omission, careful considerate omission, in a document for future times, of that which had been too hastily admitted, to meet an emergency of that time. The omission was made by persons who probably were strong in the belief that the punishment of wicked men is endless, but who did not dare to enforce that opinion upon others; above all, who did not dare to say that the words Eternal and Everlasting, which they knew had such a profound and sacred meaning in reference to God Himself, and to the revelation of his Son, could be shrivelled and contracted into this signification.

III. I have answered two of the objections at some length. I have considered how it is that the New Testament speaks more of eternal life and of eternal punishment than the Old; how the usage of the words in the New Testament explains that fact, and is explained by it; how, instead of interfering with the assertion of St. Paul, that *it is the will of God, that all men should be saved*, and of St. John, that *God is love;* without these words, the others would be inexplicable. Next, the charge that there has been a tendency throughout the history of the Church to determine the limits of God's love to men, and to speak of all but a few as hopelessly lost, but that this tendency has been much more marked and strong in Protestants than in Romanists, so that we are much more bound by the opinion than they were,—I have met by a sketch of the history of opinion upon this subject, which, however slight, I believe is accurate, and will bear examination. And I have come to the conclusion, that the deepest and most essential part of the theology previous to the Reformation, bore witness to the fact that eternal life is the knowledge of God who is Love, and eternal death the loss of that knowledge; that it was the superficial theology,—that which belonged to the Papal system as such,—which interfered with this belief; that it was the great effort of the Reformation to sweep away that superficial theology, in order that Righteousness and Evil, Love and Hatred, might stand out as the two eternal opposites; the one as the eternal life which God presents to men, the other as the eternal death which they choose for themselves, and which consists in being at war with His love. I have now to consider the third statement, that, whatever may have been the case at the time of the Reformation, theologians have in our age become entirely positive and dogmatic upon this subject; that upon it they can brook no doubt or diversity of opinion; that in fact, they hold that a man is as much bound to say 'I believe in the endless 'punishment of the greater portion of mankind' as 'I 'believe in God the Father, in God the Son, and in 'God the Holy Ghost.'

I wish that I felt as able to controvert these propositions as the others. But I am bound to admit that the evidence for them is very strong. Perhaps I may be permitted to trace some of the causes which have led to this state of feeling. They will account, I think, for the existence of it, at least under certain modifications, in very good men. They will explain what are likely to be the issues of it if it is not counteracted. They may help to show English Churchmen, and especially English Clergymen, what their standing-ground is, and what their obligations are, if they are really stewards of the everlasting Gospel.

1. Every one must be aware how much the philosophical teaching under which we have grown up, unconsciously modifies our thoughts and opinions on a multitude of subjects which we suppose to be beyond its range. Luther's first battles, as his letters show us, were with Aristotle: he found how much the habits of thought learnt from him, and consecrated in the schools, interfered with the understanding of St. Paul. He wanted his pupils to look directly at the sense of Scripture; they came with certain preconceived notions which they imputed to the Sacred writers; any one who construed them without reference to these notions was supposed to depart from their natural, simple meaning. It was not that Aristotle might not be an exceedingly useful teacher for certain purposes; but what Bacon discovered to be true of him in the investigation of Nature, Luther discovered to be true in the investigation of Scripture. His logical determinations

and arrangements, even his accurate observations, hindered the student, who was not to bring wisdom but to seek it.

What Aristotle was to the German in the sixteenth century, John Locke is to an Englishman in the nineteenth. His dogmas have become part of our habitual faith; they are accepted without study, as a tradition. In this respect he resembles his predecessor. Proscribed at first by divines for the Essay on the Understanding more than for his politics or his interpretations of Scripture, just as Aristotle was proscribed by popes in the twelfth century,—divines now assume that Essay to be the rule and measure of thought and language, even as in the thirteenth century the Stagirite Metaphysics became the rule and measure of thought and language to all orthodox schoolmen. But there is this difference. Aristotle belongs merely to the schools; Locke connects the schools with the world. He found a number of mystifications which doctors were canonising. He courageously applied himself to the removal of them. The conscience of ordinary men recognised him as their champion. He spoke to the love of the simple and practical, in which lies the strength of the English character. He asked men who were using phrases which they had inherited, and to which they attached no meaning, to give an account of them, and if they could not, to surrender them. It was evident that he had an immense advantage over his opponents, because he understood himself, and because he had determined to be faithful to his own convictions. He succeeded in persuading those who believed very little, not to pretend to believe more than they did. Who can doubt that this was a good and great service to mankind? But it involved this consequence. If men should chance hereafter to discover that some of the principles held by their ancestors, had a substance and meaning in them, however little that substance and meaning might be represented in the dialect of the day, there would be considerable difficulty in recovering the possession. It would be supposed that the good sense of a great man had settled the question for ever, and those who knew little how it had been settled or what there was to settle, would be just as zealous in discountenancing and ridiculing any further investigation, as if they were bowing to a dictator, not accepting help from one who had protested against dictation.

When any one ventures to say to an English audience, that Eternity is not a mere negation of time, that it denotes something real, substantial, before all time, he is told at once that he is departing from the simple intelligible meaning of words; that he is introducing novelties; that he is talking abstractions. This language is perfectly honest in the mouths of those who use it. But they do not know where they learnt it. They did not get it from peasants, or women, or children. They did not get it from the Bible. They got it from Locke.

And if I find that I cannot interpret the language and thoughts of peasants, and women, and children, and that I cannot interpret the plainest passages of the Bible or the whole context of it, while I look through the Locke spectacles,—I must cast them aside. I am sure Locke would wish me to do so, for I believe he was a thoroughly honest man, and one who desired nothing less in the world, than that he should become an oppressor to the spirits which he supposed he was setting free.

Here then is one cause of our present state of feeling respecting the question which I am now considering; here is a proof how much that state of feeling must affect a multitude of subjects, besides that of everlasting punishment. 'When the Scriptures speak of Eternity 'they *must* mean endlessness; they *can* mean nothing 'else. To be sure they *do* mean something else, when 'they speak of God's eternity; but we have only to put 'in also "without beginning" to that, and all is right.' The divines who use such language, are supported by those who most object to the conclusion which they deduce from it. The old Unitarian cannot give up Locke. The orthodox Dissenters have always supposed that he must be right, because Churchmen disliked him for his notions of government and toleration. Practical men suspect that some German mysticism must be near, when his decrees are disputed. And those who have no dread of this mysticism, and who know that the explorers of other nations have passed beyond the Hercules pillars, within which our navigators confine themselves, and have even affirmed the existence of islands and continents where Locke supposed there was nothing but ocean, yet ask 'what that has to do with 'old Hebrews like Paul or John? of course they knew 'nothing about these islands and continents. The 'coarsest, most material view of things is most suitable 'to them.' Nearly all people therefore in this country, who speak on such matters, are agreed that the words of the Gospel, if they were taken strictly and fairly, must have the hardest (I do not say the most awful, for I believe the sense I contend for is much more awful) meaning which has ever been given them. Only the tens and hundreds of thousands who cannot speak, dissent from that decision.

2. However hard and exclusive the Romish Church may have been,—though the great complaint we make of her is, that she excommunicates those who are members of the body of Christ as much as she is,—it is impossible not to see that she takes up a position which looks, at least, much more comprehensive than that of the Protestant bodies. She assumes the Church to represent mankind. The day before Good Friday, the Pope blesses the universe. The sacrifice which she presents day by day, is declared to be that sacrifice which was made for the sins of the whole world. We believe that the strongest witness we have to bear is, that the sacrifice

was made once for all; that our acts do not complete it, but are only possible because it is complete, that they are grounded upon our right to present that continually to the Father, with which He has declared Himself well pleased. We *ought*, therefore, to assert the redemption of mankind more distinctly than they do. But it is clear that in practice we do not seem to the world to do so, nor seem to ourselves to do so. The distinctiveness, the individuality, of Protestantism is its strength, as I have maintained before in these Essays. But close to that strength is its greatest weakness, that which we all feel,—which all, in some sort, confess,—which is the root of our sectarianism—which is continually kept alive by it; and yet, which is destroying the very bodies that it has created. What is the consequence to theology? The religious men, the saved men, are looked upon as the exceptions to a rule; the world is fallen, outcast, ruined; a few Christians, about the signs and tokens of whose Christianity each sect differs, have been rescued from the ruin. I have had to speak in almost every page of this book, respecting the habit of mind to which this opinion appertains; and to show how it is at war with all the articles of the Christian faith. I only wish to point out here, how it bears upon the subject of everlasting salvation and damnation. Damnation does not mean what its etymology would lead us to suppose that it means, what it certainly did mean to the Church in former days, amidst all its perplexities and confusions. It is not the loss of a mighty gift which has been bestowed upon the race. Men are not regarded as *rejecting the counsel of God against themselves.* God is represented as the destroyer. Nay, Divines go the length of asserting—even of taking it for granted,—that our Lord Himself taught this lesson to His disciples when He said, *And I say unto you my friends, Be not afraid of them which kill the body, and after that, have no more that they can do; but I will forewarn you whom ye shall fear: Fear him which, after he hath killed, hath power to cast into hell, yea, I say unto you, fear him. Are not five sparrows sold for two farthings? and not one of them is forgotten before God. But even the very hairs of your head are all numbered. Fear not, therefore; ye are of more value than many sparrows.* We are come to such a pass, as actually to suppose that Christ tells those whom He calls His *friends,* not to be afraid of the poor and feeble enemies who can only kill the body, but of that greater enemy who can destroy their very selves, and that this enemy is —not the devil, not the spirit who is going about seeking whom he may devour, not him who was a murderer from the beginning,—but that God who cares for the sparrows! They are to be afraid lest He who numbers the hairs of their head should be plotting their ruin! Does not this interpretation, which has become so familiar that one hears it without even a hint that there is another, show us on the edge of what an abyss we are standing, how likely we are to confound the Father of lights with the Spirit of darkness?

While this temper of mind continues, it is absolutely inevitable that we should not merely look upon the immense majority of our fellow-creatures as doomed to perdition, but that we should regard the Gospel as itself pronouncing their doom. The message which, according to this view of the case, Christ brings from Heaven to earth is, 'Your Father has created multitudes whom He 'means to perish for ever and ever. By my agony 'and bloody sweat, by my cross and passion, I have 'induced Him in the case of an inconceivably small 'minority to forego that design.' Dare we state that proposition to ourselves, dare we get up into a pulpit and preach it? But if we dare not, seeing it is a matter of life and death, and there must be no trifling or equivocation about it, let us distinctly tell ourselves what we do mean, and if we find that a blasphemous thought has mingled with our belief hitherto, let us confess that thought to God, and ask Him to deliver us from it.

3. I cannot wonder that Divines, even those who would shrink with horror from such a view of God's character and His Gospel as this, should crave for some more distinct apprehensions, nay even statements respecting eternal punishment, than might perhaps be needful in former days. It is quite clear, that the words which go forth from our pulpits on the subject, have no effect at all upon cultivated men of any class, except the effect of

making them regard our other utterances with indifference and disbelief. They do not think that we put faith in our own denunciations. They ask, how it is possible for us to go about and enjoy life if we do; how, if we do, we can look out upon the world that is around us and the world that has been, without cursing the day on which we were born? They say that we pronounce a general sentence, and then explain it away in each particular case; they say, that we believe that God condemns the world generally, but that under cover of certain phrases which may mean anything or nothing, we can prove that, on the whole, He rather intends it good than ill. They say, that we call upon them to praise Him and give Him thanks, and that what we mean is, that they are to testify emotions towards Him which they do not feel, and which His character, as we represent it, cannot inspire, in order to avert His wrath from them. Cultivated men, I say, repeat these things to one another. If we do not commonly hear them, it is because they count it rude ever to tell us what they think. Poor men say these same things in their own assemblies with more breadth and honesty, not wishing us to be ignorant of their opinions respecting us. And though these considerations, so far as they concern ourselves, may not move us, how can we help being moved by their effect on those who utter them? If we believe that the words Eternal Damnation or Death have a very terrible significance, such as the Bible tells us they have, is it nothing that they should be losing all their significance for our countrymen? Is it nothing that they should seem to them mere idle nursery-words that frighten children, but with which men have nothing to do? Is it nothing, that a vague dream of bliss hereafter into which righteousness and goodness do not enter, which has no relation to God, should float before the minds of numbers, but that it should have just as little power to awaken them to any higher or better life, as the dread of the future has to keep them from any evil?

The members of the Evangelical Alliance perceive, more or less clearly, that this is the state of things which has increased and is increasing, among us. They hear of a vague Universalism being preached from some pulpits in America and on the Continent. They think that notion must encourage sinners to suppose that a certain amount of punishment will be enough to clear off their scores, and to procure them ultimate bliss. 'You are relaxing the strictness of your statements,' they say, 'just when they need to be more stringent, 'because all moral obligations are becoming laxer, 'because people are evidently casting off their fear, 'without obtaining anything better in the place of it.' Therefore they conclude that such freedom must be checked. It cannot answer, they think, now, however it may have answered heretofore, to leave any loop-hole for doubt about the endless punishment of the wicked.

I have stated the arguments which I think may have

inclined worthy and excellent men to arrive at this conclusion; though I believe a more fatal one, one more certain to undermine the truth which is in their hearts, and which they are seeking to defend, cannot be imagined. We do, it seems to me, need to have a more distinct and awful idea of eternal death and eternal punishment than we have. I use both words, *Death* and *Punishment*, that I may not appear to shrink from the sense which is contained in either. Punishment, I believe, seems to most men less dreadful than death, because they cannot separate it from a punisher, because they believe, however faintly, that He who is punishing them is a Father. The thought of His ceasing to punish them, of His letting them alone, of His leaving them to themselves, is the real, the unutterable horror. A man may be living without God in the world, he may be trembling at His Name, sometimes wishing that He did not exist; and yet if you told him that he was going where there would be no God, no one to watch over him, no one to care for him, the news would be almost intolerable. We do shrink from this; all men, whatever they may fancy, are more appalled at the thoughts of being friendless, homeless, fatherless, than at any outward terrors you can threaten them with. I know well how the conscience confuses this anticipation with that of meeting God, with being brought face to face with Him. The mixture of feelings adds infinitely to the horror of them. There is a sense of wrath abiding on the spirit which has refused the yoke of love. This is one part of the misery. There is a sense of loneliness and atheism. This is another. And surely this, this is the bottomless pit which men see before them, and to which they feel that they are hurrying, when they have led selfish lives, and are growing harder, and colder, and darker, every hour. Can we not tell them that it is even so, that this is the abyss of death, that second death, of which all material images offer only the faintest picture? Will not that show them more clearly what life is, the risen life, the eternal life, that which was with the Father and has been manifested to us? Will it not enable us to say, 'This life is that for which God has 'created man, for which He has redeemed man in His 'Son, which He is sending His Spirit to work out in 'man?' Will it not enable us to say, 'This eternal death 'is that from which God sent His Son to deliver men, 'from which He has delivered them? If they fall into it, 'it is because they choose it, because they embrace it, 'because they resist a power which is always at work to 'save them from it.' By delivering such a message as this to men, should we not be doing more to make them aware how the revelation of God's righteousness for the redemption of sinners is at the same time the revelation of the wrath of God against all unrighteousness and ungodliness? Would not such a message show that a Gospel of eternal love must bring out more clearly than any mere law can, that state which is the resistance to it and the contradiction of it? But would not such a message at the same time present itself to the conscience of men not as an outrage on their experience, but as the faithful interpreter of it, not as disproving everything that they have dreamed of the willingness of God to save them, but as proving that He is willing and able to save them to the very uttermost?

Suppose instead of taking this method of asserting the truth of all God's words, the most blessed and the most tremendous, we reject the wisdom of our forefathers and enact an article declaring that all are heretics and deniers of the truth, who do not hold that Eternal means endless, and that there cannot be a deliverance from eternal punishment. What is the consequence? Simply this, I believe: the whole Gospel of God is set aside. The state of eternal life and eternal death is not one we can refer only to the future, or that we can in any wise identify with the future. Every man who knows what it is to have been in a state of sin, knows what it is to have been in a state of death. He cannot connect that death with time; he must say that Christ has brought him out of the bonds of *eternal* death. Throw that idea into the future and you deprive it or all its reality, of all its power. I know what it means all too well while you let me connect it with my present and personal being, with the pangs of conscience which I suffer now. It becomes a mere vague dream and shadow to me, when you project it into a distant world.

And if you take from me the belief that God is always righteous, always maintaining a fight with evil, always seeking to bring His creatures out of it, you take everything from me, all hope now, all hope in the world to come. Atonement, Redemption, Satisfaction, Regeneration, become mere words to which there is no counterpart in reality.

I ask no one to pronounce, for I dare not pronounce myself, what are the possibilities of resistance in a human will to the loving will of God. There are times when they seem to me—thinking of myself more than of others—almost infinite. But I know that there is something which must be infinite. I am obliged to believe in an abyss of love which is deeper than the abyss of death: I dare not lose faith in that love. I sink into death, eternal death, if I do. I must feel that this love is compassing the universe. More about it I cannot know. But God knows. I leave myself and all to Him.

It is of this faith that some are seeking to rob us. Have we made up our minds to surrender it? Have we resolved that the belief in Endless Punishment shall be not *a* tenet which any one is at liberty to hold,—as any one is at liberty to hold the notion that the elements are changed in the Lord's Supper, provided he does not force the notion upon me, and will come with me to eat of a feast which is beyond all notions,—but *the* tenet of the Church to which every other is subordinate; just as

Transubstantiation has become in the Romish Church since it has been declared essential to all who partake of the Eucharist? Let us consider, not chiefly what we are accepting, but what we are rejecting, before we tamely submit to this new imposition.

There is one other consideration which I would impress very earnestly upon my brethren—especially upon the Clergy, before I conclude. The doctrine of endless punishment is avowedly put forward as necessary for the reprobates of the world, the publicans and harlots, though perhaps religious men might dispense with it. Now, I find in our Lord's discourses, that when He used such words as these, '*Ye serpents, ye generation of vipers, how shall ye escape the damnation of hell?*' He was speaking to religious men, to doctors of the law; but that when He went among publicans and sinners, it was to preach the Gospel of the Kingdom of God.

Does not this difference show that our minds are very strangely at variance with His mind? Ought not the discovery to make us think and to make us tremble? I am certain that we who are in continual contact with eternal things do require to remind ourselves what danger we are in of losing these things. Spiritual pride is the essential nature of the Devil. To be in that, is to be in the deepest hell. Oh! how little are all outward sensual abominations in comparison of this! And surely to those who are sunk in those abominations, no message will avail but that which He who knew what was in man delivered. Freedom to the captives, opening of sight to them that are blind, a power near them which is mightier than the power of the Devil, a Father and a Son and a Spirit who are willing and able to bring them out of darkness and the shadow of death—this was the news which turned the circumcised and the uncircumcised, the children of God's covenant, those who were afar off, the corrupt men and women of the most corrupt period in history, into saints and martyrs. We deliberately proclaim that this method will not avail for us! What is this but saying that we have not faith in that which the Apostle declares to be the power of God unto salvation; that we have substituted for it an earthly and Tartarean machinery of our own? May God preserve us from such apostasy! May He teach us again by mighty evidence that when we preach the name of the Father, the Son, and the Holy Ghost, we invade the realm of Death and Eternal Night, and open the kingdom of Heaven!

NOTE ON THE ATHANASIAN CREED.

There are those who will say, 'Your explanation of the word *Eternal* 'in the New Testament may be the true one. It certainly accords 'with what we have been wont to think its peculiar characteristics, 'better than the one which is given in popular sermons. It even seems 'to throw a light on a phrase which is very common in those sermons, '*the loss of the soul*, which *ought* to have a spiritual sense, one would 'suppose, and which continually receives a very carnal and material 'one. And it is at least possible, that if Eternal punishment denotes 'in Scripture, Spiritual punishment, portions of its language which 'seem to contain threatenings of outward sufferings may, without 'losing their literal force, receive a new character by being referred to 'this leading principle. We can understand this; we may be glad at 'least to try your method, and see whether the words of Apostles and 'Evangelists will bear the application of it. But can you accept it 'honestly? Are you not tied by formularies which bind you to an'other maxim? Must not these be thrown aside before you can freely 'and fairly give a force to the words Eternal or Everlasting Punish'ment, Fire, Death, or Damnation, which they do not convey to the ears 'and eyes of ordinary hearers and readers?'

It will be perceived that I have already given a partial answer to this question. To the Articles one naturally turns for definitions of words, for assertions of doctrines. In the Articles we find no definition of the word Eternal or Everlasting. They are not merely silent on the doctrine of everlasting punishment. The framers of them have *refused* to pronounce upon it. But the Articles are only one part of our formularies. We have Prayers which we are expected to use daily; we have Creeds which have descended to us from the early ages—the ages of anathemas. What do these say?

First as to the Prayers. It is assumed that I am teaching a meaning of the word Eternal, which the ordinary person, the peasant or woman cannot take in, which can only be understood by the most learned theologian or metaphysician. I utterly deny the charge. I say that I have been forced into the belief of an Eternal world or kingdom, which is about us, in which we are living, which has nothing to do with time, by prayers. These common prayers which I offer up with peasants, and women, and children, have taught me that there is an Eternal Life which is emphatically a present life, (not according to a doctrine which I have listened to lately with astonishment, alike for its logic and theology—a *future* life begun in the *present*;) and that this Eternal Life consists in the knowledge of God; and that the loss of the knowledge of God is the loss of it. And I say that simple people do believe in this life, do grow in the perception of it as they pray, do cast aside, as they pray, that other notion which is so plausible to the senses and the carnal understandings, and which doctors find it so hard to escape. Negatively then, the Prayers define nothing about Eternity, for definition is not the office of prayer. Positively, they are the great means of leading thousands into a practical apprehension of that meaning of Eternity, which I have deduced from the New Testament. But these prayers carry us further still. We have no prayers, thank God! for the dead as such; how can we, when Christ says that all live to God? We have no masses for the dead. How can we? The sacrifice is complete; we cannot make it more perfect than it is. But prayer does break down the barriers between the visible and invisible world, and in prayer we cannot set it up again, however in our theories we may. Christ's sacrifice compasses the whole universe; we cannot limit the extent of its operation by measures of space or time. When we pray for '*all men*,' how dare we limit the Spirit who is teaching us to pray, and affirm that we will not pray for any but those who are in certain conditions with which we are acquainted! When we meet to hold communion with Him who has given Himself for the world, how dare we declare for whom He shall or shall not present His all-embracing sacrifice! Are we wiser or more loving than He is? Do we wish better things for mankind than He does, from whom all our good and loving thoughts proceed?

Next as to the Creeds. The negative evidence for the Apostles' and the Nicene—our daily popular Creeds—is decisive. They speak of a Judgment of quick and dead. They speak of Eternal Life. They contain no sentence about future Punishment. But the positive evidence, from their effect on those who utter them, is stronger still. They are expressions of Trust; Trust in a Father, a Son, and a Spirit. Augustine taught them to the Heathens in Africa, as witnesses that there is a God of Infinite Charity, utterly unlike the gods whom they worshipped. Our missionaries, I hope, use them for the same purpose. All who say them with their hearts feel that they are flying to God from their enemies—Death, Hell, the Devil.

But the Athanasian Creed? Does not that settle the question? I think it does. There, indeed, we find no more definition of Eternity than we do in the other Creeds. But we do find sentences about Punishment to which there is nothing corresponding elsewhere. They are such sentences as I affirm could not have been introduced and could not be repeated by any honest or Christian man, if the idea of Eternal Life, as consisting in the knowledge of God, and of Eternal Death, as consisting in the absence of that knowledge, were not practically the idea of the old time as well as of our own; however in our formal writings we may deny it.

Eleven years ago I expressed what were then my opinions on this subject, in a book not addressed to Unitarians. I said that I could not agree with Mr. Coleridge in thinking that this Creed contradicted the Nicene, on the subject of the subordination of the Son to the Father; that, if it forced me to pronounce judgment on any person, I would not have laid myself under the obligation of reading it,—whatever Church might adopt it,—because I should be violating an express command of Christ; that I never had felt myself encouraged or tempted by it to pass sentence on those who differed with me most on the subject of the Trinity; that, on the contrary, I had felt it was passing sentence on my own tendencies 'to confound the Persons, and to divide the Substance;' that these tendencies in me, I knew, had nothing to do with intellectual formulas, but with moral corruptions, from which many who are called heretics may be freer than I am; that I doubted whether we should gain in Truth or Charity by casting away this Creed, because I looked upon it as a witness, that eternal life is the knowledge of God, and that eternal death is Atheism, the being without Him.* I have not seen any cause to alter these opinions. I feel, indeed, that every year of fresh experience, as it should ground us more in principles, should make us more diffident of our own judgment on questions of expediency. Though the Creed, instead of tempting us to condemn others, has, I think, often overcome our inclination to condemn them—(for the more tremendous its language, the less we can dare to bring any individual within the scope of it), though some sentences of it, those especially concerning 'the taking of the Manhood into God, the reasonable soul and flesh, the persons, and substance,' have thrown a clear broad light into dark passages of my mind, and I doubt not, have taught my brethren more; yet if it does cause any of those for whom Christ died to stumble, if it hinders any from enter-

* 'Kingdom of Christ, or Hints to a Quaker,' vol. ii. p. 548.

ing into the mystery of God's love, I hope He will not suffer us to retain it. For that which is meant as a witness of Him, must be given up, like the brazen serpent, if it ceases to be so, or is made an instrument of turning men's eyes from Him. Still I cannot help thinking that the reasons generally urged for abandoning it are not charitable, and that submission to them will not conduce to charity. I find persons objecting, first, that the basis of our fellowship should not be laid in Theology, in principles concerning the nature of God. Secondly, that Eternal Punishment or Death *may* be denounced against those who hold certain opinions on certain subjects,—probably on the subject of the Trinity,—but should not be denounced against those who do not think 'thus' or 'thus' concerning it.

On the first proposition I have spoken much in these Essays, and have endeavoured to show that any basis of fellowship, but a Theological one,—any basis of human consciousness, or of mere materialism,—must be narrow and exclusive, one on which an edifice of superstition will certainly be reared, one which must be protected by persecution. On the second point I would observe, that if the Creed had meant that the not holding certain intellectual notions concerning the Trinity involved the penalty of everlasting death, it would consign to destruction, not heretics,—extreme or moderate,—but every peasant, every child, nearly every woman in every congregation in which it is read, seeing that these (thank God!) have formed no such intellectual conceptions, that the majority are not capable of forming them. And the few persons it would count worthy of eternal life, are a set of schoolmen, the best of whom pray every day and hour that they may become as little children, and have the faith which those have, who do not look upon the subject from a logical point of view at all. Lastly, it would directly contradict its own most solemn assertions. If we could comprehend this truth in an intellectual statement, the Father would *not* be incomprehensible, the Son incomprehensible, the Holy Ghost incomprehensible. But since there is no alternative between this utterly monstrous imagination, and that which supposes the Creed to affirm the knowledge of God and eternal life to be the same; and therefore the denial,—not in the letter, but in the spirit,—not intellectually and outwardly, but morally and inwardly,—of the Father, Son, and Spirit, to be eternal death,—I cannot help thinking that, with all its fierce language, it has a gentler heart than some of those who get themselves credit for Toleration, by wishing the Church well rid of it. *They* leave us free to judge occasionally, to assume a portion of God's authority, only protesting against any excessive intrusion into it. The Creed obliges us to give such a meaning to eternal life,—or rather to adhere so closely to our Lord's explanation of it,—that we have no power of saying, in any case, who has lost it, or incurred the state which is opposite to it.

If I am asked whether the writer did not suppose that he had this power, I answer; When you tell me who the writer was, I may possibly, though probably not even then, be able to make some guess whether he supposed it or not. At present, I am quite in the dark about him and his motives. If I adopt the theory, which is as reasonable as any other, that he lived in the time of the Vandal persecution, I think it is very likely, that along with a much deepened conviction of the worth of the principle for which he was suffering, he had also a mixture of earthly passion and fierceness, and that he was tempted to show his opponents, or those who were apostatising, that there were more terrible penalties than those of scourging the back or cutting out the tongue. In that case, I should say I was giving up that part of his *animus* which he would wish me to give up; that part which was not of God, and could not be meant to abide; and was clinging to that which made his other words true and consistent with themselves, when I interpreted his Creed in conformity with our Lord's sentence. I should not be imitating the treatment which Mr. Ward (in his Ideal of the Church) applied to our Articles, (I have no doubt he is one of those on whom Romanism has conferred a benefit by making him at least respectful to the formularies by which he is bound,) when he maintained that a non-natural sense might be put on them, because the compilers of them meant to cheat Catholics, and Catholics might pay them in their own coin. I should apply just the opposite rule. If I found a general scope of meaning which was important and precious, and which belonged to all times, I should not sacrifice that for the sake of a portion which belonged to the circumstances and feelings of a particular time or a particular man. To use Mr. Canning's celebrated simile, I should not follow the example of those worshippers of the Sun, who chose the moment of an eclipse to come forth with their hymns and their symbols.

This rule is necessary, I suspect, that we may do justice to the Church of the Fathers generally, and prove our reverence for it. I cannot honour that age too much, for its earnestness in asserting and defending theological principles. I believe no other age has had precisely the same task committed to it. Of course, I have most sympathy with those (like him to whom this Creed is erroneously attributed) who fought at fearful odds for that which was dear to them, who exposed themselves to imperial, episcopal, and popular indignation, for the sake of it. It is not only more pleasant to contemplate them than the prosperous men,—and them in their adversity than when they were threatening and excommunicating others; but their weak time was certainly the time in which all their chief work was done. Nevertheless,

I cannot say that their anathemas were indications of a cruel spirit, that these did not show, like their endurance of persecution, how much they were in earnest, and how precious the truths which they had realized were to them; or that the distinctions which were the excuses for them were not very valuable for Theology and for Humanity. *There*, I believe, they were wiser than we are, unless we are willing to profit by their wisdom. But there are points on which I know we ought to be wiser than they were. They could not foresee how God would govern His world, what methods He would see fit to use for bringing His truth to light. We ought to see that doubts, questions, partial apprehensions, denials of one principle for the sake of affirming another, have been, through His gracious discipline, means of elucidating that which would otherwise have been dark. Would the sentence of the Nicene Council have sufficed to illustrate the faith of Athanasius? Was not a century of strife in the Empire,—three centuries of Arianism among the Barbarians,—needful for that purpose? And if I find this to be so, and find also much horrible sin among the orthodox mixed with their excellences, many virtues among the heretics mixed with their denials and contradictions, I am bound to believe God was using both. I dare not deny History any more than the Theological truth, which, I believe, History has expounded. That truth will suffer if I do. How was the noble heart of Dante crushed by the thought that his dear master, and all the men whom he reverenced in the old world, were outcasts, for not believing in the Trinity! That thought evidently shook his faith in the Trinity. And it would shake mine, because it would lead me to suppose, that Truth only became true when Christ appeared, instead of being revealed by Him for all ages past and to come; so that, whoever walked in the light then, whoever walks in it now, seeking glory and immortality, desirous to be true, has glimpses of it, and will have the fruition of it, which is Life Eternal.

I have spoken of the possible animus of the *writer* of this Creed; but I must repeat that I know nothing of him, and therefore my guesses are good for very little. The *animus imponentis* concerns us, as all casuists admit, much more; and of that we have no right to pretend ignorance. Our Church has given us great helps for understanding what her meaning is, and what spirit she wishes us to be of. So long as I am commanded to repeat her prayers, no one shall compel me to put a construction upon this formulary which contradicts them, and makes me consciously false in the use of them. And I will add once for all in reference to those who wish to bind us by the current and floating opinions of this age, on the topics I have discussed in these Essays; I hold to that which I have confessed already; I hold to the prayers in which I find that confession made living and effectual for me and for all my brethren. If you say my faith is not distinct enough, bring forth your substitute for it. Do not talk about a perfect Atonement, or a divine Satisfaction, or an Eternal Death; these I believe in as much as you can do. Put forth distinctly before your own consciences, and before the conscience of England, the meaning which you attach to these words. See whether what you intend is not either that assertion of God's infinite Charity, which is contained in St. John's express words, in the whole Bible, in our forms, or something so flagrantly in contradiction with that, as to make the duty of rejecting it, and protesting against it, one from which no Churchman and no man ought to shrink.

THE END.

R. CLAY, PRINTER, LONDON.

A Second Edition, with a new Preface and other Additions,

THEOLOGICAL ESSAYS.

"They are valuable as a complete exposition of his views of Christianity—the views of a man who is powerfully influencing his generation, and who profoundly believes in revealed religion as a series of facts disclosing God's plan for educating and restoring the human race."—*Spectator*, August 6, 1853.

"Mr. Maurice is aiming at a high object. He would reconcile the old and the new. He would disencumber what is popular of what is vulgar, confused, sectarian, and preserve and illustrate it by disencumbering it. He calls on us not to be afraid of the depths and heights, the freedom and largeness, the 'spirit and the truth' of our own theology. It is a warning and a call which every age wants. We sympathise with his aim, with much of his positive teaching, with some of his aversions and some of his fears. We do not respect him the less for not being afraid of being called hard names. But certainly such a writer has need, in no common degree, of conforming himself to that wise maxim which holds in writing as well as in art, 'Know what you want to do, then do it.'"—*Guardian.*

"Throughout these Essays runs a large-hearted, truthful, and earnest spirit, which provokes a similar warmth of feeling in the reader. Their candour and straightforwardness, the anxiety evinced to put the best construction upon dissentients and not to escape from any just charge against ourselves, are as rare in Christian and Church Advocates as they are valuable in their cause. Even those who may not be able to agree with Mr. Maurice throughout, will certainly admire the charity and forbearance he displays in dealing with difficult and delicate subjects: none can well be other than gainers by witnessing a treatment of them so remarkable in respect both of temper and ability."—*Clerical Journal.*

"Every author of real mark has a purpose in writing a book, without a knowledge of which it cannot be fairly appreciated, and by it should be estimated the method of his reasonings, illustrations, and phraseology. This plain canon of writing might, we think, help to absolve Mr. Maurice from some of the weightier accusations which have been brought against him."—*Church of England Quarterly Review.*

AN ESSAY ON ETERNAL LIFE:

And the Preface to the New Edition of "THEOLOGICAL ESSAYS," crown 8vo. sewed.

This will be published separately for the Purchasers of the First Edition.

WORKS OF THE REV. F. D. MAURICE.

---

1. **PROPHETS AND KINGS OF THE OLD TESTAMENT.**
10*s.* 6*d.*

2. **THE KINGDOM OF CHRIST.**
2 vols. 21*s.*

3. **LETTER TO DR. JELF.**
1*s.*

4. **MORAL AND METAPHYSICAL PHILOSOPHY.**
Part I.—Ancient. 5*s.*
II.—Modern. First Six Centuries.

5. **ON THE EPISTLE TO THE HEBREWS.**
7*s.* 6*d.*

6. **CHRISTMAS DAY, AND OTHER SERMONS.**
10*s.* 6*d.*

7. **ON THE RELIGIONS OF THE WORLD.**
5*s.*

8. **ON THE OLD TESTAMENT.**
6*s.*

9. **ON THE PRAYER-BOOK.**
5*s.*

10. **THE CHURCH A FAMILY.**
4*s.* 6*d.*

11. **ON THE LORD'S PRAYER.**
2*s.* 6*d.*

12. **LAW'S REMARKS ON THE FABLE OF THE BEES.**
4*s.* 6*d.*

www.ingramcontent.com/pod-product-compliance
Lightning Source LLC
LaVergne TN
LVHW021310110826
845150LV00003B/542

* 9 7 8 1 4 2 5 5 5 8 2 5 3 *